To
Bob Gutkowski,
A unique & special
leader who brought
Mike Tyson and many
other great events to MSG.
The sports world thanks
you for all you have done!
Jim Thomas

# THE
# HOLYFIELD
## WAY

WHAT I LEARNED
ABOUT COURAGE,
PERSEVERANCE,
AND THE BIZARRE
WORLD OF BOXING

James J. Thomas II

with commentary by

**Evander Holyfield**

**SPORTS
PUBLISHING
L.L.C.**

www.SportsPublishingLLC.com

ISBN: 1-59670-019-X

Publishers: Peter L. Bannon and Joseph J. Bannon Sr.
Senior managing editor: Susan M. Moyer
Acquisitions editor: John Humenik
Developmental editor: Elisa Bock Laird
Art director: K. Jeffrey Higgerson
Dust jacket design: Kenneth J. O'Brien
Interior layout: Kenneth J. O'Brien
Imaging: Kenneth J. O'Brien
Photo editor: Erin Linden-Levy
Vice president of sales and marketing: Kevin King
Media and promotions managers: Nick Obradovich (regional),
        Randy Fouts (national), Maurey Williamson (print)

Printed in the United States of America

Sports Publishing L.L.C.
804 North Neil Street
Champaign, IL 61820

Phone: 1-877-424-2665
Fax: 217-363-2073
Web site: www.SportsPublishingLLC.com

# CONTENTS

# PREFACE

**W**hat follows is my account of my years at Evander Holyfield's side as his attorney, boxing management adviser, friend, and confidant. I have attempted to provide the reader with a candid insight into the public and private lives of a truly extraordinary man, the bizarre and fascinating business and sport of boxing, what it is like to work and play with some of the world's best-known celebrities, and most of all, what I learned about succeeding through courage and perseverance from one of the greatest warriors in sports history.

I have made every effort to be as accurate as possible. I have not intentionally fabricated, exaggerated, or enhanced any of the facts, and the perceptions and opinions are my true perceptions and opinions as an eyewitness. These are solely my observations. My guess is Evander would be too humble to tell the stories as I have, but I believe my version is more accurate than his more modest account might be. In the statements in the book that I have attributed to Evander, I have done my best to paraphrase what he said to me at the time or what he recounted to me as having happened in his life before we began working together many years ago. The statements I have attributed to others also reflect my best effort to paraphrase the substance of what was said but may not be exact quotations. All accounts of fights in this book reflect my honest opinions of what occurred, but they are inevitably just that—opinions. Boxing is one of the most subjective of all sports, and victory is very often in the eye of the beholder.

While I have recounted many of Evander's amazing triumphs and outstanding character traits, I have not attempted to idealize him. Evander is most certainly human. He has flaws and makes mistakes, and many of those flaws and mistakes are included in this book. In my estimation, Evander Holyfield is not only an extraordinary athlete, but also an extraordinary man, not *in spite of* his mistakes and failures, but in large part *because* of them. Evander believes and has convinced me that success is not measured by proximity to perfection but rather by one's determination to overcome the inevitable failures in life. To Evander Holyfield, a *warrior* is someone who absolutely refuses to give up, whether that means finishing 15 grueling rounds in the ring or, as his mother did, raising nine children as a single mother with virtually no worldly resources. By that measure, Evander Holyfield is truly the ultimate warrior in and out of the ring. By allowing readers to learn more about Evander in these pages, I hope to inspire others, through his example, to become warriors and to believe, as he so often says: "A setback is nothing but an opportunity for a comeback."

# Chapter 1

# THE TWO SECRET HOLYFIELD VERSUS TYSON BOUTS AND HOW THE THIRD ONE THAT SHOCKED THE WORLD CAME ABOUT

I n 1996, my friend and client, Evander Holyfield, told me he wanted to fight then-current Heavyweight Champion of the World Mike Tyson and told me he was absolutely sure he would beat Tyson if I could get him the fight. I asked Evander why he thought he could beat the so-called "Baddest Man on the Planet" when none of the other top heavyweights was able to last even a few rounds. Evander corrected me and told me he did not *think* he would beat Tyson; he *knew* he would beat him, and the reason was simple. Unlike the other heavyweights, Evander was not afraid of Tyson, and Tyson knew it. When I asked Evander why he didn't fear Tyson and how he knew Tyson knew he wasn't afraid of him, Evander told me two stories about his first encounters with Tyson that very few people had heard.

Evander and Tyson met in the ring in early 1984, as top-rated amateur boxers in the United States gathered in Colorado Springs at the Olympic training facility for the boxing trials to determine who would represent the United States at the 1984 Olympics in Los Angeles. One of the heavyweight prospects was the extremely muscular, powerful, fast, and talented 18-year-old Tyson, who was already gaining attention as a fighter to watch. Not surprisingly, none of the prospects for the Olympic team wanted to risk injury by sparring with the fierce young heavyweight from Brooklyn, New York. None of them, except for one.

Evander was a light heavyweight prospect from Atlanta, Georgia, a quiet, polite, lean, muscular, 175-pound 21-year-old "Southern boy." When Olympic coach Pat Nappy had trouble finding someone willing to spar with Tyson, Evander eagerly volunteered. Coach Nappy was reluctant to allow Evander to spar with Tyson because Tyson had about a 25-pound weight advantage, but Evander was insistent, and Coach Nappy finally allowed it, assuming the fighters would go half speed. When the bell rang, however, Evander let Tyson know immediately that he had not come to spar; he had come to fight. Two of the most competitive and physically fit fighters in the Olympic camp held nothing back and went after each other as if it were for the Heavyweight Championship of the world. As the intensity escalated, Coach Nappy could see that neither man was going to back off.

"Stop! Get out of there before somebody gets hurt," he shouted at both of them.

Evander reluctantly climbed out of the ring, but not before joining a very, very exclusive club—fighters who were not afraid of Mike Tyson. And Tyson knew it.

## HOLYFIELD

*There was no reason to fear Mike Tyson. He was very good and very powerful, but he was just a man like me. My mother taught me to fear no one but God. Besides, I was pretty sure Mike couldn't hurt me any more than my big sister Eloise had when I was growing up. Eloise could fold a heavy bag in half, and I had survived her punches. The fact that I was much lighter than Mike made no difference to me. Mike had a lot of power, but so did I.*

A few weeks later, the Olympic team had been selected and was in Gonzalez, Texas, to prepare for the Olympic Games coming up that summer. Evander had surprised the United States amateur boxing community by beating the favorite in the light heavyweight division, a talented and vicious thug from Detroit named Ricky Womack, to win a spot on the team. Tyson had lost to Henry Tillman for the heavyweight spot. As the runner-up, though, Tyson was in camp as a heavyweight. One night at camp, most of the fighters were in the rec room taking turns on the pool table. The protocol was for guys who wanted to play to line up to play the winner, while the loser dropped out or went to the end of the line. The protocol, however, did not seem to apply to Tyson, who had developed the obnoxious habit of taking the next game whenever it suited him. There were very few fighters able to credibly challenge Tyson, and none willing to do so. Except for one. Evander was on deck to play the winner of the current game, but when the game ended, Tyson walked over and grabbed the cue ball.

"Tyson's gonna take your game," some of the guys behind Evander whispered.

"He ain't takin' my game," Evander shot back without hesitation and loud enough for Tyson to hear.

Tyson was still holding a cue ball, potentially a very effective weapon. Evander, being not only brave and tough, but also no fool, grabbed a cue stick and turned it upside down as he walked toward the pool table—just in case. He walked confidently to the table and locked eyes with Tyson. When Evander reached the table, he stopped. Tyson looked at him, put the cue ball back on the table, and backed off to allow Evander to play. Whether Tyson backed off because of his sparring session a few weeks earlier with Evander, no one will ever know, but for some reason, Tyson decided any effort to intimidate Evander would be futile, because Evander was genuinely unafraid of Tyson, which may well have made him unique.

**HOLYFIELD**

*Even back in 1984, I realized there was a good chance I might fight Tyson some day. I knew that if we ever confronted each other, the one who flinched would be at a psychological disadvantage when that day came.*

Twelve years later, when Evander asked me to get him the opportunity to face Tyson in the ring for the Heavyweight Championship of the World, Evander's experience from 1984 gave him the confidence to seek a fight many felt could only end in serious injury to Evander or worse. As of the spring of

1996, Holyfield had already won and lost the heavyweight championship twice and had assured himself a place in history as one of the best heavyweights of his era. But he was considered a distant second to Tyson, who was the current champion. Furthermore, Evander had looked old and tired in his last two fights, and although I completely disagreed, many so-called experts believed he was "shot." For Evander to establish himself as the best heavyweight of his era and one of the best of all time, he would have to do what most people considered impossible—shock the world by beating Tyson. But first, the terms for the Tyson versus Holyfield bout would need to be agreed upon, and that would be nearly as hard as winning the fight.

On May 30, 1996, Evander and I were on a plane on our way to Toronto knowing that the next 24 hours were likely to determine Evander's legacy in boxing. At that point, Evander was considered by many to be an overachieving, blown-up cruiserweight who had won the heavyweight title more by courage and determination than by extraordinary talent and devastating power. The outcome of this trip would determine whether Evander would have the opportunity to change that assessment and establish himself as one of the greatest heavyweights of all time.

## HOLYFIELD

*I knew this was our last chance to make a fight with Tyson, but I wasn't really worried about it. I believed God had a plan for me and my boxing career, and that His will would determine whether I got the chance to fight Mike Tyson and become the only fighter other than Muhammad Ali to win the Heavyweight Championship of the World three times.*

On the way to Toronto, I reflected back on the stories Evander had told me over the past five years about how he had gotten into boxing and how he had gotten to this point in his career.

Evander's boxing career began in 1971, in Atlanta, Georgia, when he was eight years old. Evander was the youngest of nine siblings born to Annie Mai Holyfield, who raised her children with love and faith but few worldly resources. When Evander, ironically nicknamed "Chubby" after his mother's best friend, started to show signs of getting into trouble while out of school for the summer, his mother took him to the Warren Street Boys Club in an effort to dissipate his energy in a constructive manner. There Evander was immediately attracted to the rhythmic noise of the speed bag in the gym. Evander approached the coach of the boxing team, a kind, dedicated white man in his 60s named Carter Morgan, and asked whether he could hit the speed bag. Coach Morgan told Evander he could hit the speed bag only if he joined the boxing team. Evander, who received at least one "whooping" a day from his iron-willed, iron-handed mother and others from his eight older siblings, had no interest in getting hit by anyone else, so he declined Coach Morgan's invitation. Day after day, however, the insistent "ba-da-ba, ba-da-ba, ba-da-ba" of the speed bag became more irresistible, and finally Evander joined the boxing team.

Evander got to hit the speed bag, but he also had to learn to box. In his first bout, with gloves nearly up to his elbows, Evander received his prefight instructions.

"Son, I want you to go in there and hit that boy right in the face," Coach Morgan told him.

When the bell rang, Evander did exactly what he was told. His opponent, also eight years old, immediately began to cry. The bout was stopped, and Evander had his first technical knockout.

Later that day, Coach Morgan pulled Evander aside, and he told Evander something that I have heard Evander recount so many times I feel like I was there.

"Evander, you have a natural talent for boxing, and you've got lots of courage. If you work hard and never quit, you could become the Heavyweight Champion of the World."

"What's the Heavyweight Champion of the World?" the little boy asked.

"You know, the best heavyweight boxer in the world. Like Muhammad Ali."

"But Coach, I'm only eight years old."

"Evander, trust me, you won't always be eight years old."

Coach Morgan gained a good measure of credibility with Evander on this point, because Evander knew that within about a week, on October 19, he would turn nine, but another flaw in the plan quickly occurred to Evander.

"But Coach, I only weigh 65 pounds."

"Evander, I assure you, you will not always weigh 65 pounds."

Again, what Coach Morgan prophesized rang true. Evander was playing on the 65-pound-and-under Boys Club football team, and he was having trouble keeping his weight under 65 pounds.

"Coach, do you really think I could become the Heavyweight Champion of the World?"

"Evander, if you work very, very hard and never, ever give up no matter what, you will be the Heavyweight Champion of the World."

This was exciting stuff, but it seemed a little far fetched, so Evander decided to take it to the ultimate authority on all things, his mother.

"Mama, Coach Morgan told me if I work hard and never give up, I could someday be the Heavyweight Champion of the World, like Muhammad Ali. Is that true?"

"'Chubby,' he left one thing out, but what he said is true. If you work hard, never give up, and trust in God, you can do anything you set your mind to do."

Every message Evander had received up to that point in his life from outside his home told him that a poor kid from the public housing projects could never amount to anything. Now, a man who had no reason to lie to him and seemed very sincere was telling him that wasn't true, and his mama, who would never lie to him, said that man was right. That was probably the single-most important day of Evander's boxing career and perhaps his life, because suddenly anything was possible if he worked hard, trusted in God, and never gave up; things were entirely within his own control. That night, Evander went to the bathroom in his crowded home, made sure no one was in the immediate vicinity, looked in the mirror, held his fists up with his elbows at a 90-degree angle, flexed his less-than-bulging biceps, and said the words he would hear from an announcer in a ring in Las Vegas 20 years later: "Evander Holyfield … Heavyweight Champion of the World."

Evander won all of his boxing bouts as a nine-year-old, and at 10, he was scheduled to fight a white kid named Cecil Collins. The other members of the Warren Street Boys Club Boxing Team were envious and kidded Evander about his great fortune in getting to fight a white kid, because everyone knew white kids couldn't fight. Evander fought Collins and suffered the first of many setbacks in his boxing career. Collins was awarded the decision in the bout. Evander had lost for the first time—and to a white kid. Evander was humiliated, and the humiliation got worse when he couldn't stop himself from crying.

Evander rushed home, told his mother he had lost, and announced that he was quitting the boxing team. His mother was totally unambiguous.

"I did not raise a quitter," she said emphatically. "You'll go back and beat that boy, and if and when you do, you can quit the team, but only after you reach this goal. You'll quit on top or not at all."

Evander would have argued, but he knew it would do no good, and he had already taken one beating that day and had no interest in another from his mother. Going back and facing Collins again was intimidating, but nothing compared to defying his mother.

Several months later, Evander had the opportunity/obligation to fight Collins again. The white boy beat Evander again. Evander cried again, and this time he didn't care what his mother said. He was going to quit boxing forever and never suffer this kind of embarrassment again.

When Evander got home, he told his mother what had happened, and this time he was adamant. No matter what his mama said, he was done boxing. Evander's mother was not the kind of woman to be dictated to, especially by one of her children. With no doubt whatsoever about her resolve to be obeyed, she explained the situation to Evander at sufficient volume so that he could not escape her meaning.

"I thought I told you I didn't raise a quitter!" she responded. "You are going to fight that boy as many times as it takes to beat him. Then, and only then, will you quit!"

Once again, Evander chose not to defy his mother and thereby lived to fight another day—or another—or another for as long as it took, so he could quit boxing.

Months later, Evander had a third chance to fight Collins almost a year after their first encounter. Fortunately for Evander, during that year he had grown, become stronger, and developed his boxing skills. This time he soundly beat Collins. Evander was ecstatic and rushed home to tell his mother and be smothered with praise.

"Mama, I beat the boy!"

"Uh-huh."

"No, Mama, you don't understand. I beat the boy who beat me twice, the one you said I had to beat."

"That's good. Now that you've reached your goal, you can quit."

"But, Mama, now I don't want to quit."

That may well have been the second-most important day of Evander's boxing career and perhaps his life.

From that point, Evander got bigger, stronger, and better, and compiled an excellent amateur record in Georgia and the South but did not immediately win any national awards or acclaim. Then, in 1983, Evander began to get some attention at the national level by winning the tournament to select the representatives for the United States at the Pan-American Games in Cuba. The next year, in the trials to make the U.S. Olympic team, Evander was one of the top contenders, but he was considered a decided underdog to a brutally tough fighter from Detroit named Ricky Womack. Womack started the war for the light heavyweight (175-pound limit) spot on the U.S. Olympic team by stomping on Evander's foot as hard as he could at the prefight weigh-in. But Evander stunned the amateur boxing world by defeating Womack twice to win the spot on the Olympic team. Evander went on to the Olympics, and Ricky Womack eventually went on to a lengthy prison sentence for armed robbery and an untimely death in 2002 at age 42.

At the Los Angeles Olympics in 1984, Evander was simply spectacular. In amateur boxing, safety gets high priority. The boxers wear heavily padded gloves and headgear and at that time boxed only three three-minute rounds per bout, as opposed to the current four two-minute rounds. Consequently, knockouts in amateur boxing were, and still are, rare. Through the first four rounds of competition, Evander was the only fighter in the Olympics who had knocked out all four of his opponents. That put Evander into the semifinals. Of the four boxers left in the light heavyweight division, the two winners of the semifinal bouts would fight for the gold and silver medals, and the two losers would each win a bronze medal.

In the first semifinal bout, the Yugoslavian fighter defeated his opponent and would therefore face the winner of the bout between Evander and Kevin Barry of New Zealand. Evander was a heavy favorite to beat Barry, and there was no question that the Yugoslavian fighter, his teammates, and his countrymen were hoping Barry would somehow miraculously beat Evander, clearing the way for the Yugoslavian to win the gold medal.

Under these circumstances, it was incredible, in retrospect, that the referee assigned to Evander's bout was from Yugoslavia. Soon after Evander's bout against the New Zealander began, it became apparent that Evander had superior skills and power and it would be just a matter of time before Evander claimed his fifth straight knockout victim and moved on to the finals to fight for the gold medal. And that is exactly what happened. Evander dropped Barry with a clean, hard left hook. Barry could not recover, and the Americans began to celebrate. But then the Yugoslavian referee called a foul, claiming that Evander's knockout punch came after the referee had given the fighters a command to break. The punch was replayed on television, and it was clear that although the punch had landed literally a split-second after the command was given, it was begun before Evander could have possibly responded to the command. Furthermore, at the time the command was given, Barry was holding Evander around the head so that the ear holes on Evander's headgear were blocked. Evander could not have heard the command, and if he had, he could not have stopped the punch that knocked out Barry.

In accordance with the rules, a foul should not have been called, and virtually the entire boxing world was outraged. Even the Yugoslavian fighter, who was awarded the gold medal in a walk-over against Barry—Barry was prohibited by the rules from fighting for the gold medal because he had been knocked out by Evander—recognized that Evander had been robbed. At the medal ceremony, in a very classy display of sportsmanship, the Yugoslavian fighter pulled Evander up onto the gold medal level of the platform and held Evander's hand up. The greatest display of sportsmanship, however, was by Evander. No one would have blamed Evander if he had fumed, ranted, or pouted, but he did none of that. Evander accepted the unfair result with such grace and equanimity that he became the darling of the Olympics, and his popularity soared. The world had just seen the trademark behavior of Evander Holyfield that would, over the years, make him one of the most popular athletes in the world.

After the Olympics, Evander turned professional. After only four bouts at light heavyweight (175-pound limit), he moved up in weight to become the greatest cruiserweight (190-pound limit) champion in history. Then, unwilling to accept the fact that Tyson was making 10 times the money he was making because Tyson fought as a heavyweight, Evander moved up to the heavyweight division despite a consensus by critics that he was simply too small to be a serious heavyweight threat. On October 25, 1990, almost exactly 20 years after Coach Morgan and his mother told him he could do it, Evander knocked out Buster Douglas to become the undisputed Heavyweight Champion of the World. It was at that point that I began representing Evander and attending his fights.

Evander then successfully defended his title against George Foreman and agreed to face Tyson in his next title defense. A rib injury sustained while training by Tyson delayed the fight. Then, Tyson was indicted on charges that he raped a beauty pageant contestant in Indianapolis, causing Holyfield versus Tyson to be canceled. After successful defenses against Bert Cooper, who substituted for Tyson, and former heavyweight champion Larry Holmes, Evander put his title on the line and faced the young, talented, powerful, quick, and huge Riddick Bowe in November 1992. In that fight with Bowe, Evander allowed his courage to overrule his reason, causing him to lose one of the greatest slugfests in heavyweight history. A year later, Evander came back to beat Bowe to become heavyweight champion for the second time. In April 1994, however, fighting with a severely injured left shoulder, Evander lost his championship in a close decision to Michael Moorer.

Immediately after the Moorer fight, suffering from the pain of severe trauma to his injured shoulder, Evander was taken to the hospital, drugged, treated for symptoms of cardiac distress, and flown to Atlanta. The next day Evander was diagnosed with a serious heart disorder and told he could never fight again. After several weeks of rest, Evander felt well enough to train and was re-evaluated and found to have no significant disability. After a legal battle to win the right to fight again, Evander began his comeback in May 1995, more than a year after the Moorer fight, with a victory over the very tough "Merciless" Ray Mercer.

In November 1995, Evander faced Bowe in a rubber match in the next step of his comeback. Not wanting to postpone the fight, Evander fought Bowe while still suffering from the effects of a bout of hepatitis A, probably brought on by bad food. After having Bowe all but knocked out, Evander hit the wall and was defeated by technical knockout. Evander then fought a former light heavyweight champion named Bobby Czyz, and although Evander won, he looked so bad that there was a nearly universal cry for his retirement.

That was where Evander's career stood as we flew to Toronto for negotiations to fight Tyson. If it had ended then and there, Evander would have been remembered as one of the best heavyweights of his era, but Evander and I believed he was much more than that and was not finished. He just needed a chance to prove it.

Evander and I understood that the loss by knockout to Bowe and the unimpressive win against Czyz were not indicative of his ability at that point in his career. Evander had no interest in any more meaningless fights, like the

Czyz fight. He wanted to go straight to the top and fight the current champion and so-called "Baddest Man on the Planet." I also wanted that for him, because I fully believed Evander could, and would, beat Tyson if given the opportunity.

## HOLYFIELD

*After my fight with Bobby Czyz, most people thought I was finished as a fighter, but I knew there were reasons for my recent struggles in the ring, and I believed I was still the best heavyweight in the world when I was at my best. My mother taught me that God works in mysterious ways and that all things happen for a reason. Looking back, I can see now that the only reason I had any chance to fight Mike Tyson and become the WBA heavyweight champion for the third time was that I looked like a "shot" fighter against Bowe and Czyz in my previous two fights. If I had been at my best, Don King would not have even considered letting me fight Tyson. I knew this was all part of God's plan, and I was absolutely sure I could and would beat Tyson if I could just get the chance.*

At that time, in early 1996, Don King Productions had the exclusive contractual right to promote Tyson's fights, and Main Events, a rival promoter, had the exclusive rights to promote Evander's fights, although Evander could terminate those rights. On Evander's behalf, I had asked Dino Duva, the president of Main Events, and Pat English, the outside general counsel for Main Events, to try to reach an agreement with King and make the fight between Evander and Tyson happen. Unfortunately, the long-running feud between the Duva family and King, including a recent litigation battle between Main Events and its fighter Lennox Lewis, on the one hand, and Don King Productions and Tyson, on the other, had made negotiations between the two promoters extremely difficult, at best. Previous efforts at negotiations, which I attended as Evander's personal representative, had deteriorated almost immediately into angry accusations.

Tyson was under an exclusive television rights contract with Showtime. Although not under an exclusive contract, Evander preferred at that time to fight on Showtime rather than HBO, the other major television distributor of boxing. As I became increasingly frustrated with the inability to make happen the only fight Evander wanted, I had turned to Showtime's executive producer, Jay Larkin, a longtime friend and supporter of Evander, to brainstorm strategies to get an agreement despite the Duva–King feud. Larkin, an affable and gregarious guy but also a shrewd businessman, knew all of the parties well and had suggested that I personally meet with King and explore the possibility of a Tyson–Holyfield fight. When I agreed, Larkin had arranged a meeting between King and me in King's office in Deerfield Beach, Florida, with Larkin in attendance.

## HOLYFIELD

*Ever since I turned pro in 1984, Main Events had always negotiated my contracts. They had done a good job, and I had no desire to go around them, but in this case, the feud between Main Events and Don King was an obstacle, and I was watching my chance to regain the heavyweight title slipping away. We had to try another way, and I took Jay Larkin's suggestion to send Jim to meet with Don King to explore whether a deal could be made if we removed the problems between King and Main Events from the negotiations.*

I had met Larkin at King's offices, and King had kept me waiting for over two hours while he reconnected with the great Puerto Rican fighter, Felix Trinidad, from whom King had been estranged. I had swallowed the insult of the wait without showing any reaction because I wanted the Tyson fight for Evander so badly. I also did not want King to believe he could get to me with such tactics, which I had watched him employ very effectively on others years earlier.

I had met King before on several occasions and had watched him operate in various contexts, but I had never been in a one-on-one situation with him where I could meet the "real" Don King, as opposed to the public persona. My impression of King going into the meeting was of a pompous, superficial con artist, who won most confrontations by bluster and intimidation. In that first private meeting with King, I discovered a much more complicated man. He was certainly physically intimidating and in some ways seemed larger than life. Publicly he was a walking, talking malapropism, but privately he was thoughtful and disarming. In that first private meeting with King, I had learned that he can be almost whatever he wants to be to suit his purpose, and anyone who underestimates him will pay a very high price for doing so.

In that first meeting, the players in attendance had been King; Larkin; King's longtime friend and lawyer, Charlie Lomax, who had been with King since the mid-1970s and was one of the first African-Americans to become a partner in a major American law firm, Sidley & Austin of Chicago; and me. As we sat at opposite ends of a 10-foot table, King told me that although we had met many times, until recently he did not know much about me. He said he had learned that I had graduated as the outstanding law graduate in my law school class at William & Mary and had served as editor-in-chief of the law review. He said he knew I was a senior partner in one of the country's best law firms. As I listened quietly, King said that he had very little formal education and no training in the law and would appreciate my going slowly with him as we talked about business matters because of my vast superiority in education.

When it was clear that King had completed his opening statement, I responded. I told King that I began working at age 10 as a dishwasher in my grandfather's diner, standing on a milk crate to wash dishes. I told him that I was still an anonymous lawyer who achieved acceptable results by working harder than my opponents. I told him that I was not accustomed to dealing with celebrities like himself and the people he consorted with and asked him to indulge me if I seemed a bit naïve and unsophisticated.

When I had finished, he chuckled, looked me in the eye, and said, "I think we can do business together."

King then suggested that we get down to the business at hand. He said he understood from Larkin that I was there because I wanted Evander to fight Tyson. I corrected him by telling him that I was there because Evander wanted to fight Tyson. Attempting to explore whether I knew something he did not, King asked whether I thought Evander could win the fight. I avoided the temptation to tell him I was sure Evander would win by telling him my job was not to determine who would win but to maximize Evander's income, and that Evander was growing older and needed and deserved a big pay day. King seemed to accept my answer at face value, perhaps because it reflected his own approach to the fight business and his assessment of Evander's chances to defeat Tyson—slim to none.

King then told me there were a few things I would need to understand and accept, because otherwise we were wasting each other's time. First, I needed to understand that as a non-negotiable condition to further discussions, if Evander somehow won the fight, he would be promoted by Don King Productions for as long as he was heavyweight champion. He asked whether that condition could be accommodated. I explained that although he preferred not to do so for reasons of loyalty and a history of solid service, Evander had the right to terminate his promotional contract with Main Events. Second, King said that Evander could make any financial arrangement he wished with Main Events, but King would deal directly only with me, and he had some rather harsh and profane comments about Duva and English. I told King I would discuss that condition with Evander but assumed we could find common ground. Third, he said that he would not pay Evander more than he was paying the current WBA champion, Bruce Seldon, to fight Tyson, which was $5 million. I told him that was a big problem and if it was truly non-negotiable, we probably could not make a deal. King said that if the other conditions could be met, there might be room for negotiation on the purse but not much. At that point, we had accomplished all I had set out to achieve in this initial meeting, and it was time for me to leave. King, Larkin, and I all agreed we would begin telephone discussions within the next few days to explore the possibility of reaching an agreement.

In the following days, Larkin had attempted to mediate an agreement between King and me. I spoke daily with Larkin and Evander and with English and/or Duva. At times, it seemed as though we were making progress, but the process was very frustrating, as King sometimes retreated from certain positions, and English and Duva consistently opined that I was being too accommodating to King's demands and conditions, especially about promotional rights in the event Evander beat Tyson. Because Evander truly wanted the Tyson fight and because I doubted there would be another chance to make the fight, I was willing to indulge positions that I would otherwise not have tolerated. Despite my efforts to be flexible, eventually the negotiations stagnated and then reached deadlock. Larkin and I commiserated by telephone but eventually were on the verge of conceding defeat. I was tempted to give up, but, by that time in my life, my own lessons of winning by perseverance had been so dramatically bolstered by Evander's creed of never giving up, that quitting was not an option. In late May, Larkin telephoned with an idea. He said that he and other Showtime representatives would be in Toronto over the weekend of May 31 and June 1 for a boxing convention with King and his lawyers. Larkin suggested that if Evander and I came to Toronto without Main Events, he would prevail upon King to meet with us in one final attempt to reach agreement on Tyson versus Holyfield.

Evander and I arrived in Toronto on the night of May 30. At about 9 a.m., we met with Larkin and Roy Langbord of Showtime and with King, Lomax, and a new young lawyer for DKP, John Wirt, in King's suite at the Four Seasons Hotel. King began the meeting by making sure Evander understood that if he won the fight, DKP would be his promoter while he was champion. Evander said I had already explained that point and he would accept it to get the fight. King then stated that he was prepared to pay Evander $5 million, what the current champion Seldon would be paid to fight Tyson. I told King that would not be nearly enough. We had heard reports that Tyson would be paid as much as $30 million to fight Evander, and the split was unacceptable. King argued that Evander had looked terrible in his last fight and had no further drawing power, whereas Tyson was the biggest current draw in boxing and maybe the biggest draw ever. I told King he had already indicated to me that he would come off the $5 million figure and asked him not to waste our time but instead just tell us the real number. After some further argument and discussion, King eventually said he would overpay Evander the sum of $10 million to fight Tyson, but "not one penny more—take it or leave it." At that point, Evander wanted to speak to me alone.

## HOLYFIELD

*I knew that the trip to Toronto was my last chance to make a deal to fight Tyson any time in the foreseeable future, and I was willing to be flexible to get the deal done, but I was not going to agree to anything I felt was totally unfair. I was willing to accept a 2:1 split, which would mean Tyson would get $30 million and I would get $15 million. I felt that $10 million, or a 3:1 split, was unfair, and I was not going to agree to be treated unfairly by anyone, including Don King. I very much wanted the Tyson fight, but I did not feel that I needed the Tyson fight.*

JAMES J. THOMAS II

Evander and I went into an adjacent room and closed the door.

"I'm ready to leave," Evander said. "Let's go."

"Of course I'll go, but would you mind telling me why we're leaving?" I responded.

"It's obvious King is not willing to be fair about the money. I should be getting at least one-third of the total purse. If Tyson's getting $30 million, I should be getting $15 million."

"I'm sorry," I said. "It's my fault we wasted two plane tickets to get here. I thought you understood we had no leverage, and with no leverage, we never had any chance of getting a fair deal from King."

"I do understand that now," he insisted. "It's not your fault, but I still want to go."

"That's fine, but before we go, do you mind answering one question first? Can you beat Tyson?"

"Of all the people in the world, I thought you knew better than anyone whether I can beat Tyson," Evander replied annoyed.

Partly because I knew about the sparring session and pool game in 1984 and also because I had come to know and believe in Evander, I was absolutely sure Evander could and would beat Tyson, so I pushed him toward the fight the best way I knew how.

"Oh, I still have no doubt, but I'm wondering about you."

"What are you talking about?" Evander said with an edge in his voice.

"You and I are the only people in the room who know you are going to win the fight against Tyson. King will insist upon a rematch clause in the event that you somehow win. Whatever we give up in the first fight, we'll make up in the rematch. If you're going to lose, then don't fight Tyson unless the money is right, but if you're going to win, look at it as a two-fight deal and don't worry so much about how much you get for the first fight. When you're the champion, we'll have a lot more negotiating leverage."

Evander smiled his great big, warm smile.

"Jim, I'm gonna leave, but you go in there and make the best deal you can. Whatever deal you make, I'll sign. I'm gonna beat Tyson."

## HOLYFIELD

*I really hadn't focused on the rematch issues. But, of course, King would insist on a clause in the contract requiring me to give Tyson a rematch if I won. When I realized Jim was asking me to believe in and bet on myself, I was excited, and the decision was easy. I would fight Tyson for free, if I needed to, in the first fight if all I needed to do was beat him to get paid what I was entitled to in the rematch.*

Evander and I re-entered King's suite and announced that Evander was going to leave but I would stay and negotiate on his behalf. Evander then left, and the detailed negotiations began. First, King wanted to know whether we were settled on a purse of $10 million to Evander. I told him we wanted $15 million, and he said that would never happen. I asked whether $10 million was a drop-dead position, and King said there could be a little bit of room depending on whether I accepted everything else. He said, for example, if Evander won, Evander would need to fight Tyson in a rematch in his next fight for a purse of $20 million. We then negotiated long and hard on the $20 million figure for the rematch, and King would not budge at all and swore he never would. At that point, I suggested that King and his lawyers give me a proposed draft of the contract they would accept and let think about whether we would have serious problems with the proposed terms. We agreed that we would all break for lunch and that Lomax and Wirt would give me a proposed draft in an hour or two.

By mid-afternoon, King's lawyers had completed a proposed draft of a contract for the Tyson fight. The contract provided for a fixed purse to Evander of $10 million and an obligation to fight a rematch, in the event Evander won, for a fixed purse of $20 million to Evander. The contract also provided that if Evander won, Don King Productions would have the exclusive promotional rights to all of Evander's fights as long as Evander remained Heavyweight Champion of the World. The draft also required a written documentation that the promotional contract between Evander and Main Events was terminated. Of course there were countless other provisions in the 15-page document, but those were the most critical.

For the next two hours, I studied the proposed contract in detail and drafted various proposed revisions. I also called English of Main Events and explained to him what was happening, that Evander wanted to take the fight, and that a condition was that we terminate the Main Events contract. Although

I was confident we had the right to terminate the Main Events contract, English, Duva, and I all knew that if Main Events raised a dispute over this issue, it could kill the Tyson versus Holyfield fight. I asked that English and Duva please cooperate so that Evander could have the fight he wanted so badly. English then called Duva to discuss the situation and called me back. To their great and everlasting credit, English and Duva were very understanding and supportive, and we mutually agreed to terminate the Main Events promotional contract and pay Main Events a consulting fee for the Tyson fight. I then confirmed this agreement with a fax, and with this unpleasant task accomplished, I gave a status report to Evander and asked where I could find him later to update him on progress in the negotiations. Evander said he would be dancing at a nightclub called White Dove, four blocks down the street from the hotel.

It was now about 7 p.m., and I spent the next couple of hours working with King's lawyers on contract language, technical legal issues, and relatively minor disputed points. At that point, about 9 p.m., the real negotiations began between King and me, with Larkin, Langbord, Lomax, and Wirt in attendance. There were still a number of relatively minor substantive issues in dispute, along with three major issues: the purse for the Tyson bout, the obligation to fight a rematch, and the purse for the rematch. Of all of the open issues, the only one I really cared about was the obligation to fight the rematch.

For the next five hours, King and I engaged in very tense and sometimes heated negotiations, with the Showtime representatives generally acting as mediators, and King's lawyers were becoming increasingly tired of what they characterized as my unreasonable positions. From time to time, especially after midnight, King threatened to terminate the negotiations and kill the deal. I persistently directed the negotiations to the money issues, taking the position that because Evander was almost sure to lose, he needed to be paid enough to make the fight worth taking. Although I had authority from Evander to take the $10 million purse that was on the table, I continued to insist on a compromise between $10 million and $15 million. King would not budge off of the $10 million guaranteed purse, but eventually we began working on a potential upside depending on the level of pay-per-view buys. Around midnight, I asked for a break, purportedly to report to Evander, but really because I just needed a break after working for about 15 hours. Once again, there was a great temptation to declare an inability to reach agreement the next time King threatened to kill the negotiations, but I was not a quitter, and my client was the greatest non-quitter in history. I did walk down the street a few blocks to the White Dove, where I found Evander dancing, pulled him reluctantly from the dance floor to the great dismay of the horde of women competing for a chance to dance with him, reported briefly on our progress, and told him we still had work to do. Evander confirmed that he would sign whatever deal I felt comfortable with, and he went back to the dance floor to the delight of the waiting ladies, and I went back to the negotiating table.

Eventually, King and I reached agreement on a guaranteed purse in excess of $11 million. In addition, we reached agreement on a pay-per-view upside that brought Evander's potential purse to about $15 million. I then indirectly broached the issue I really cared about. I wanted to eliminate the obligation to fight a rematch. I told King I would compromise on every other issue, but I could not allow Evander to sign a contract that legally obligated him to fight a rematch with Tyson if Evander won. Perhaps because it was almost 2 a.m. and we were all very tired and/or perhaps because King had never intended to compromise because he had all the leverage and felt I had pushed him too far, he exploded, jumped up from the table where he was sitting, declared the negotiations terminated and the deal off, and stormed past me. In the process, King knocked me backward onto a sofa.

King was about six foot four (not counting the height of his hair), weighed about 300 pounds, and had been convicted and imprisoned for allegedly killing a man in a fight. I was five foot nine and 175 pounds, but I had successfully fought a lot of men much larger than me in karate and kickboxing bouts, and King was 20 years older than me. My instinct from a lifetime of fighting bullies was to attack King and beat him to a pulp or get beaten to a pulp myself. At the time, after more than 15 hours of putting up with King and his lawyers in a negotiation in which I had no leverage, either scenario seemed preferable to going on with the negotiations. Fortunately, however, I had one urge stronger than instant gratification or suicide, and that was doing whatever it took to get the Tyson fight for Evander. And, like Evander, I would rather die than quit. I was in enough emotional control to realize a physical confrontation with King, regardless of the outcome, would forever kill the chances of the one thing in the world I wanted most at that time. There was a bit of a gasp from everyone, but I got up, brushed myself off, smiled, and apologized for being so clumsy. Everyone breathed a sigh of relief.

I then asked Larkin and Langbord to ask King to meet with me privately to see whether we could resurrect the deal, and eventually King agreed to do so.

I explained that Evander was not just my client, but also a very close friend, that I cared very much about Evander and his children and that Evander was like a younger brother to me. I reminded King that Evander was nearly 34 years old, had been diagnosed with a very serious heart disorder, had been knocked out by Bowe recently, and looked completely shot against Czyz less than a month earlier. I acknowledged that Evander would be a huge underdog. But, ironically in light of later events, I asked rhetorically what might happen if Evander were being badly beaten but Tyson did something to get himself disqualified. I explained that I could not, and would not, under any circumstances, allow Evander to be in the position in which he was likely to be badly hurt or worse if he fought a rematch but would be liable for millions of dollars if he did not. I pointed out that King and I both knew that under those circumstances, Evander would insist on fighting. I reiterated that I could not allow that scenario to take place and that it was the only absolute deal breaker as far as I was concerned. King looked at me for a while. Then we joined the rest of the group, and King instructed Lomax to insert the language I had requested expressly allowing Evander to retire if he beat Tyson, with no liability whatsoever. This provision later proved to be extraordinarily valuable.

At that point, King told me in no uncertain terms that he was finished negotiating, and I could either take the deal or leave it, but it was not going to change anymore. I quickly conceded and told King that I would go get Evander at the White Dove and recommend he accept the deal as it stood. I did exactly that, and at approximately 3 a.m. on Sunday, June 1, 1996, the Tyson versus Holyfield contract was signed. Later that morning, as we got off the plane in Atlanta, I told Evander I had done my part and now it was his job to get ready to beat Tyson. He responded with characteristic simplicity, but to my great satisfaction: "Thanks, you did a good job," which is high praise from Evander. It is not that Evander is unappreciative, but he attempts to hire the best people in their respective fields to be a part of his team and he, therefore, expects excellent work, so he doesn't feel the need to lavish too much praise. I came to understand that continuing to have the opportunity to work for Evander in itself meant he thought I was performing at the highest level.

On my way home, I thought back to how I came to know Evander and how our relationship had grown to the point where he would trust me enough to put himself in my hands to secure the most important fight of his career.

# CHAPTER 2

# THE FIRST YEAR AS CHAMPION: A YEAR OF LITIGATING DANGEROUSLY AND LEARNING THE STRANGE BUSINESS OF BOXING

Evander won the title of undisputed Heavyweight Champion of the World on October 25, 1990, in Las Vegas, by knocking out Buster Douglas, who had knocked out Mike Tyson, the so-called "Baddest Man on the Planet." The next day, on the plane back to Atlanta, ambassador Andrew Young spoke to Evander, who was then 28 years old and had very little business experience, about his future. Ambassador Young told Evander that Evander was now an ambassador for Atlanta, and Young did not want Evander to end up destitute like too many fighters and other athletes before him. He recommended to Evander that the first thing the fighter should do was hire a good lawyer with a top-quality business law firm. Evander asked whether he had any suggestions, and Ambassador Young suggested, among others, my partner, Jesse Spikes, and our firm then named Long, Aldridge & Norman. Ambassador Young explained that Spikes, who is African American and a Dartmouth undergraduate, Rhodes scholar, and Harvard Law School graduate, was a man of impeccable character and that our firm was a full-service business law firm and one of the best in Atlanta. Evander said that all sounded good and got Spikes's telephone number.

## HOLYFIELD

*I did not have a lot of business experience when I became undisputed Heavyweight Champion of the World in 1990, but I knew I would make a lot of money, and it was just common sense to me that earning the money was just half the battle; the other half was keeping the money I made and using it to make more money. Ambassador Young's suggestion—to start with a top-notch law firm and let them help me choose and watch the other people who worked for me and make sure they were putting my interests first—made sense to me, and that is what I decided to do.*

Evander met with Spikes and the chairman of our firm, Clay Long. The meeting went well, and Evander engaged Long, Aldridge & Norman in November 1990, with Spikes as his principal lawyer. The first major legal problem facing Evander was a litigation matter. Spikes, who was not a litigator, had to select a lawyer within the firm to handle the current and any future litigation matters for Evander, and I was the logical choice. I was one of the most senior litigation partners in the firm with substantial experience in representing athletes and almost 15 years of experience as general counsel to the Professional Karate Association. I was also recognized throughout the firm as a certifiable sports nut. I had played football and wrestled in high school and college, was a champion black-belt karate fighter, had fought a professional kickboxing match against one of Evander's sparring partners, and had followed Evander's ring career closely.

The immediate problem was boxing litigation, which I was to learn over the coming years, is an extremely significant part of the business of boxing. In this case, Don King Productions, Mike Tyson, and the World Boxing Council were suing Evander and his promoter, Main Events, and were seeking to enjoin Evander from fighting George Foreman and force him, instead, to fight Tyson. Because Evander was the No. 1-rated heavyweight contender at the time he defeated Douglas, he should have been allowed, pursuant to the rules of the WBC, to fight any fighter rated in the top 10 in his first title defense. His mandatory obligation to fight the No. 1-rated contender should not have been due until one year after his victory over Douglas.

King, Tyson, and the WBC had contended in their suit that Douglas's knockout of Tyson was tainted because, earlier in the fight, Tyson had knocked Douglas down, and Douglas had been given a long count, allowing him to get up before the referee had counted to 10. According to the WBC Championship Rules, if a fight is determined to be "highly irregular or controversial," the WBC may order what is called *an indirect rematch*, which means that the winner of the highly irregular or controversial bout (Douglas) is entitled to one title defense against another opponent (Holyfield), but the winner of that bout (Holyfield) must then fight the loser of the highly irregular or controversial bout (Tyson).

In this case, the plaintiffs had contended that the Tyson versus Douglas bout was highly irregular and controversial due to the alleged long count and that the WBC had properly ordered the winner of the Douglas versus Holyfield bout to fight Tyson next. Evander was scheduled to fight Foreman in April 1991 for $20 million in a fight Evander was very likely to win. If he were forced to fight Tyson first—and were to lose, he would make about the same purse as for fighting Foreman, but he would lose the opportunity to fight Foreman and the additional $20 million that went with it. On the other hand, if Evander fought Foreman first, the Tyson fight would still be there for him and, if anything, would be larger because Tyson would have beaten someone and restored his status while Evander was fighting Foreman. Therefore, the outcome of the WBC case was potentially a $20 million issue for Evander.

As I familiarized myself with the case, I very much looked forward to meeting Evander and getting to know him as we prepared for the WBC case. I had seen Evander many times and had followed his career from a distance, but I wanted to know more about what he was really like. What I knew about him was that he was an incredibly fierce fighter in the ring and seemed to be a gentle and genuinely spiritual man outside the ring. That combination intrigued me. As I prepared to meet with him, I had no idea he would become one of the most important, and inspiring, people in my life. I expected to respect and admire Evander, but I never expected to feel as close to and as protective of him as I became over the coming years.

When I met with him, we hit it off right from the start. Evander looked around my office and noticed that instead of diplomas, I had my fourth-degree black belt, my samurai swords, and my Dai Nippon Butoku Kai (Japanese) Hall of Fame plaque displayed. We talked about my karate career, including my undefeated tour of Japan. Because I represented the Professional Karate Association and attended all of its major professional kickboxing events, I knew Evander was a fan of PKA kickboxing because I had seen him at many of the events. We talked about Jerry Rhome's devastating knockout of "Bad Brad" Hefton to win the World Heavyweight Kickboxing Championship, and I showed Evander pictures of me fighting Rhome in an earlier bout. Evander told me he knew Rhome well because he was one of Evander's sparring partners. My last picture showed Rhome knocking me out, ending my short career as a kickboxer.

"At least you got in there with him," he said after looking at the photograph.

We then talked for a while about boxing in general and about Evander's career specifically. I asked Evander what he thought was his best fight ever, and he turned the question around and asked my opinion, perhaps as a test. I told him I thought his 15-round fight with Dwight Muhammed Qawi in 1986 might have been the best fight ever and was certainly the greatest fight I had ever seen in person. Evander lit up, and we talked about that fight at some length, including the fact that, halfway through the fight Evander felt "like I was trying to swim across the Atlantic Ocean, and halfway across, I knew I couldn't make it, but I knew there was no way to go back." Evander explained that in the last few rounds, he was no longer focused on winning. His goal was to survive and not quit. If he could do that, he would accept whatever decision the judges made. This was one of those pivotal moments in Evander's life when not quitting was a kind of victory in itself. I asked Evander whether it was really true that he lost 15 pounds in that fight, had to be hospitalized, and seriously considered never fighting again, and he said it was true.

## HOLYFIELD

*When I met Jim Thomas for the first time in early 1991 to discuss the WBC case, I was surprised and pleased to have a lawyer who understood firsthand what I did for a living. It was obvious to me that Jim had the kind of mental toughness I wanted in the guy who was going to fight for and defend me in court, and I liked that he knew so much about boxing, which would give him an advantage in boxing-related cases. I was also pleased that Jim knew a lot about me and my career and truly appreciated what*

*I had accomplished and how much work and courage it took to get there. Because he was an athlete himself, Jim has great respect for athletes, and that helped us establish a good relationship right from the start.*

Eventually, we turned to the WBC litigation. I explained the plaintiffs' theory of the case and the procedural status of the case, including the plaintiffs' request for a preliminary injunction against the Holyfield versus Foreman fight and that we would be seeking to stop the litigation and exercise our contractual right to have the case decided in arbitration. I explained to Evander that because Main Events was also a defendant in the case and because Pat English was very experienced in boxing litigation, one option was to allow English to represent both Main Events and Evander. I explained that although the interests of Main Events and Evander were consistent in many respects, they were not identical in my opinion. I explained that Evander had much more at stake in the case than Main Events. Evander said he had already discussed this issue with Spikes and that from now on Evander wanted his own lawyers representing his interests, and he wanted me to represent him in the WBC litigation.

**HOLYFIELD**

*One of the first things I decided when I became the champ was that I was going to take and keep control of my own destiny. That meant that the people who were supposed to be working for me would work directly for me and answer only to me. I did not want someone else's lawyers working for me. I was beginning to realize that there are a lot of conflicts of interest in the game of boxing, and I was determined to avoid those problems by making sure the people around me answered only to me and looked out only for my interests.*

The WBC litigation was on a fast track. The Holyfield versus Foreman fight was scheduled for April 19, 1991. The WBC had voted to strip Evander of his title if he did not fight Tyson next. English, on behalf of Main Events and Evander, had already filed a preemptive suit in the Superior Court of

Sussex County in Paterson, New Jersey, where English had filed other boxing-related cases and had achieved favorable results from Judge Amos Saunders. The suit sought to enjoin the WBC from stripping Evander if he fought Foreman before fighting Tyson. Judge Saunders had entered a preliminary injunction, stayed proceedings in the case, and ordered the disputes between the parties resolved by arbitration. When Evander engaged me to represent him in the case, I entered my appearance on his behalf and took over his representation, working closely with English, who continued to represent Main Events.

The first thing I did was to embark upon a crash course in the business of boxing—not only the written rules, but also the customs of the industry—learning as much as I could as fast as I could. In other words, I wanted to know how things were supposed to work and how they actually worked. Of course, the first thing I needed was a program so I knew who the players were.

Boxing is a worldwide sport, and there are worldwide governing organizations that rate fighters, sanction bouts (for a fee) as championship fights, and recognize champions. I was not particularly surprised that such an organization existed. After all, baseball, basketball, football, and hockey were governed by MLB, the NBA, the NFL, and the NHL, respectively. What was surprising was that there was not one sanctioning body in boxing, but instead three major recognized bodies and several more bodies attempting to become widely recognized. Furthermore, the Big Three sanctioning bodies, the World Boxing Association (WBA), the World Boxing Council (WBC), and the International Boxing Federation (IBF) were often antagonistic competitors. The WBA, WBC, and IBF each had a detailed Constitution and Rules and Regulations, which, although similar, differed and conflicted in many significant respects. In addition, due to the various timing requirements in each sanctioning body's Rules and Regulations, compliance with one organization's requirements often made it impossible to comply with another organization's requirements. Finally, anyone recognized as a champion in one organization would not even be recognized in the others' rankings.

Most states in the United States that allow professional boxing have their own boxing regulatory body with the legal authority to regulate all boxing bouts within the state. In 1991, each regulatory body was totally independent of the others, and the rules and regulations varied greatly. Furthermore, their rules and regulations often contradicted the rules and regulations of the sanctioning bodies. Finally, the quality of the rules and regulations and of their administrators varied greatly from state to state.

Promoters dominated boxing events. As of 1991, there were three major promoters, and many less significant promoters. The Big Three were: Main Events, then headed by Dan Duva; Top Rank, headed by Bob Arum; and Don King Productions, headed by Don King. The promoters were theoretically neutral parties, who basically produced the boxing show and took the financial risk of its success or failure. As neutral parties, they were not permitted to have legal affiliations with managers of boxers. The fact was, however, that most of the promoters had relationships of varying degrees with the managers. Finally, rather than having no stake in the outcome of fights they promoted, the promoters regularly signed fighters to exclusive promotional contracts prohibiting the boxers from fighting in any bout sponsored by any other promoter. This was especially curious to me because, at the time, the Nevada State Athletic Commission's Regulations prohibited such contracts.

Almost every boxer had a manager, who purportedly guided, defended, and protected the fighter. The managers, of course, were supposed to put the interests of their fighters first. Unfortunately, I saw too many situations in which the manager appeared to be more concerned with his relationship with a promoter than with the interests of his fighter. I found nothing inherently wrong with the reality that the promoters generally tried to maximize their own income to the detriment of every other party, particularly the fighters. After all, Hollywood producers try to pay the stars in their movies as little as possible, and baseball owners try to pay their players as little as possible. The fairness and balance lies, at least in theory, in the protection the actor or ballplayer receives from his agent. In boxing, I did not always feel that the managers fought as hard as they should with the promoters on behalf of the fighters. In fact, there were widespread rumors of managers who had surreptitious business relationships with promoters.

Other major players in the boxing business were the television companies. Earlier this meant the broadcast companies, but by 1991, at least the upper end of boxing in North America was distributed to at-home consumers by one of two companies: HBO and its pay-per-view arm, TVKO, and Showtime and its pay-per-view arm, SET. Although these companies certainly benefited the boxing industry by helping generate much more revenue, they also complicated matters by signing fighters to exclusive television contracts. The matter was further complicated by the tendency of some promoters to have at least strategic alliances and sometimes exclusive or other types of confining contracts with HBO or Showtime. And all of these entanglements were exacerbated by the intense rivalry between HBO and Showtime. Finally, there were foreign television distributors all over the world, such as BBC and Sky, in Great Britain, Canal+ in France, and Premiere in Germany, to name just a few.

Another group of major players were the various boxing sites. These consisted principally of casinos in Las Vegas and Atlantic City (and later, on Native-American reservations and so-called riverboat sites) and Madison Square Garden. The reason casinos became the dominant sites was simple. Due to the gambling revenues that could be generated from bringing in big-time gamblers for fights, casinos could afford to pay promoters site fees far beyond the revenues that would be generated by ticket sales. One problem that could arise from the sites was that if the fighters or promoters signed exclusive contracts with particular sites, as, for example, Tyson did with the MGM Grand in Las Vegas, there could be one more hurdle to get over to make a fight.

One other group that I found had a strong influence on boxing was the boxing news media—the newspaper reporters and the television and radio commentators. This was a group of almost all men with drastically varying degrees of knowledge of, and love for, the sport of boxing. Most tried to be objective in a very subjectively judged sport. Others seemed to have one ax to grind or another. Most knew a lot about boxing, and others only thought they did. Some still loved the sport, and others had become entirely too cynical and jaded and seemed to resent deeply anyone who profited from the sport in any way, especially fighters, promoters, and managers, who were sometimes less educated, but better paid, than the reporters were. Most were gentlemen; most were guys with whom one enjoyed having a drink or two and one could trust with a secret. A few were not like that at all.

Finally, last and, unfortunately, perhaps least, came the fighters. I realized that I was strongly biased by my background as an athlete, but on the whole, I found the fighters I met to be courageous, extremely hard-working, dedicated athletes, who all too often received much too little of the revenues they generated. Every promoter operated differently, but on the whole, they paid a fixed amount to a fighter for a given bout. Even when a manager was trying to get the biggest purse possible for his fighter, the promoter could all too often appear to justify lower winnings by manipulating numbers and not including certain revenue streams such as foreign television sales, which were extremely hard to verify. If a promoter had revenues of $10 million for a fight and promotion costs of $4 million, there was nothing to stop the promoter from offering to pay the fighters a total of $3 million and keeping $3 million for himself, particularly if the manager, for whatever reason, was helping convince the fighter the pay-out was adequate and the fighter had never dreamed of making that much money. In such a scenario, from those winnings, the fighter needed to pay his trainers, various other expenses, a sanctioning fee, and his manager's fee, which was often 33 percent.

My crash course in boxing immediately raised many questions in my mind. When I posed these questions to boxing insiders, the answer I usually got was, "You just don't understand the business." Eventually I realized that I was in the midst of a game of "The Emperor's New Clothes" in which too many people pretended to see fairness where none existed so that the very lucrative status quo could be maintained for everyone involved. Lucrative, that is, for everyone but the fighters. Most of the promoters were making big money on boxing promotions while paying the fighters a small percentage of the profits, and most of the managers were going along to get along, hoping to have the promoters guide fighters to them for management. So the cycle continued. The emperor was buck naked, but everybody talked about what a nice new suit he was wearing. With that said, it would be completely unfair to omit the fact that in each category of the major players in boxing I found genuinely good and honorable men (and some women), who truly wanted to make the sport better, cleaner, and more fair for the fighters.

## HOLYFIELD

*I have found that the boxing industry is like every other industry. There are crooked people in boxing, but there are a lot of really good people, too. It seems to me it's the same to some extent in all parts of life. Boxing may be a little worse than some because it is not very regulated, but steps are being taken to change that, and I am in favor of the recent reforms aimed at weeding out the crooked people and crooked practices. In the boxing business, I've met some of the best people I've ever known, along with a few of the most crooked.*

Back to the WBC case. The arbitration proceeding, in which many hearings took place at the Gateway Hilton in Newark, New Jersey, was expedited in an attempt to have them concluded before the Holyfield–Foreman fight, but that did not happen, and we were able to keep the injunction in place through that fight, which, to a large extent, was victory in itself. The case needed to proceed, however, because there were still issues about whether Evander was obligated to fight Tyson at all, and the WBC still had the ability to strip Evander of the WBC title and give it to Tyson, should the WBC, King, and Tyson prevail in the case. I spent a long spring and summer in Newark, with Evander present for some of the hearings but absent for many more because his presence was not necessary, and he needed to train for the Foreman fight.

The case was suspended for the Holyfield versus Foreman fight in Atlantic City on April 19, 1991. Spikes went in earlier, and I arrived on the night before the fight in time for a star-studded dinner hosted by Donald Trump and Marla Maples. Spikes was gracious enough to have a seat added at his table for me, and I met many celebrities that night, including Trump and Maples, Dennis Hopper, Will Smith, and many others. At this time, I was merely a faceless, nameless hand to shake, but I met most of these people on other occasions during the next decade, and I always remembered this night as the beginning of this fun perk of working with Evander.

At the fight, I shook the hand of the man on my left and introduced myself, and he said his name was Isom Coley. I told him that I did not believe I had ever seen a hand as large and powerful as his, and I asked his connection to the fight. He said he was Evander's father. He said he had only recently met his son and was very happy and proud to be invited to see his first title defense. I remarked to Coley that he must have been a very powerful man in his youth, and he told me he still was, but he could no longer pick up trucks. I asked what he was talking about, and he told me that, back in Atmore, Alabama, where Evander was born and Coley still lived, he was often broke. He said when that condition occurred, he would generally try to find some guys who didn't know him and bet them each $1 he could pick up the back end of a pickup truck, which he never failed to do.

## HOLYFIELD

*I never met my father until I was grown up, and when I did finally meet him, one thing that had always been a mystery to me finally made sense. All my life I had always been exceptionally strong for my size. When I met my father, I understood where that unusual natural strength came from. My father is one of the most physically powerful men I have ever met. I have big, strong hands, but my father's hands are even bigger and stronger. I never would have used steroids no matter what, but I was blessed not to need anything other than great genes and lots of hard work to be exceptionally strong.*

Evander beat Foreman in a great 12-round decision, and the celebration at the post-fight party was really tremendously fun. I was amazed to see Evander come in and do the Electric Slide on the dance floor as if he had not done anything that night. I later learned that if Evander is not unconscious and has no broken bones, he can dance all night.

**HOLYFIELD**

*The Foreman fight was a really tough fight. Other than my sister Eloise, who can fold a heavy bag with her punch, George is probably the hardest puncher I had ever faced, and he came in to the fight in great shape. I usually use my shoulders against my opponent's body to create some space if my opponent is trying to hold me, but with George, it was like banging my shoulder against a brick wall. The fight went 12 rounds and took a lot out of me, but because I've always been in great shape, I recovered quickly, so it was only natural that I would dance at the post-fight party. We always danced at home when I was a kid, and it's one of my favorite things to do. When I was an amateur boxer, dancing was part of my training routine. I would dance all night and then go run real early in the morning before I went to bed. Then I'd get up and do my boxing workout, take a nap, and go dancing again.*

While the WBC case continued, a very difficult and urgent issue arose that had to be resolved quickly. There had been discussions between Duva and King regarding a first-ever Holyfield versus Tyson fight, but the discussions were bogged down. The alternative for Evander was a rematch with Foreman. Spikes asked whether I would participate in a meeting to discuss this issue and provide my opinion to Spikes and Evander on the litigation implications of the decision, such as whether we could win the case if the WBC tried to strip Evander again. Duva, English, Shelly Finkel (who at the time was Evander's manager), Evander, Spikes, and I attended the meeting, and there was a lot of discussion about projected revenues from a Holyfield versus Foreman fight as opposed to a Holyfield versus Tyson fight. The proposition was that Evander would make more money in a rematch with Foreman than in a fight with Tyson, because Tyson and King would demand much more than Foreman and his promoter, Bob Arum. Therefore, the smart move was to fight Foreman in a rematch, a fight Evander was very likely to win, and keep Tyson and King waiting to soften them up for future negotiations. At this point in the discussion, we all took a break.

During the break, I secretly pulled Evander down the hall and into an office. I told him that I knew he grew up without much money and so did I. I told him that I doubted that the relatively small differences in such huge sums of money being discussed were very meaningful to him, because they meant very little to me.

"You're right," he said with a smile.

"Evander, athlete to athlete, if everything else is equal, who do you want to fight?" I asked.

"Definitely Tyson."

"I was sure of that, so why don't you just go ahead and fight him?"

"But they're saying—"

"Evander, this is your career, not theirs," I interrupted him, "and they all work for you, you don't work for them."

"You know, you're right."

When we reconvened, Evander said he had been thinking, and he decided he wanted to fight Tyson. There were protests, but Evander firmly gave the directive to try to make the Tyson fight.

## HOLYFIELD

*My mother taught me to be polite and respect my elders, and I grew up doing that, so it was natural for me to accept the advice of people older than me who were experts in their professions.*

*When Jim reminded me that I was in control of my own life and career and that the people around me worked for me, I was able to see things in a new light. Ever since that time, I have always listened respectfully to the advice of my advisers, but I always remember that I have the right and responsibility to make my own decisions about my own life and career.*

Wanting to make the Tyson fight and making it happen were two completely different things. Under the rules of the sanctioning bodies, if an agreement could not be reached between the champion (Evander) and the highest-rated available challenger (Tyson), the fight would go to what is called *a purse bid* for which any promoter could bid to put on the fight by offering a total purse for the two fighters. That purse would be split with 75 percent going to the champion and 25 percent to the mandatory challenger. Everyone on both sides understood and acknowledged that in the case of these two fighters, the fight would never be made with Evander making three times the winnings of Tyson. Our side was willing to compromise at 2:1, but King was insisting on an even split, to which we were never going to agree. In addition, the ongoing arbitration case fanned the flames of enmity between Main Events and King and made discussions slower and more difficult.

When planning a pay-per-view event, such as a major boxing card, a great deal of thought must go into the timing of the event. Obviously, one would not schedule a pay-per-view bout against the Super Bowl or the World Series, but even lesser events can hurt pay-per-view sales. Major college sporting events must be considered as well as the public's cash flow. For example, mid-December is a bad time for pay-per-view, because people are using discretionary funds to pay for holiday gifts, and January is the month when holiday credit card bills arrive. Furthermore, in the summer many people are away from their homes and do not have access to pay-per-view cable boxes. One of the best weekends for a major pay-per-view boxing event has been the second weekend in November, when not much else is going on, and that was the target date for Holyfield versus Tyson or the Holyfield versus Foreman rematch if the Tyson fight could not be made. Add that to the fact that a major pay-per-view event needs at least 90 days and preferably 120 days of lead promotion time, and it was clear that by late July, we were running out of time to make

Holyfield versus Tyson, and everyone in the Holyfield, Tyson, and Foreman camps knew it.

Consequently, Duva began discussions with Arum for a contingency plan to fight Foreman in a rematch if we couldn't make the Tyson fight, and an agreement appeared to be reachable. Then there appeared to be a possible breakthrough in the deadlock between Duva and King. Jose Sulaiman, president of the WBC, agreed to host a meeting in New York between the Holyfield and Tyson representatives to discuss a settlement of all disputes and an agreement on a Holyfield versus Tyson fight. Although Duva, English, and Finkel were extremely skeptical, they felt obligated to accept the invitation or lose the public relations battle for who was to blame when the fight did not happen.

English and I were at the Gateway Hilton in Newark for a hearing in the arbitration case when English got a call from Duva about the meeting. I called Spikes, and we agreed that I needed to attend the meeting as Evander's personal representative. Although I did not know it at the time, Duva and English were close to making a deal with Arum on a rematch with Foreman. I later learned that Duva had told Arum that a meeting had been called to make one last effort to agree on Holyfield versus Tyson but that Duva doubted that King was sincere and predicted an agreement would not be reached. Duva had said he felt King was just trying to keep us from making the Foreman fight until it was too late. Consequently, Duva apparently had told Arum to go ahead and have papers drawn up for Holyfield versus Foreman so we could move quickly if the meeting with King went as Duva predicted.

Duva, Finkel, English, and I met in the lobby of the Parker Meridian Hotel in midtown Manhattan to discuss our strategy for the meeting. I said that I was very encouraged about Evander getting the fight he truly wanted. Duva, Finkel, and English all were a bit amused by what they perceived to be my naïveté. They explained that King was just trying to prevent our making a deal for the Foreman fight and that our goal was to demonstrate a willingness to compromise with King and preserve, as well as we could, our ability to put the blame for a lack of agreement on King. English told me that King would almost certainly try to work on me directly and separate me from our group, as divide and conquer was one of King's most consistent tactics. Duva told me I needed to understand that Sulaiman was not the neutral party he purported to be but instead was there to help King.

King was also in the lobby of the Parker Meridian at a table with Lomax and Mike Tyson's personal representative, his co-manager John Horne. When the time for the meeting approached, we all went to the elevator to go to Sulaiman's suite, which was the designated site for the meeting. After some consideration of taking separate elevators, King jovially suggested that we were all friends and ought to travel together, and so we did. In the elevator, King repeatedly referred to one of the prominent boxing writers named John Saraceno as "Saracenovitz," and laughing his deep, extraordinarily loud, laugh. I had no idea what he was doing, but when I got off the elevator and saw how angry Finkel, who is Jewish, was, I understood that King had begun to go to work.

Once we were in Sulaiman's suite and the obligatory pleasantries were exchanged, we got down to business. The game appeared to be for King and Duva to debate in front of Horne, Sulaiman, and me in an effort to convince the WBC and the representatives of the two fighters which promoter was being unreasonable and preventing the fight the two boxers wanted. King seized the initiative and began by complimenting me about my fine reputation and then feigning total shock at how Spikes and I were breaching our fiduciary duties to Evander by allowing Main Events and Finkel to prevent the fight Evander wanted just because they were afraid he would lose. I tried to keep a poker face but smiled inwardly at how the prediction of the divide and conquer strategy had already been fulfilled. I looked King in the eyes and told him I understood my fiduciary duty to Evander very well and took it extremely seriously but thus far was of the opinion that it was either King or Tyson who was being unreasonable. I now had both sides calling me naïve and, in response, I promised King I would listen carefully with an open mind and report accurately to Evander on what occurred in this meeting.

Duva then asked for a few minutes to explain the objective basis for his negotiation position. Duva then launched into an extremely impressive analysis of the projected revenues and expenses of the Holyfield versus Tyson fight. As it became clear to me that Duva was very persuasive and appeared to be entirely reasonable, I caught something out of the corner of my eye. King had pulled his trouser leg of his very expensive suit all the way up to his upper thigh, and was methodically scratching his bulky, hairy, bare thigh. It was like watching *The Jerry Springer Show*, too gross and disgusting to watch but difficult to turn away from. When I finally pulled my eyes away, I looked around at the group and saw that no one was paying attention to Duva, and everyone's attention was focused on King. After a while, King looked up.

"I'm sorry," he said slyly. "I didn't mean to interrupt."

The tactic worked well, and Duva's flow was entirely disrupted. That incident taught me a lot about King. First, he was obviously smart, clever, and manipulative. Second, there was nothing he was unwilling to do to gain an advantage.

King then responded with his own equally impressive presentation of the revenues and expenses projected for the fight. He was just as well prepared as Duva and equally persuasive. But for my bias in favor of my own teammates, I would not have been convinced either side was being unreasonable but would have concluded that they disagreed on financial projections. It appeared to me that each promoter had succeeded in defending the reasonableness of his position, and a compromise was unlikely. At this point, Horne called for a break to talk to King.

We took a 30-minute break while King and Horne left the room. When they returned, King made a lengthy and hyperbolic speech about his love of boxing and of the American people and that sometimes one needed to sacrifice his own interests for the greater good. King announced that to bridge the gap and make the fight possible, he would sacrifice his own extremely fair and reasonable share of the revenues, accept Duva's proposal, and agree to terminate the arbitration case. I could almost hear "God Bless America" in the background.

After some closing pleasantries and congratulations all around, Duva, English, Finkel, and I left. It was about 10 p.m., and we decided to get something to eat and discuss our next move. We took the short walk to Mickey Mantle's Restaurant on Central Park South. Once we had ordered, I proposed a toast and expressed my appreciation on behalf of Evander for getting him the fight he wanted on such favorable terms. They looked at me with amusement and explained that we had not reached agreement on anything. They said they knew King—and I did not—and that he was merely trying to kill our deal with Arum, and then he would renege on the deal. I expressed my doubts and said it looked to me like Tyson sent Horne to make sure King did whatever was necessary to make the deal. They explained that even if I were right, King would kill off the Foreman fight and then renegotiate the Tyson fight from strength. Even though I was not as skeptical as the others, we all agreed that King had us in a difficult position. Duva and King had reached an oral agreement, and considering both public relations and potential liability, we could not afford to appear to be the side that reneged.

English suggested the strategy we all agreed upon. We would find King and tell him the deal was open only until 9 a.m., at which time we would make the Foreman fight if our deal, or at least a written outline of our deal, was not signed by then. This would smoke out King's intent and preserve the Foreman option for a few more hours. We had heard that King was on his way to one of his favorite New York restaurants, the Palm Too, to celebrate the deal. Duva reached him there and made the proposal, and King and Duva agreed that English and King's outside lawyer, Bob Hirth, of the law firm of Sidley & Austin, would work through the night to paper the deal. I offered to stay with English, but he said he would not vary from the provisions of the Foreman fight we had approved months earlier without calling me, and I should just be on call in my hotel room.

By 9 a.m., a deal was signed, and we had a written agreement for Holyfield versus Tyson. Duva then called Arum and told him that to our amazement, we had reached an agreement. Arum was not a happy camper. I reported to Spikes, who reported to Evander. The fight was scheduled for November 9, 1991. We were all very pleased, and I thought we had successfully resolved a very difficult situation. In this I now admit I was a bit naïve about the world of boxing. Within days, Arum and Foreman filed suit in the Superior Court of Harris County, in Houston, Texas, where Foreman lived, claiming that Duva had agreed orally to a Holyfield versus Foreman fight and that Main Events, Finkel, and Evander were now breaching that agreement by fighting Tyson. They sought immediate injunctive relief and, in lieu of injunctive relief, huge monetary damages. When the suit was served, English was out of the country on a rare and well-deserved vacation with his family and could not return immediately. I quickly hired local counsel in Houston to help represent Evander, and I helped English arrange local counsel for Main Events, Duva, and himself. I immediately left for Houston.

## HOLYFIELD

*When I heard that we had a deal for the Tyson fight, I was very happy, because that was the fight I wanted. When I heard a few days later that Foreman and Arum were suing to prevent the*

*Tyson fight, I was a bit disturbed, but I was confident Jim would be able to handle it and, in any event, there was nothing I could do about it. I have always tried to have the strength to work on things I can do something about, the patience to accept the things I cannot do anything about, and the wisdom to know the difference, as taught in a famous prayer, and this was no exception.*

After a preliminary hearing, at which the judge scheduled the case for trial on a very fast track, both sides agreed to a day of mediation to try to resolve the dispute. In preparation for the mediation hearing, I met with Evander to prepare him to tell his part of the story to the mediator. As any careful litigator does, I wanted to take Evander through a certain critical conversation he had had and to make sure he presented the facts in the most favorable light possible consistent with the truth. I explained this to Evander. He said he needed to eat before we began work, and then when he was finished eating, he told me he needed to lie down while we talked. As I talked, Evander appeared to fall asleep, and each time I woke him up, he fell asleep again. I told him I had been up almost all night preparing and needed his cooperation. He laughed.

"Jim, anybody ever tell you you're a little too intense?" he chuckled.

I realized he had been playing with me. He sat up and turned serious.

"I know you're doing your job, but you don't need to worry about me, I remember exactly what was said."

"But Evander, there are millions of dollars at stake."

"What difference does that make? If it's $1 or $1 billion, my mama taught me one thing I know is true: The truth can only hurt you one time, but a lie can hurt you for all eternity."

Although I still insisted that Evander at least tell me what he remembered so I could be fully prepared, the sincerity of his conviction touched me and confirmed my initial conclusions that I was dealing with a very rare and special person.

**HOLYFIELD**

*Many people have principles they say they live by, but when the money gets big enough, they find ways to justify giving up their principles. Because I truly believe in the Word of God as revealed in the Bible and because of my respect for my mother and what she taught me, it doesn't occur to me to twist the truth just because the consequences of telling the exact truth might be severe. As my mother taught me, a lie is an offense against God and will hurt you for eternity, but the truth can only hurt you once. I knew Jim wasn't trying to get me to lie, but I wanted him to understand that I would not be willing to twist the story even a little bit no matter how much was at stake.*

Eventually, after a lot of hard work, some long nights, and cooperation from a number of people, we were able to work out a mutually agreeable and beneficial settlement of the case. With a contract signed for Holyfield versus Tyson and the WBC case and the Foreman case settled, we all breathed a sigh of relief and assumed we had a clear and unobstructed path to Holyfield–Tyson. This proved to be unduly optimistic and failed to take into account the volatile and unpredictable opponent we had selected. Several weeks before the fight, we were informed that Tyson had incurred an injury to his rib cage while training for the fight.

**HOLYFIELD**

*Of course, I was disappointed when I heard the Tyson fight would be postponed because it would mean stopping training and then starting over, but injuries and postponements are a part of boxing, and this delay was just one more thing I would need to accept as God's will. I consoled myself with the fact that a few weeks wouldn't make much difference and would go by quickly and then I would have the fight I was looking forward to.*

Then, a few weeks later, the other shoe dropped. Tyson was indicted for allegedly raping a Miss Black America pageant contestant named Desiree Washington in Indianapolis while he was attending the pageant. Washington alleged that she went to Tyson's room late at night and that he forced her to have nonconsensual sexual relations. Tyson denied the charges. Due to a number of different factors, this meant that Tyson would be unavailable to compete in the ring until the criminal rape case was resolved, which would take, at a minimum, several months.

## HOLYFIELD

*When I found out Tyson had been accused of rape and that he would be unavailable to fight at least until his trial ended, I was very disappointed, but once again, I needed to move on. When I realized I then had the opportunity to fight someone else, I really wanted to try to bring the fight to Atlanta so my fans there would have a chance to see me fight. Most of them would otherwise never have a chance to see a heavyweight title fight, and this was a chance for me to give something back to the community that had been so supportive of me.*

Suddenly, Evander had no opponent, and no one knew whether or when Tyson might be available again. The decision was made to go forward with Evander's title defense on November 23, with a new opponent in Atlanta at the Omni Arena. The new opponent was Francesco Damiani of Italy, a very large, strong-looking, relatively slow fighter of unexceptional skill but with a good enough record and punching power to be a credible opponent. All good fighters train specifically for the next opponent, and Evander trained against sparring partners who resembled Damiani in size and style.

Damiani arrived in Atlanta for the typical prefight promotional activities and to become acclimated to the site of the fight. Suddenly and inexplicably, Damiani allegedly suffered an injury that put him on the next plane back to Italy. There was some speculation that Damiani's injury was somehow related to his watching Evander train. In any event, the tickets and the television airtime and advertising had been sold, and efforts were made to find a last-minute emergency substitute for Damiani. Typically, it is hard to find a quality opponent who just happens to be in shape to fight for a world heavyweight title with virtually no advance notice. For better or worse, such an opponent was found in Bert Cooper. Cooper was a tough, feisty, very quick, short, compact veteran reminiscent in style of Smokin' Joe Frazier. In other words, the polar opposite of Damiani, for whom Evander had been training.

**HOLYFIELD**

*It was risky for me to accept an opponent like Bert Cooper when I had trained for a guy who was pretty much the opposite, but I didn't want to disappoint my fans in Atlanta, so I agreed to go forward. Some fighters might have made the mistake of looking past a guy like Cooper, who did not have a big name, but I had already learned that there is no such thing as an easy fight for me. Maybe it's because I'm not a particularly big heavyweight, or maybe it's because I do not belittle or try to intimidate my opponents, but for some reason, most guys I fight end up fighting one of the best fights of their lives. I knew I had to stay focused, and I expected Cooper to fight a great fight. Otherwise, I risked disappointing everyone in Atlanta in addition to losing the titles I had worked so hard to get and keep.*

On the night of the fight, the Omni was sold out, and virtually everyone in attendance was there to watch Evander knock out Cooper, who was a heavy underdog. Cooper, though, continued a tradition that started before him and has continued through the present, and that is the tendency of underdogs to fight the best fights of their careers against Evander. Cooper had no intention of lying down for Evander before the home crowd. After four competitive rounds, Cooper rocked Evander with a hard shot to the head, and Evander staggered against the ropes. The referee called a technical knockdown, which he had the discretion to do if he determined that Evander would have been on the canvas but for being held up by the ropes. The referee stopped the bout to give Evander the knockdown count, which some people opined allowed Evander to clear his head. Evander survived and went on to win a technical knockout in the seventh round. Atlantans got to see their champion win a heavyweight title bout, but not without a scare. Years later, when I referred to a potential fight as a relatively easy fight, Evander reminded me that, for him, there are no easy fights.

With the successful conclusion of the Cooper fight, Evander was 2-0 in the ring and effectively 2-0 in the courtroom for 1991. An unforgettable year of litigating dangerously and learning the strange business of boxing came to an end with a very merry holiday season, made a bit merrier by Evander having earned more than $25 million that year.

# CHAPTER 3

# 1992 TO 1994:
# THE ROLLER-COASTER
# YEARS IN WHICH EVERY
# SETBACK WAS AN
# OPPORTUNITY FOR A
# COMEBACK

In early 1992, it appeared as though Mike Tyson was not going to be available within the foreseeable future, so another opponent needed to be selected. That opponent was Larry Holmes, one of the greatest heavyweight champions of all time. After holding the heavyweight title for more than seven years, Holmes lost it in September 1985 but had launched a comeback. By June 1992 Holmes had defeated his last six opponents, including the then-undefeated tough ex-Marine heavyweight, Ray Mercer, and the only two fighters who had ever defeated Holmes were world champions Michael Spinks and Tyson. Although by no means at his peak, Holmes was still skillful and dangerous.

**HOLYFIELD**

*It was disappointing to me that the boxing press would criticize me for deciding to fight Larry Holmes in the spring of 1992. They said I was being protected because my first three title defenses were against two old fighters [Foreman and Holmes] and one journeyman [Cooper]. The truth is that in each decision I chose the best available opponent. George Foreman was obviously not over the hill when I fought him in 1991, as was proven by the fact that he won the heavyweight title from Michael Moorer three years later. I then chose to fight Mike Tyson and would have fought him if he had not become unavailable. When Tyson became unavailable and the first replacement backed out of the fight, Bert Cooper was the best guy available on such short notice. Then I chose to fight Larry Holmes, who had only two losses— both to world champions—and who had just beaten Ray Mercer, who three years later fought Lennox Lewis in a fight many experts thought Mercer won. Holmes was not at his peak when I fought him, but he was, without question, still one of the 10 best heavyweights in the world and probably in the top five.*

Evander won a unanimous decision against Holmes and, predictably, was given little credit for having done so. The press once again clamored for Evander to fight the best available contender.

In mid-1992, Riddick Bowe was a 25-year-old, six-foot-five, 250-pound fighter with perhaps the best skills of anyone his size in heavyweight history. Bowe was almost universally recognized as the best heavyweight contender in the world, and many felt his size, skill, and youth would be too much for Evander to handle.

**HOLYFIELD**

*After Holmes, I chose to fight Riddick Bowe, who was considered by almost everyone to be the best heavyweight contender in the world. The press wrote that I was finally fighting the best available guy, but the truth was that I had always tried to fight the best available guy. I was looking forward to the challenge of fighting Bowe and to finally getting the respect and credit from the press I deserved.*

When he was younger, Bowe had been one of Evander's sparring partners, and the two were friends. Then, Evander could handle Bowe with relative ease, but now Bowe declared he was going to be too big and too strong for Evander. Bowe, aided by the press, did a good job of baiting Evander into a slugfest.

Bowe repeatedly said he knew Evander would run from him, rely upon speed, and fight him exclusively from the outside in an effort to steal a decision, and the press opined that that was the only way Evander could beat Bowe. Evander, who usually does not allow what others say to influence him, was inclined to prove in this case that he was a complete fighter who could beat any other boxer any way the opponent wanted to fight, including proving he could beat Bowe in an up-close and personal toe-to-toe war.

On November 13, 1992, Evander fought Bowe at the Thomas & Mack Center in Las Vegas in one of the great fights in heavyweight history. From the outset, Bowe was talking trash, hitting low and after the bell, and otherwise trying to anger Evander—and it worked. Evander abandoned his original game plan of boxing and moving and settled into a power-punching contest with the much bigger Bowe. It was not as if Evander had no rationale in taking this alternative approach. He remembered the younger Bowe, growing into his body and lacking stamina. Evander gambled that if he were willing to take the punishment of a slugfest, Bowe would eventually tire and become vulnerable.

## HOLYFIELD

*My strategy was influenced to some degree by Bowe and the press telling me I couldn't beat Bowe toe to toe, but that wasn't the key factor. I had been in the gym with Bowe, and I knew he wasn't a real hard worker. He was one of those guys who was so big and talented that he didn't think he needed to work that hard. I felt sure that he would not work hard enough to get in shape to go 12 rounds. I fought Bowe toe to toe partly because he was hitting me low and after the bell and talking too much, but the main reason was that I was sure he would get tired if we fought a war. I knew I could take the punishment, and when Bowe tired, I would take him out. My whole strategy was based on the assumption that Bowe couldn't go 12 rounds. In that sense I was wrong, and I left the fight in his hands instead of fighting my best fight.*

The fight was an absolute war. Round after round Evander traded punches with Bowe, and remarkably Bowe did not seem to tire. Although Bowe was slowly but surely winning the war of attrition by using his great size advantage, Evander refused to change to a hit-and-run outside boxing strategy. As I sat at ringside and watched the fight, I was sad and disappointed to see Evander losing, but I could not have been more impressed with his courage. Early in the legendary 10th round, Bowe caught Evander with a devastating punch, and Evander was hurt badly. Bowe followed up with more power shots. Evander fought on, nearly out on his feet, with pure courage and a relentless and almost superhuman refusal to quit. It looked like it was only a matter of time until Evander was knocked out, and a part of me wanted it to be sooner rather than later to stop the punishment. Bowe knocked Evander all over the ring, and somehow Evander stayed up. I had never before, and have never since, seen a fighter take more punishment and refuse to go down or quit. Suddenly, a truly unbelievable thing happened. Not only had Evander survived the pounding from this devastating puncher, but with 30 seconds left, Evander became the aggressor and was hitting Bowe hard with his own power shots. When the bell rang, everyone in the arena rose for a wild standing ovation for these two courageous warriors and especially the smaller guy with the biggest heart in boxing. It was the greatest single round of boxing I have ever seen, and many boxing historians count it as one of the best rounds ever. The battle continued through the 11th and 12th rounds, and Evander later said he wished there had just been one more round because he was about to take Bowe out. At the end of the fight, the two battered warriors stood in the ring to await the decision while they received another thunderous standing ovation.

When Michael Buffer announced Bowe to be the winner of the bout, Bowe was mobbed by everyone in the ring. He was ecstatic, and Evander was dealing with the first loss of his professional career. Bowe was immediately proclaimed by virtually everyone in boxing to be the next great heavyweight champion, in the league with Joe Louis and Muhammad Ali, expected to reign for many years to come with his insurmountable combination of youth, size, power, and boxing skills. Bowe was seen as the prototype of the huge modern heavyweight champion.

Evander also received a great deal of praise but with more than a hint of condescension. Evander was praised for his courage and indomitable spirit, but the implication was that he should be very proud to have been heavyweight champion at all, being an overachieving blown-up cruiserweight. It was on this night that I realized a very peculiar phenomenon in boxing. At any given time, with only rare exceptions, the boxing media acknowledge only one or two heavyweights as being great, and all others are varying degrees of bums. The fact that Evander had taken Bowe 12 life-and-death rounds and had lost a very close decision did not earn him the respect of being a great heavyweight and at that moment, the second best in the world. Instead, Evander was written off and almost universally advised, if not implored, by the boxing media to retire. Generally speaking, in boxing if a boxer is not the champ, he is either a bum, not ready for prime time, or over the hill. If golf were boxing, Tiger Woods would be champ, and Phil Mickelson, Ernie Els, Vijay Singh, Retief Goosen, and Sergio Garcia would be considered a bunch of bums.

## HOLYFIELD

*When the decision went against me in the Bowe fight, I experienced something that I had never experienced as a professional and had not experienced at any level in eight years. I had lost. The fight was a close competitive fight, though, so I had nothing to be ashamed of, but you would have thought all I had done before that fight had suddenly disappeared. I felt invisible. That night I learned that, in boxing, at any given time, it's all or nothing. You're either on top, or you're just one of the guys in line trying to get there.*

On the flight back to Atlanta, Evander thought long and hard about what he was going to do, and he came to the conclusion that he should retire. Evander arrived at his home, just south of Atlanta, intending to announce his retirement. When he met with his then-eight-year-old son, Evander Jr., however, to discuss the Bowe fight and how Evander lost, Junior cried and reminded Evander that he had told Junior no one could beat him. Evander consoled Junior and told him he just fought the wrong fight and that he could beat Bowe. When Junior did not seem to be completely convinced, Evander said he was going to teach Junior the most important lesson of his life. He was going to prove a man could do anything if he works hard enough and never quits. He was going to go back and beat Bowe for the sake of Junior and his other children and children all over the world.

## HOLYFIELD

*If it had not been for my intense love of my children, I would have quit boxing after that first Bowe fight. I had been the champ and made a lot of money, and I could have gone on to other things, but I needed to teach my kids, and especially my oldest son, Evander, the most important lesson about life I knew. If you never give up and you work hard enough, you can accomplish anything. To teach Evander and his brothers and sisters this lesson in the best way I knew how, I decided I would come back, beat Bowe, regain the title of undisputed Heavyweight Champion of the World, and then retire.*

When Evander announced his plans to remain in boxing and to regain the undisputed heavyweight championship, there was a cry of protest from mostly well-meaning people who thought he was on the way down and should retire. Evander, however, had his mind made up that he would regain his titles. Bowe made the quest to regain the undisputed title a bit harder. Bowe faced a mandatory bout against the WBC's highest-ranked challenger, Lennox Lewis. When Lewis insisted on his right to fight Bowe next or have Bowe stripped, Bowe beat Lewis and the WBC to the punch and gave up the WBC title, literally throwing it in a trashcan at a press conference. Lewis took advantage of the mandatory rules and was allowed to fight Tony Tucker for the vacant WBC heavyweight title, which Lewis won, splitting the three major heavyweight titles for the first time since they had been united by Mike Tyson in 1987 when Tyson ironically beat Tucker.

**HOLYFIELD**

*When Bowe refused to follow the rules and fight his mandatory challenger, I was very disappointed. Tyson had worked hard to unify the heavyweight titles, and I had worked hard to keep them together. Now Bowe was acting like he was bigger than boxing. When Bowe gave up his WBC title and Lennox Lewis won the vacated WBC title, I readily recognized Lewis as the WBC champ, because no one man is bigger than the game, and part of being the champ is fulfilling your obligations by following the rules.*

In addition to planning a strategy to regain his titles, Evander had to deal with the difficult psychological issues of the change in his status in the sports world. As I later witnessed firsthand from attending events with Evander and many of the world's best athletes in every sport, any fighter recognized as the legitimate heavyweight champion is truly the king of the sports jungle. The top athletes in baseball, football, basketball, hockey, golf, and tennis all pay homage to the champ, especially if the champ has been around for a while and commands respect by his behavior, like Evander. I do not know why this is. The sport of boxing has nowhere near the respect among the sports media and the public as the major team sports, but the athletes themselves still put the champ on top. I have witnessed this personally over and over, with the most popular athletes in the world. My speculation is that even the greatest team sports stars are not sure they would have the courage to take the kind of punishment the champ takes over and over, all alone, with no protection but his own hands. Whatever the reason, the position of Heavyweight Champion of the World commands respect, admiration, and sometimes embarrassing displays of hero worship by otherwise sensible people, and the fall from being the champ to being someone who used to be the champ is a huge drop. Suddenly, the former champ needs to wait in line, and even pay for things, for the first time in years. Due to his faith and the love and support of his family, Evander handled the disorientation better than most, but even for him it was hard. One of the things Evander did was to reassess some of the people around him. During the year following his loss to Bowe, Evander dropped his trainers, Lou Duva and George Benton, and hired Emanuel Stewart as his new trainer. Also in 1993, Evander decided not to renew his management contract with Shelly Finkel. Finkel was one of the people who opined that Evander should retire. Although Finkel's motive was presumably pure and reflected a genuine concern for Evander, Evander did not want people around him who did not truly believe in him and his vision of his future.

## HOLYFIELD

*I believe in God and His plan for me, but I have never required that anyone else share my religious beliefs. I believe, of course, that belief in Jesus Christ is the pathway to heaven and everlasting life, and I wish that for all people, but I have never tried to impose my beliefs on others who are not open to receiving them. Each person has the right to believe whatever he wants about God and anything else, but when it comes to my boxing career, I do not want anyone around who does not share my belief about the out-*

*come of my next fight. If someone does not believe in me and my
success, he should not be part of my team.*

Unfortunately, one of the people who jumped into the vacuum when
Finkel's contract was not renewed was someone who, in my opinion, either did
not have Evander's best interests at heart or did not have the knowledge to represent Evander in boxing matters. Although no contract was signed, Evander
allowed the recording star once known as M.C. Hammer, and later called simply Hammer, to act as his manager beginning in 1993. In my opinion, Hammer
knew very little, if anything, about the world of boxing but convinced Evander
he could do the job because he knew show business. To say that Hammer projected an aura of self-importance would be a huge understatement. I felt that
Hammer was interested only in promoting his own interests and posed a threat
to Evander. To say we did not get along is another understatement.

On the other hand, Evander was wise and fortunate enough to keep one
constant on his team. Tim Hallmark had been Evander's strength and conditioning coach since 1984. Hallmark was truly dedicated to Evander and was an
innovator in developing strength and endurance for boxing. Hallmark was
then, and to this day has always been, looking for the best training techniques
for Evander. While all sorts of other changes were occurring, he was there to
keep Evander on track to come back and fulfill his vision of regaining the
heavyweight championship.

**HOLYFIELD**

*In Tim Hallmark, I have been fortunate to have a man who truly
cares about me. He is always trying to help give me an advantage,
and he really knows his business. Tim cares enough about me to
push me and even argue with me, and sometimes that is what I
need. Partly because of Tim, I knew that every time I stepped in
the ring, I would be in the best shape possible.*

Generally, before a rematch is set up between two fighters, it is best for
each to take an interim bout to restore the loser's prestige with a win. With the
hope and expectation of a rematch between Evander and Bowe later in 1993,
Evander took a bout with a tough journeyman Alex Stewart, and Bowe fought

both Michael Dokes and Jesse Ferguson. Evander and Bowe won their bouts, and soon thereafter, the rematch between Evander and Bowe was scheduled for November 6, 1993. This time, however, Evander was a heavy underdog, but Evander planned to fight a fight he could win. He planned not only to outbox Bowe but to outthink him as well.

## HOLYFIELD

*The first time I fought Bowe, I allowed myself to rely on something outside my control. I assumed that, if I fought Bowe toe to toe he would eventually tire, and then I would be able to take him out. That was an assumption, and assumptions are often wrong. The assumption that Bowe would not be able to go 12 hard rounds turned out to be a mistake. For the rematch, I was not going to rely on any weaknesses in Bowe. Instead, I would rely on my own strengths. That way, victory would be in my own control. I planned to do things I could do better than Bowe, moving in and out and "dancing" around the ring.*

The Holyfield versus Bowe rematch took place almost exactly one year after the first bout in an outdoor arena erected behind the host hotel, Caesar's Palace, on the Strip in Las Vegas. Typical weather in early November in Las Vegas is warm days and cool evenings. Because Vegas fight times need to be coordinated with the Eastern time zone, the main event of a Vegas fight comes on between 8 p.m. and 8:30 p.m. Vegas time or 11 p.m. to 11:30 p.m. Eastern time. Although the temperature drops rapidly in the dry desert air, we assumed that the temperature would not be a problem as early as 8 p.m., especially under the intense lights around the ring. But on that evening the temperature was dropping unusually fast, and by the time the main event came on, it had become quite cool even though I was wearing a sweater and sport coat. By the time all of the celebrities were introduced, the fighters made their respective ring walks, and the preliminary ceremonies had taken place, the air around the arena was no longer cool; it was cold—breath-seeing cold.

When the fight began, a different dynamic was immediately apparent. Evander was not trying to outbomb Bowe. He was sticking and moving, throwing combinations and dancing away. At the halfway point in the 12-round fight, Evander was clearly leading, and the crowd began to sense a surprise.

They had no idea. Between the fourth and fifth rounds and again between the fifth and sixth rounds, I, along with others around me, began to watch what appeared to be a hang glider hovering several hundred feet above the arena. It seemed to be nothing more than a curiosity, but it was odd and disturbing.

In the seventh round, Evander continued to outbox Bowe, and Bowe was becoming frustrated and impatient. By mid-round, Evander had Bowe in trouble after landing a series of power shots, and it appeared that the huge young champion might not make it out of the round. Then suddenly I caught something out of the corner of my left eye, and an instant later a guy with a hang glider and a fan motor crashed into the lights at ringside near Bowe's corner. Everyone was shocked, and the fight was stopped. I was stunned by the appearance of the Fan Man but more angry and upset that Evander's momentum had been stopped. Then a group of angry spectators decided to punish the Fan Man. In fact, they jumped on him and hit him with every object they could grab, and he was fortunate not to have been killed. Caesar's security took him out on a stretcher, and the whole time Evander stood soaking wet from sweat in the cold air. Although Bowe was obviously also exposed to the cold air, he was also recovering from the beating he had been taking. It would have been so easy for Evander to condemn his bad luck and feel sorry for himself, but instead he kept his faith and his focus and prepared himself to begin again. When the fight resumed more than 20 minutes later, Evander picked up where he had left off, and at the end of 12 rounds had clearly beaten Bowe in a stunning upset. Evander had stunned the boxing world.

"And once again, the Heavyweight Champion of the World, Evander 'Real Deal' Holyfield!" ringside announcer Buffer shouted.

Within almost exactly 12 months, Evander went from the top of the sports world, to a precipitous plunge where he was written off as someone who never deserved to be there, to the top once again.

### HOLYFIELD

*Before the fight, a minister told me that there would be a distraction in the fight and that I needed to stay focused when it occurred. When the fight was stopped because of the Fan Man, I was disappointed because I had all of the momentum and I had Bowe in trouble. Then I remembered the warning I had received, and I knew that warning was God's way of telling me not to get upset or distracted, so I calmly waited until the fight could be resumed and then I went right back to work, doing what I had been doing before the interruption. Although others were surprised I beat Bowe, I wasn't surprised at all. I had told my son, Evander, I would beat Bowe to show him and his sisters and brothers that a man can do anything with enough faith and hard work, and I never had any doubt I would keep that promise.*

By beating Bowe, Evander inherited Bowe's obligation to fight the IBF's mandatory challenger, Michael Moorer. Rather than attempting to delay the Moorer fight, Evander agreed to take that very tough fight instead of first taking a break for a relatively easy voluntary defense. In training camp leading up to the Moorer fight, Evander sustained a serious injury to his left shoulder. Evander had terminated his relationship with Emanuel Stewart and hired Don Turner, who had trained Larry Holmes, as his new head trainer. Turner was worried about Evander's shoulder, but rather than reporting the injury and postponing the fight, Evander opted to go forward, as scheduled, believing he could beat Moorer, injured or not.

**HOLYFIELD**

*Obviously, I was taking a risk fighting Moorer with an injured shoulder, but I didn't want to postpone the fight. I had fought many times when I had injuries, and I had never in my life ever postponed a fight. I have often said that if I postponed my fights every time something hurt, I would never fight. Looking back, the shoulder injury was not just a nagging pain. It was a serious injury, and it was a mistake not to postpone the fight to allow it to heal.*

The fight took place on April 22, 1994, with Evander as the favorite. After a round of the two fighters feeling each other out, Evander landed a left hook in the second round and tore a ligament in his shoulder. Instead of accepting the fact that he could not continue, Evander insisted on going forward. Hallmark later confirmed that Evander could not lift his left arm to throw a jab or block a right jab from the left-handed Moorer. Nevertheless, Evander insisted on staying in the fight, believing he could and would win no matter what.

At the end of the fight, the judges scored the fight for Moorer by the narrowest possible margin, not giving Evander the usual 10-8 score when he knocked Moorer down. One of the judges actually scored that round 10-10.

Characteristically, rather than making excuses, Evander accepted the loss, but after the fight, he was in severe pain due to the torn ligaments in his left shoulder. He was taken in an ambulance to Valley Hospital in Las Vegas for treatment. Evander was treated with various drugs for pain and for some reason, put on a plane to Atlanta. When he landed, he was examined by a doctor who did not have the benefit of an accurate medical history and concluded that he had fought with a serious heart defect and should never fight again. Evander accepted the news with his typical equanimity and announced his forced retirement. Evander accepted the medical determination that he should retire as the will of God and expressed gratitude for the great career he had had, the many blessings he had received as a result, and the support he had been given.

## HOLYFIELD

*It was a huge disappointment to be told I could never box again, especially after being declared the loser in a fight I felt I had won. I had been fighting for more than 20 years. I loved the sport, and I still felt I was the best heavyweight in the world. But it seemed to be God's will that I stop, and I felt lucky to have this heart problem discovered without suffering any serious problem. I was told I could expect to lead a normal life but could never box again. The news could have been a lot worse, so I prepared myself to move on to other things. I had had a great career in boxing and had made a lot of money, and it was time to find out what God had in store for me next.*

Between November 1992 and April 1994, a period of less than 18 months, Evander had gone from the top of the sports world, to being a has-been, to once again being at the top, to being finished. Evander's ability to handle this exaggerated roller coaster was a preview of his unprecedented ability to live out his belief that "every setback is an opportunity for a comeback." It is one thing to state an inspirational slogan, but it is quite another to live it when the chips are down. As much as any other, this phrase captures the very essence of Evander Holyfield.

# CHAPTER 4

# MID-1994 TO MID-1996: A SECOND COMEBACK

E vander truly accepted as God's will his forced retirement in mid-1994, but soon thereafter, he attended a revival hosted by televangelist Benny Hinn, who was believed by his followers to have the power through touch to heal even the most serious infirmities. At the revival, Evander was touched by Hinn and was declared healed. Later, Evander began to feel as though there was nothing wrong with his heart and questioned whether he was really impaired. When tested, Evander's heart showed no significant impairment. Whether due to a misdiagnosis in the first place or a cure at the Hinn revival, Evander's heart was not defective by late 1994, and he was declared physically capable of resuming his boxing career.

## HOLYFIELD

*Following my fight with Michael Moorer, my heart was not working properly, and then, after much prayer and attending the Benny Hinn revival, my heart was once again working properly. In that sense, I had been "healed." I don't know exactly how I was healed, but I know that I was healed by the hand of God.*

At the end of 1994, Evander made one other change in the team around him, a change that had a huge impact on my life. Evander decided he wanted to work directly with me as his principal attorney. With Evander not having another manager, but instead being self-managed, my new role meant that I would handle most, if not all, of the tasks handled for other fighters by their managers. To define my role in this regard, Evander and I settled on the title boxing management adviser. Although I have often been called Evander's manager in the press and have even been nominated for Manager of the Year by the Boxing Writers Association of America, I have been careful not to call myself Evander's manager but instead to call myself his management adviser to emphasize the fact that Evander managed his own career and made all final decisions.

My first order of business as Evander's legal counsel and boxing management adviser was to work with Main Events on developing a plan to resume Evander's boxing career. First, an appropriate opponent needed to be found and convinced to take the fight. Evander's comeback fight was scheduled for May 1995, which meant that he would have been out of the ring for over a year. Conventional wisdom in boxing would dictate selection of a very easy, or soft, opponent. On the other hand, Evander was a former two-time Heavyweight Champion of the World, was accustomed to fighting for very large purses, and did not want to drop back too far in the amount he made. These two goals— taking an easy comeback fight and making a lot of money—were directly contradictory. Evander, contending that for him there are no easy fights, insisted on keeping his market price up and fighting whatever opponent was necessary to do so. As a result, the opponent selected for Evander's comeback fight was the very tough and highly regarded "Merciless" Ray Mercer. At the time Evander agreed to fight Mercer in Atlantic City in May 1995, Mercer was probably one of the five best heavyweights in the world and by no means a typical comeback opponent.

## HOLYFIELD

*Even though I did not get the decision in my fight with Michael Moorer a year earlier and had not had a fight in over a year, I still felt I was the best heavyweight in the world, and I did not want to start my career over by dropping back and fighting a mediocre opponent. I knew Ray Mercer was one of the toughest*

*guys out there, and that was exactly the kind of opponent I want-*
*ed to establish that I was back.*

Mercer fought a very tough fight, but midway through the scheduled 10-rounder, Evander knocked Mercer down. It had to be a hard shot, because that was the first time Mercer had ever been knocked down in his life. Evander clearly won the closing rounds, was awarded a unanimous decision by the judges, and his latest comeback was launched.

At that point in time, the heavyweight division of boxing was in disarray. When Bowe refused to fight his WBC mandatory bout after winning all three major titles in November 1992, the belts began to split up and continued on that course. In May 1995, when Evander beat Mercer in the first step of his comeback, Mike Tyson had recently been released from prison and was beginning his own comeback against Peter McNeeley in August 1995. Lewis had lost his WBC title to Oliver McCall by way of knockout the previous September, and McCall had just successfully defended the WBC title against Larry Holmes. Michael Moorer had lost his WBA and IBF titles to George Foreman in November 1994, but Foreman then was stripped of his WBA title, which was won by Bruce Seldon in April 1995 in a knockout of Tony Tucker, for the vacant WBA title. Meanwhile Foreman defeated Axel Shultz in a controversial decision to retain his IBF title but refused to fight Shultz in a mandatory rematch and lost his IBF title, which was vacant and would be awarded to the winner of a bout between Moorer and Shultz.

The bottom line as of the time Evander began to decide who to fight next after Mercer was that the WBA champion was the relatively unknown and lightly regarded Bruce Seldon; the WBC champion was Oliver McCall, who had five losses and was generally considered to have beaten Lewis with a lucky punch when Lewis got careless; and the IBF title was vacant and would be contested by two fighters, Shultz and Moorer, who had recently been beaten by Foreman. In short, there were no attractive title bouts available to Evander in the fall of 1995. But there was a big and meaningful fight that could be made: a third fight with Bowe. HBO favored the fight because it would either re-establish Evander or re-establish Bowe at or near the top of the heavyweight division. Either way, HBO won, and to increase the benefit, HBO promoted the bout as the fight between the two best heavyweights in the world for a

People's Championship and arranged for the New York *Daily News* to offer a People's Championship belt to the winner.

On the night before the Bowe fight, I stopped by Evander's suite. He was sitting at the dinner table with Tim Hallmark talking, and I joined them. Evander is always remarkably loose going into a fight, and this night was no exception. There was, however, one unusual occurrence. While we were talking, Evander got up and looked at the thermostat, which showed the temperature as normal.

"It's so hot in here; I'm burning up," he said.

Hallmark and I looked at each other with some concern, because we were not hot at all. I did not say anything else, because the last thing you would want to do with a fighter on the night before a bout is tell him he must be sick. Little did I know, everyone who was in camp in Houston already knew Evander recently had been seriously ill with hepatitis A for several weeks. Apparently the others had been told by Evander not to tell me.

## HOLYFIELD

*After the fight, it was obvious that I had made a mistake by not postponing the fight to allow me to recover from the bout with hepatitis. My doctor advised me to postpone the fight, and I should have listened to him, but Mike Tyson had recently postponed a fight due to a hurt hand and had been severely criticized by the boxing media. I didn't even have anything to point to as a reason for a postponement except that I didn't feel well. If I postponed fights every time I didn't feel well, I'd hardly ever fight. Part of being a fighter is overcoming the urge to make excuses to allow yourself to avoid fighting. But sometimes this way of thinking can go too far. I had fought two of my last three fights with serious physical problems both times with disastrous results, and I vowed never again to allow my courage to overrule my judgment in deciding when to postpone a fight.*

The next night Evander fought Bowe at the outdoor arena behind Caesar's Palace where they had fought two years earlier. Early in the fight Evander completely outclassed Bowe.

At the end of the first round, I thought, "That may be the best round I've ever seen Evander fight."

In the sixth round, Evander continued to dominate, then hurt Bowe with a combination, and toward the end of the round had Bowe nearly out on his feet. Bowe was defenseless, and one more punch or maybe a slight breeze would have knocked him out. I was ecstatic and thought the fight was over. Then, I couldn't believe what I was seeing. Evander just stood in front of Bowe without moving. He did not throw the one punch needed to knock Bowe out, and eventually the round ended. Evander Holyfield, one of the best finishers ever who had always had a tremendous killer instinct when his opponent was hurt, let Bowe survive.

During the break between rounds, I was disappointed, but only slightly, because it was obvious that Evander would take Bowe out in the next round. When the next round began, however, it was clear to me something was very wrong with Evander. He was doing almost nothing, and as the round went on, Bowe began to recover. The fans in attendance seemed stunned at Evander's passivity. In the eighth round, Bowe hit Evander with a hard shot on the shoulder, knocking him down. Although Evander was not badly hurt, he was so slow and awkward in trying to get back up that the referee stopped the fight, awarding a TKO to Bowe.

At first I was crushed, because it looked like Evander's comeback had failed. Then I began to worry about a more serious consequence. Was there really something wrong with Evander's heart that all of the tests had somehow missed? Had I helped Evander get back in the ring when he should have retired? Would he recover? Did his heart suffer serious or irreparable damage in the fight? As I walked through the crowd, I heard many of the people expressing the same sort of concerns. Many were saying there must be something wrong with Evander. Some others opined that Evander was simply and obviously over the hill.

One of the collateral consequences of fighting Bowe in Las Vegas while in a weakened state was that new questions were raised about Evander's health, and the Nevada State Athletic Commissioners were upset that Evander looked like there was something wrong with him, making them look bad for allowing the fight to proceed even though he had been diagnosed with a serious heart problem after his last fight in Nevada. When they heard the rumors that Evander had concealed an illness, they were even more upset. Although there was no formal action, several of the commissioners, along with the official commission doctor Flip Homansky privately suggested to me that Evander might never be allowed to fight in Nevada again.

Where Evander would fight his next fight was only part of the problem. Losing two of his last three fights, having been (technically) knocked out for the first time in his career, and looking impaired in his most recent fight, Evander was, from a marketing point of view, damaged goods. To get Evander back into the ring, Main Events promoted a tripleheader heavyweight card in May 1996. Evander would fight former light heavyweight champion and more recently cruiserweight contender Bobby Czyz in a bout some boxing writers sneeringly called a battle of two over-the-hill blown-up cruiserweights. Lewis, attempting to rehabilitate his image after being knocked out by McCall, would fight Evander's opponent from one year earlier, Ray Mercer. Former heavyweight champion Tim Witherspoon was scheduled to fight Jorge Luis Gonzalez. Partly due to the concerns expressed in Nevada about Evander's health, the triple-header card was booked at Madison Square Garden. After some debate and much testing, we were able to get Evander licensed to fight in New York, with English, who represented Main Events and knew the local authorities better than I did, taking the lead.

Although Holyfield versus Czyz was the feature fight, some of the boxing press suggested it was the least intriguing of the three heavyweight bouts. There was a lot of dialogue among so-called boxing experts about whether Evander was far past his prime and ought to retire. There was nearly universal agreement that Evander needed to look spectacular against Czyz, who was not highly regarded as a heavyweight, if Evander was to become once again a serious player in the heavyweight picture. The prevailing wisdom was that, unless Evander dominated Czyz and looked good doing it, his career as a marquee fighter would be over.

To prepare for the Czyz fight, Evander traveled to Houston. While he was on his way to Houston, Evander's mother and sister, Eloise, were involved in a car accident. Evander's mother slipped into a coma and although she regained consciousness briefly, eventually died. The funeral was extraordinarily sad for those of us who knew how much Evander loved and respected his mother. For Evander, however, it was apparently much less painful than for some others due to his genuine faith. I was amazed to watch as a number of people who had fainted were carried out of the church service for Evander's mother by prearranged nurses, but Evander himself was remarkably strong and calm. He spoke at the service and called upon the entire family to pull together and love each other as his mother would have wanted. It was a beautiful and heartfelt dedication to a mother he clearly loved, who had gone on to heaven.

## HOLYFIELD

*My mother was the most important and influential person in my life and was largely responsible for my success in life, and obviously I did not want to lose her. But I was not crushed by her death, because I knew it was God's will, and I was happy for my mother because she was finally with God. My only concern was about the other members of my large family. My mother had always been the head of the family and kept all of her children in line. Now, I decided I needed to take on that role.*

At the Czyz fight, Evander had his older children in attendance for the first time ever. This was supposed to be a relatively easy fight, and Evander wanted his children to share the victory with him. I sat with the kids and, my best friend, former Atlanta Falcons quarterback Kim McQuilken, and Bowe. Just before Evander's fight with Czyz, Lewis fought Mercer. Bowe and I compared notes throughout the Lewis versus Mercer fight, and when it ended, we both felt strongly that Mercer had beaten Lewis. To our surprise, Lewis was awarded the victory, but it was clear that Evander's victory over Mercer a year earlier deserved more respect in light of Mercer's performance against Lewis.

When Evander and Czyz came into the ring and I looked at the two of them, Evander as chiseled as a human can be and Czyz looking like the bulked up cruiserweight he was, it seemed obvious that Evander would win easily and quickly. But when the fight began, it did not go as expected. Czyz fought very carefully, trying to avoid being knocked out. It is a truism in boxing that a fighter who is merely trying to survive is hard to knock out. Evander faced this situation many times. After the first few rounds, the crowd was restless, and Evander did not look good. Although Evander was winning, he was not dominating Czyz as expected. After the fourth round, Evander came back to his corner and rather than sitting down, leaned on the ropes facing outward with his mouthpiece dangling from his mouth. Boxing writers wrote the next day that it was "obvious" that Evander was exhausted and had gotten old. When Evander leaned on the ropes looking out, he was directly in front of me and at one point looked directly at me. I was certain he was not tired, but instead was more bored or perhaps disgusted.

## HOLYFIELD

*After the fourth round of the Czyz fight, I was totally disgusted. I was fighting a guy who was not trying to win but instead was trying not to get knocked out. I couldn't see the point of the whole thing, and I was embarrassed that I was fighting a guy who wasn't even a true heavyweight, and I couldn't knock him out.*

In the fifth round, Evander managed to get some hard shots in on Czyz, and Czyz was clearly shaken. During the break after the fifth round, Czyz went back to his corner and told his trainers he could not continue. The trainer told him it was his eyes that were bothering him. Czyz argued that it was not his eyes, but the trainer continued to insist it was his eyes. Czyz then failed to come out for the sixth round, and Evander was awarded a TKO. Czyz's corner then claimed that some caustic substance had gotten into Czyz's eyes, which forced him to quit. The implication, if not outright charge, was that Evander or his trainers had used some substance to cause Czyz's eyes to be burned.

## HOLYFIELD

*The claim that I had put something on my gloves or body so it would get in Czyz's eyes was crazy. First, I had been successful my whole life without cheating, and if I won by cheating, I would be cheating myself of true victory. Also, going into the fight I was absolutely sure I would beat Czyz easily. Why would I take a chance of using some burning substance when it could just as easily have gotten in my eyes as his?*

Czyz's camp protested the fight on the grounds that Evander and/or his corner used an illegal substance that got in his eyes, but when the New York State Athletic Commission listened to a tape of Czyz's corner after the fifth round, the commission advised the Czyz camp to drop his protest, lest the inquiry go in a direction they would not welcome. The Czyz camp withdrew the protest, but Czyz never did apologize to Evander for the false accusation his corner made.

Although Evander won the Czyz fight, the inescapable fact was that he looked bad doing so. It looked like something was wrong with him in November 1995 against Bowe, and it looked like something was wrong with him against Czyz in May 1996. The consensus among all of the boxing "experts" was that Evander had gotten old, was over the hill, and needed to retire. Although there was a hue and cry for Evander's retirement, much of it well intentioned, Evander knew he was not done, and he thoroughly convinced me he still had his best work ahead of him. Tyson had recently won the WBC title by defeating Frank Bruno, and he was scheduled to fight Seldon for the WBA title in September. Evander wanted to regain the title of undisputed Heavyweight Champion of the World, and fighting Tyson was the fastest way to do so. Evander wanted Tyson, and Tyson was promoted by King.

# CHAPTER 5

## HOLYFIELD VERSUS TYSON I: SHOCKING THE WORLD

S oon after we reached agreement in Toronto on the terms of Holyfield versus Tyson, word that the fight had been made leaked to the press, and soon after that we had a press conference in New York at the Rainbow Room at the top of Rockefeller Center to formally announce the fight, which was named "Finally" and would be held at the MGM Grand in Las Vegas. While Evander and I sat on one side of the dais and Tyson and his co-managers, John Horne and Rory Holloway, sat on the other side, we were forced to endure the rantings and ravings of Tyson's highly paid professional motivator, Steve Finch, better known as "Crocodile." Crocodile kept up an incessant stream of extremely high-volume threats and predictions of all of the horrible and humiliating things Tyson was going to do to Evander. Although this tactic had been very effective at intimidating Tyson's opponents in the past, Evander was merely amused.

### HOLYFIELD

*The idea that some guy, who was going to be safely outside the ring when the fight started, thought he could scare me by hollow threats about what some other guy was going to do made me laugh. I truly believe in God, and no man on earth can ever scare me in the least, especially a guy who wasn't even going to get in the ring with me. It did make me wonder, though, why Tyson needed a motivator. If one of my people would have yelled threats at Tyson, I would have ordered him to stop immediately. I don't see how anyone could get motivation from people around him acting tough. I sure wouldn't.*

After the usual hype, stories, mixed metaphors, malapropisms, and newly invented words from Don King, the fighters and their representatives were asked to speak to the hundreds of members of the press in attendance. Because Tyson was the WBA champ, Evander's side spoke first, which meant that I spoke, followed by Evander. I was respectful and low key, complimenting Tyson as a great fighter but who I believed would be beaten by Evander. There were snickers and rolling eyeballs from the Tyson side and many of the media members. Evander then spoke. As always he first gave glory to God. He then thanked Tyson for giving him the opportunity to fight for the WBA title. Evander then simply and matter-of-factly stated that he was certain he would win.

Next the Tyson side spoke, which meant Tyson's co-managers, Horne and Holloway, followed by Tyson himself. Horne and Holloway were, in my opinion, outrageous and abusive. I thought their behavior was despicable, and when I was later asked to describe them and called them "thugs in Armani suits," I intended the remark to be off the record rather than in *USA Today*, where it appeared, although the phrase accurately reflected my opinion. They falsely stated that Evander had called Tyson a rapist and in retaliation Tyson was going to rape Evander. Tyson then spoke briefly and after promising to punish Evander, announced disdain for the boxing press, noting that the only use he ever made of their articles was to "wipe himself." In a word, the tone and behavior of Team Tyson was disgusting to me and to a lot of others.

As usual, after the statements from the fighters and their representatives, the floor was opened to questions from the press. In response to a question to Horne and Holloway about when Evander had called Tyson a rapist, I responded that the answer was never. Horne asked how I knew that, and I explained that I was at the press conference at which Evander had commented on Tyson's arrest and had said he had no idea whether Tyson was guilty but that rape was a serious crime and anyone who committed it should be punished. This led to an argument from Horne. Evander then took the microphone from me.

"You know what, Mike, no matter what happened and no matter what anyone says, you and I are still going to fight, and that's all that matters," he said.

Evander received robust applause from most people in the room, and I believed he had just won his first psychological battle with Tyson.

### HOLYFIELD

*I knew Tyson's people were trying to get him pumped up by telling him I had called him a rapist. I knew I had never done that, but I didn't feel like arguing about it. It didn't matter who said or did what in the past. The simple fact was that Tyson had to fight me alone in the ring, and his motivators were not going to be in there with him, and I decided to remind him of that. I was actually more sure I would win after hearing all this irrelevant talk. It meant to me Tyson was not sure he would win and was trying to talk himself into being confident, but talk can never make anyone confident.*

After the questions from the press, the fighters were asked to pose for the traditional press conference photograph facing each other. Tyson and Evander stood up and faced each other. Tyson had a very menacing look on his face and aggressively stepped up to Evander's face, almost touching it. Unlike most others before him, Evander did not back up, flinch, or react in any way but simply stared right into Tyson's eyes. The tension was palpable. I was right next to the pair of fighters, and I must admit I was very tense and not at all sure this would end peacefully. Evander remained totally calm and motionless, and after a few seconds while the press called for the fighters to face them, Tyson looked away first, and Evander scored another small victory. Leaving the press conference, I was even surer Evander would beat Tyson. I knew Evander was superior mentally and spiritually and would win if he could prepare himself physically to match Tyson's raw power and ferocity.

## HOLYFIELD

*I could see that Tyson was disappointed that he couldn't intimidate me as he had almost everyone else he had ever fought, but he should have known I would not be afraid of him, because I had never been afraid of him even when almost everyone else in the Olympic camp was.*

After the press conference, Evander began preparations for his training camp in Houston. Evander's typical prefight training period was eight to 10 weeks. For this fight he planned to train for 16 weeks. Sixteen weeks of training at the pace and level Evander trains was a tremendous commitment and demonstrated how serious Evander was about this fight and how much he respected Tyson as a fighter. Before he could leave for camp, however, he needed to solve one very serious logistical problem. He needed someone to take care of his children while he was away. At that time, Evander Jr. (age 12), Evette (age 11), and Ewin (age 6) lived with Evander full time. Ebonne (age 9) and Eden (age 1) split time between Evander and their respective mothers. Emani (age 4) lived in California with her mother and visited with Evander on holidays and whenever he was in Los Angeles.

A few years earlier, Evander had met a woman named Janice Itson, who was a recent medical school graduate from Chicago. Janice was a Bible scholar, and she and Evander talked frequently on the telephone. Evander admired Janice's intellect and her knowledge of the Bible, and he frequently consulted with her by telephone on a wide range of issues in his life. With Evander scheduled to leave for camp in Houston soon after his annual July 4 party at his estate and still no one to take care of the children, Evander asked Janice to come to Atlanta and take care of his children until the fight took place on November 9, and Janice eventually agreed when Evander offered to pay her to do so.

Janice moved into Evander's house, and Evander went to camp in Houston, returning to Atlanta each weekend to see his children and the woman he was dating, Jennifer "Sandy" Bryant, who was living in Mississippi and came into Atlanta on weekends to spend time with Evander. At one point, Evander had contemplated marrying Sandy and even had my firm prepare a prenuptial agreement, but things were on hold for the time being. From my perspective, not much seemed to have changed. Evander and I talked almost daily, and I knew there was a woman named Dr. Itson at the house to take care of the children, but I did not meet her. I met with Evander on weekends, and if I saw anyone else at the house, it was the kids and Sandy.

Immediately after the press conference, I was primarily occupied with the project of getting Evander licensed to fight in Nevada. In Nevada, licenses are valid until December 31 of the year in which they are granted. Evander had had a license for his November 1995 fight with Riddick Bowe, but it had expired. The problem was that there were serious questions about Evander's health in 1994, and those issues were renewed and exacerbated when Evander "hit the wall" in his fight in Las Vegas against Bowe in November 1995. At that time, there was some suggestion that Evander would never be allowed to fight in the state again.

Evander's doctor, Chris Vaughns, and I developed a strategy for regaining Evander's license. First we would make absolutely sure to our own satisfaction that Evander was fit to fight. Vaughns performed a full battery of tests and was completely convinced Evander's health in all areas was superior to almost every other person he had ever examined. We then selected one of the most prestigious medical centers, if not the most prestigious medical center, in the world—the Mayo Clinic in Rochester, Minnesota—to examine Evander. The Nevada State Athletic Commission (NAC) agreed to accept the findings of the clinic if they were clear and unambiguous, and the NAC gave us a list of tests it wanted performed.

Although Evander had undergone some of these tests at the Mayo Clinic to get his license for the Mercer fight in 1995, we agreed to have them performed again, along with additional tests, because the Bowe fight in 1995 had occurred after those tests. While I was working on getting Evander licensed in Nevada for the Tyson fight, there were numerous articles written suggesting that the people around Evander (meaning primarily me) were not giving him the advice he needed, which was to retire. The consensus was that Evander was going to get hurt or worse and only the people he trusted could stop the carnage. One article even suggested that I should be prosecuted for facilitating the fight by working to get Evander licensed for it. I would be less than honest if I said these opinions had no effect on me. They did make me stop and think. In the end, though, I trusted Evander, Dr. Vaughns, the Mayo Clinic, Don

Turner, Tim Hallmark, and my own instincts more than people who knew far less about the facts, and I pressed forward to get Evander what he wanted.

Evander had all of the tests performed that the NAC wanted, and finally it came time for me to receive the results. Because this was a legal issue as well as a medical issue, I asked the head of the Mayo Clinic, John Scott, not to issue a written report until he had given me an oral report. When the day came for the oral report, I called Dr. Scott feeling hopeful but nervous.

"Jim, I have determined that Evander does, in fact, have an abnormal heart… " Dr. Scott began.

My own heart sunk; I could not believe my ears.

Fortunately, Dr. Scott quickly continued, "Evander has one of the strongest hearts we have ever tested at the Mayo Clinic to my knowledge; our normal testing protocol cannot even test his limits."

He also told me everything else looked great. To minimize the chances of anyone trying to find a problem where none existed, I drafted a letter for Dr. Scott to sign that listed each test performed and concluded that, having performed each of the foregoing tests, Evander was fit to fight with no restrictions rather than just sending the test results to Nevada. The NAC, with the guidance of Dr. Flip Homansky, agreed to license Evander but not before making me promise that, from now on, any medical problem Evander had going into a fight in Nevada (such as the illness before the Bowe fight) must be reported immediately to the NAC.

## HOLYFIELD

*All of the medical tests were unpleasant and inconvenient, but they actually helped me. Being the most intensely tested athlete ever made me more sure than any other athlete that I was in superb health and condition and could push myself beyond any limits without any danger.*

During July and August, Evander worked with Hallmark on getting his body into the best shape it had ever been in. In September, Evander began his actual boxing training, including sparring. One of Evander's sparring partners was a very tough guy from the projects in New York City named Gary Bell. Bell was as strong as a bull and able to simulate Tyson's fighting style and aggression. Unfortunately, for the first few weeks, Evander was not dominating Bell the way he should have been able to dominate an unranked, relatively inexperienced heavyweight. On more than one occasion when I called Evander to ask how things were going, he sounded frustrated. Turner, assistant trainer Tommy Brooks, and Hallmark were genuinely concerned, and Evander was discouraged. There were truly times when Evander began to wonder whether all those who thought he was well past his prime were right. But the lessons planted indelibly in Evander's character by his mother at an early age would not let him quit.

## HOLYFIELD

*During the early weeks of sparring before the Tyson fight, I was at first disappointed and then frustrated that I could not handle Gary Bell the way I thought I should be able to. I knew Tyson would be much tougher than Gary, and if I couldn't handle Gary, I would be in deep trouble against Tyson. There were times when I began to get down and doubt myself, but then I reminded myself that faith and hard work and a refusal to quit can overcome anything. I kept believing, kept working, and refused to quit, and gradually I got better and stronger.*

About a month before the fight, Evander, who was in Atlanta for the weekend, called me one afternoon and said he needed the prenuptial agreement we had prepared previously. I naturally assumed that plans for the marriage to Sandy were back on, and I was happy for Evander and Sandy. I reminded Evander that we were going to the Braves playoff game the next day and suggested we meet at my firm's offices in downtown Atlanta where I could give him the prenuptial agreement, and we could then go on to the game. Evander said that would work.

The next day, Evander and I met at the firm's offices. I gave Evander the prenuptial agreement, and we left in my car for the Braves game. On the way, I congratulated Evander and told him I was happy he had worked things out with Sandy.

"The agreement is not for Sandy; it's for Dr. Itson," he explained.

At first, I was stunned as I realized Evander was planning to marry someone I had never even met. Then I felt a bit hurt as I realized so much must have happened about which I knew nothing. There were a few awkward moments of silence.

"How well do these agreements work if you're already married?" Evander reluctantly asked me.

I nearly wrecked the car. When I pulled myself together, I was finally able speak.

"Evander, what are you talking about?"

"Well, last night I got married to Dr. Itson," he answered.

I then went from stunned to truly frightened for my friend.

"Congratulations, don't worry about it," I said, trying to sound convincing. "Let's just enjoy the game, and we'll talk about this on Monday morning after I've thought about it."

We went to the game, but I was extremely worried, and I could tell Evander sensed my concern.

The tension between us was broken by an incident at the game that demonstrated how genuine Evander's confidence was about the outcome of the Tyson fight. Everyone around us was trying to get Evander's attention, and he had to ignore the calls or he would have missed the game entirely. But when a Coke vendor repeatedly called out to Evander, he responded, because Evander had sold Cokes at Braves and Falcons games years earlier.

"Mr. Holyfield, you've got to beat Tyson; I've bet my house on you," he said.

It was generally known that the betting odds on the fight were, at that time, 17 to 1 against Evander, so there was some concern in the crowd for the man who was likely to lose his house.

"That's great. In November you'll have 17 houses," Evander nonchalantly responded to the delight of the vendor and those around us.

On the following Monday, October 6, I did some research and consulted with my partner, Debby Ebel, who heads our domestic relations practice, and then called Evander in Houston. I told him there were problems with an agreement signed after a marriage, and I explained the legal issues to him. I provided several alternative strategies along with the advantages and disadvantages of each. Finally, Evander said he did not want to follow any of the strategies because he was sure he would never get divorced from Janice.

**HOLYFIELD**

*I realized, of course, that some people would think I had made a mistake by getting married without a prenuptial agreement. When I talked to Jim, I realized I was not legally protected, but I didn't want to do any of the things he suggested, because I was determined to make all of these legal issues irrelevant by doing whatever was necessary to make my marriage to Janice work.*

Later that day, I called Janice, introduced myself, and congratulated her on her marriage to Evander. Although I continued to be wary, I wanted very badly to like Janice and determine that she would be good for Evander. Soon afterward I met Janice, and we pledged to work together closely to help Evander in every way possible. I found Janice to be bright and very energetic, and we did, in fact, work together closely as she got up to speed on all of Evander's business activities, except for boxing, which Evander and I continued to handle exclusively.

Evander continued to progress in camp and began hurting sparring partners and, in some cases, sending them packing. Eventually, Evander was even dominating Bell, and the mood in the camp became very optimistic. At various times during October, I spoke to Turner and Hallmark and they told me Evander was looking better than ever. On Saturday, October 19, Evander turned 34 years old, and I took him a birthday present, a special club to help his golf game. I told Evander that day he looked stronger and more confident than I had ever seen him, and I meant it. He said he felt better than ever, and I believed him.

Two weeks later, Team Holyfield assembled in Las Vegas on Sunday, November 3, 1996, six days before the fight. While many champions have had, and continue to have, huge entourages, Team Holyfield was a small, close-knit group of people, every member of which has always had an important function. Turner, Brooks, and Hallmark had obvious roles as Evander's trainers and corner men. Sharon Steuart was Evander's massage therapist. Mike Weaver and Eddie Gilbert handled all of the many logistical duties involved in setting up and maintaining a training camp. Sharon's husband, Alan, made sure we had no security problems while in camp. Dr. Vaughns made sure Evander's health was optimal. Jim Strickland came in for the fight to serve as the cut man in the event Evander got cut. I handled all legal issues, boxing business issues, regulatory issues, press relations, and the many details that most boxers' managers handle. Our entire entourage consisted of only 10 people, probably the smallest of any major heavyweight champion in boxing history. Every one of us had a purpose, we respected each other as some of the best in the business at what we each did, and we were very much like a family.

## HOLYFIELD

*I have lots of friends, and before I fight I let them stop by and say hello and talk, but when it comes to my actual team, I don't want anyone around who doesn't have a specific job, and I want each team member to be the best there is at what he or she does.*

Fight week was exciting for me. I had never seen this level of media attention for a fight, and, the truth is, there had been few, if any, fights in history with as much coverage. Although the consensus was that Evander was certain to be destroyed by "the Baddest Man on the Planet," there was still the recognition that one of the greatest warriors in the history of boxing would go down fighting with all he had. We had the traditional final press conference on Wednesday, the production meeting with the television announcers on Thursday, and the weigh-in and rules meeting on Friday. Throughout the week, I tried to keep the press off of Evander as much as possible, but he was more than willing to make himself available whenever anyone got by me. It was truly amazing how calm, even tempered, and confident Evander remained throughout the entire week.

On Thursday evening, November 7, 1996, two days before the fight, knowing that the next day Janice and Evander's family would arrive and there would be a frenzy of activity, I asked to meet privately with Evander to discuss something that was on my mind. We went to Evander's bedroom in the *Rain Man* suite (named after the suite featured in the Tom Cruise–Dustin Hoffman movie) at Caesar's Palace, closed the door, and Evander asked what I wanted to discuss. I told him that I had dreamed that he beat Tyson on numerous occasions but that now I could meditate and see it happen in my mind while I was still awake. I told Evander I could see him standing over Tyson while Tyson was in a sitting position in the ring and it seemed almost like it had already happened.

"Jim, you need to have faith," he said very calmly. "It has already happened. I just need to go out there on Saturday and do it, but the outcome is already known."

"I believe it, and because I do, I want to ask you to think about something. On Saturday night, your whole world will change one more time. You will once again be king of the sports world. People who have written you off will suddenly be saying they knew all along you would win. Think about who is here now, on Thursday, and truly believes in you, because it will be much harder to sort out the real friends from the pretenders on Sunday."

"You know, I'm glad you said that, because you're right," he responded with a smile. "That is going to be the focus of my prayers tonight."

Although the fight was at the MGM Grand and Evander had a beautiful two-level suite there, the team stayed at Caesar's Palace because Tyson had a multifight deal with the MGM and the MGM was essentially Tyson's house, and Evander did not want to stay in Tyson's house. There were widespread stories about Tyson supporters intimidating opponents and their camps by knocking on doors all through the night and other tactics. Although it would have been easier on the night of the fight to simply take the elevator down from the suite at the MGM to the arena instead of taking limos from Caesar's over to the MGM, it was worth the inconvenience to be away from the Tyson circus.

On the day before and the day of the fight, I tried to shield Evander from any further interviews. Because the various radio, television, and print reporters could not get to Evander, they asked me for my comments, observations, and predictions. I asked Evander how he felt about this, and he told me to do the interviews. In each case, I boldly predicted a Holyfield victory, and in each case I was laughed at to one degree or another. I consoled myself with the thought that "he who laughs last, laughs best."

Because main event fights need to start as close to 11 p.m. Eastern time as possible, they must start as close as possible to 8 p.m. Pacific time. Consequently, we were expected at the MGM Garden Arena by 6 p.m. and needed to leave Caesar's in our limos by 5:30 p.m. because of traffic. On fight day, Evander acted like it was just another day until 3 p.m., when he took a nap. He got up at 5 p.m. and got ready to leave. When he came out of his room, he was a different man from the one who went in at 3 p.m. He was not tense, but he was focused. In the limo on the way to the arena, he was quieter than usual, and the whole team was quieter than usual, but no one was scared, and everyone was upbeat and confident.

We arrived at the arena a little after 6 p.m. and settled into the locker room to watch the preliminary bouts on television. Various celebrities stopped by to wish Evander well during the next hour, and Evander remained very calm. A little after 7 p.m., the NAC and WBA officials paid a visit, and a little later, reporter Jim Gray did an interview with Evander from the locker room for Showtime. Then the referee, Mitch Halpern, visited the locker room, confirmed the rules, and asked for a good, clean fight. One of my jobs was to keep in touch with the Showtime people to determine as closely as possible when we would leave the locker room based on what was going on in the preliminary bouts. At about 30 minutes out, Evander's hands were wrapped and gloved with a Tyson representative present. Then Evander got into his trunks and shoes, and Hallmark stretched him and warmed him up. The team then assembled in a circle and held hands, and Hallmark led us in a prayer. With 20 minutes to go, Evander threw combinations at the hand pads held by Brooks and with 10 minutes to go, broke a sweat.

All through this warmup process, Evander was playing gospel music at moderate volume. A fighter's ring music is an important part of the pageantry of a fight, and Evander planned to enter the fight to Fred Hammond's "Spirit of David." In the locker room, about five minutes before we were to leave, "Spirit of David" was playing. Janice went over to Evander.

"Remember what David did when he faced Goliath; he danced before the Lord," she said.

I learned later that Janice had also mentioned this to Evander privately before we left Caesar's. At that point, Evander told Weaver to turn up the volume, and he began to dance almost euphorically. I cannot adequately describe my feelings at the time, but suffice it to say, there was a very spiritual feeling in the room. Maybe I was lightheaded from the excitement, but everyone seemed to be floating a bit, and there was a strange pink aura in the room. Suddenly, there was a knock on the door, and we were told we had one minute before we left. I walked out with Evander at the head of the group, and I was still reeling from the experience in the locker room. I was told by many people and I must admit from looking at videotape that when we came out of the locker room, Evander looked like he was going to a party and I looked like I was going to face Tyson. At that moment, however, I absolutely guarantee that if I had had a deed to my house and there had been a bookie outside the locker room, I would have joined the Coke vendor at the Braves stadium in betting my house.

## HOLYFIELD

*When we left the locker room, I knew for sure in my heart that the Lord was with me and that I had already won and just needed to go out and finish the job.*

We walked through the frenzied crowd, and Evander, Turner, Brooks, Hallmark, Strickland, and I entered the ring. Standing in the ring for a heavyweight championship fight was an exhilarating experience. No matter what critics may say about boxing, there is nothing more electrifying than a big fight when the bell rings and the announcer begins to introduce the fighters. There is a sense of anticipation unmatched in sports when the ring is cleared. I was still confident of the outcome but tremendously aware of how much easier it was for me to feel confident than for Evander to stay in there all alone and fight for his pride, the title, and his life. Suddenly, this all seemed more real than it had for the past five months.

The fight began with a huge right hand landed by Tyson on Evander's head in the first five seconds. Many competent heavyweights would have set a record for the fastest knockout in history, but Evander merely looked at Tyson unfazed. I will always believe that was one of the most significant cracks in the Tyson wall that night. Having weathered the famous first onslaught of Tyson, Evander began to surprise everyone by holding his own. Then it appeared that Evander was actually outfighting Tyson. Evander fought brilliantly with a near-perfect strategy.

## HOLYFIELD

*I knew that Tyson beat his opponents by intimidation and a relentless forward attack, but I also knew that because most other opponents were intimidated, Tyson had very little experience fighting while going backward. I was absolutely determined to show him right from the start that he could not intimidate me, that I was stronger than him, and that I would not back up no matter what. Most guys who fought Tyson tried not to get hit, which caused them to go backward, but that was not my strategy. I decided that if I didn't back up, I would get hit, but Tyson would be backing up when he hit me causing a loss of power, and I was going to hit Tyson twice for every time he hit me. Finally, I made sure that when he hit me, I had no reaction at all, and I knew that rattled him and further shook his confidence.*

Tyson was unaccustomed to anyone not backing off when he charged. He just assumed that the space in front of his head was his. As a consequence, Tyson's and Evander's heads inevitably collided during the bout. There is a big difference between an intentional use of the head to strike a blow, which is a foul and is properly called a *head butt*, and an unintentional clash of heads caused by two fighters trying to occupy the same space at the same time. Logically, the term *unintentional head butt* makes no more sense than an accidental punch, but the term is used in boxing. A better differentiation would be to call an intentional strike with the head a *butt* and an unintentional collision of heads a *clash*. In any event, Tyson later claimed he had been head-butted, but a review of the videotape shows that his head clashed with Evander's. In the third round, one such head clash resulted in a cut to Tyson's head, which seemed to bother him more than expected.

In the sixth round, Evander floored Tyson with a solid shot to the chest. Rather than screaming and jumping up and down like everyone around me, I calmly thought to myself, "There it is; that's what I saw in my vision." From that point on, the fight went Evander's way. The crowd, beginning to realize it was about to see one of the most stunning upsets in boxing history, began to chant "Ho-ly-field, Ho-ly-field." In the 10th round, Evander pummeled Tyson, and I knew it was effectively over. It was one of the happiest moments of my entire life. Finally, in the 11th round, Evander hit Tyson with a barrage of unanswered shots, and Halpern was forced to stop the fight to protect Tyson from serious damage. The team and I celebrated in the ring, hugging each other, but Evander was much more calm.

### HOLYFIELD

*I realized my team was excited, and that was fine, but I truly believed I had already won before I got in the ring, so I was not surprised at all that I won. I was pleased that I fought so well, but I was not surprised.*

We went to the locker room where there was a whirlwind of activity, with print and electronic media reporters everywhere, all competing for an interview. Also, friends of Evander and various celebrities streamed in to congratulate him. I distinctly remember one of Evander's former business associates, who had told me emphatically only hours earlier that day, "Tyson will kill Evander; this fight should not be happening." Now this man was hugging Evander and telling him repeatedly, "I knew you would do it. I just knew it." I caught Evander's eye as this was going on and tapped my forefinger to my temple to remind him of what I had told him would happen when he won, and Evander nodded in recognition, smiled, and peeled the man off of his neck.

While Evander was showering, giving his post-fight urine sample, and dressing, I stepped out of the locker room for some fresh air. Thirty feet down the hall on a bench outside Tyson's locker room sat King, who was obviously very disappointed. To my surprise, though, he was very gracious. I walked over to him; we shook hands.

"Congratulations, I didn't think he had that left in him," he said. "We need to talk [about the rematch provision] but not tonight. You and Evander deserve to enjoy this."

I sincerely thanked him and returned to the locker room. It was a classy thing for him to say and proved King is either a complicated man—and not the one-dimensional evil person many of his detractors say he is—or that he is even smarter than everyone says he is.

Eventually, we made our way to the post-fight press conference. As Evander and I sat together at the dais waiting for Tyson and his managers to arrive, I put my hand on Evander's shoulder.

"You may have just saved boxing," I told him.

I meant this to be a private comment, but either the microphone in front of me was already on and picked it up or someone was a good lip-reader, because that statement was widely repeated and attributed to me in the press.

King praised both fighters effusively, and recognizing the new champion, reversed the order of speaking from the previous press conferences. Horne and Holloway were uncharacteristically restrained and respectful although they did allege a head butt in the third round had seriously affected Tyson. The real surprise of the conference was Tyson. There was no trace of the sneering, hateful bully. Instead Tyson was incredibly complimentary and respectful, almost like a boy talking to his hero. He finished by saying he just wanted "to touch" Evander and reached across me to touch Evander's hand, which was caught in a photograph seen all over the world and which hangs prominently on my wall at home.

Next it was my time to speak. I praised Tyson's courageous performance in the ring as well as his exemplary sportsmanship in accepting the loss. I then spoke about Evander. I praised him as an athlete but concluded by saying he was not just one of the greatest heavyweights of all time but also one of the best human beings I had ever known. This last statement drew a standing ovation for Evander Holyfield, the man. Evander then spoke. Of course, he began by giving thanks to God, and he then spoke with his characteristic humility, demonstrating what a great champion he is.

Evander and I and the rest of Team Holyfield got in our limousines and went back to Evander's suite at Caesar's Palace, where we had a very low-key non-alcoholic party of friends and relatives talking and joking. After a couple of hours, Evander retired to his bedroom and everyone left. Evander left early the next morning for Atlanta.

The next day, I got a call from a radio sports talk show for whom I had done an interview only hours before the fight. The hosts wanted to know how I knew Evander was going to win the fight when every boxing "expert" in the world predicted a very easy knockout for Tyson. First, I reminded them that not every expert had picked Tyson to win. One boxing writer in the world, Ron Borges of *The Boston Globe*, had predicted a Holyfield victory. Second, I told them I knew Evander would win because I knew about the incident back in 1984 in which Evander had demonstrated that he was absolutely unafraid of Tyson. I knew that when Tyson confirmed with his own eyes what he already knew in his heart—that Evander was not afraid of him, his confidence would collapse.

It was with great frustration and disappointment that I realized many people could not accept the simple fact that Evander was better than Tyson and had simply beaten him physically and psychologically. For weeks after the fight, I heard people who seemed to be truly convinced that the fight had been fixed so that a rematch could be held to make more money for everyone. These people could not bring themselves to believe that the Bible-toting Evander Holyfield could defeat the mean, hip, exciting "Baddest Man on the Planet." I guess they had no way of knowing that there was no amount of money that could be paid to either Evander or Tyson that would have caused the other to allow himself to be beaten.

Although there is much terribly wrong in the sport and business of boxing, I can honestly say that, with only one exception, I am unaware of any fight about which I have personal knowledge being fixed. Maybe fights are fixed at lower levels than championship fights. I wouldn't know, but even if one assumed a motive to fix a fight at the highest level, there is so much to be gained in winning a major heavyweight bout that there is no rational economic model for fixing a fight, at least with top-ranked fighters. In any event, anyone who was on the inside of the Holyfield versus Tyson fight knows beyond the shadow of a doubt that neither Tyson nor Evander would have taken a dive for any amount of money, and because the fight ended in a knockout, there is no need to delve into the obligatory analysis of whether the judges were competent and honest.

On the first few days after the fight, Evander was inundated with requests for appearances and interviews. We went to New York for a series of back-to-back interviews on various television shows. One incident that made me laugh was when I got a request for Evander to be interviewed by Ru Paul. I asked Evander whether he wanted to fit this interview in.

"Isn't that the guy who looks like a woman?" he asked.

When I confirmed it was, Evander, reflecting his inherent conservatism on some topics, said, "I think I'll do that one by telephone."

And he did.

Back in Atlanta, Mayor Bill Campbell, a great supporter of Evander, was planning a major parade for him. In a great show of respect and appreciation for his team, Evander insisted that each of us had our own open car in the parade. I was allowed to have my then six-year-old daughter, Chelsea, join me, and it was a great thrill for her—and, I must admit, for me. At the end of the parade route, a stage had been erected in the park, where about 10,000 people congregated to hear Evander speak. Mayor Campbell spoke and then Earvin "Magic" Johnson, a friend of Evander's, introduced Evander as one of the greatest warriors in sports history. Evander then spoke about his past, his mother, and his great affection for his community, and the crowd adored him.

# CHAPTER 6

# CONFIRMING GREATNESS: THE REMATCH

It wasn't too long after the Mike Tyson fight before Don King called me and said we needed to meet to discuss the rematch. He suggested I meet him in New York, where we could also meet with the Showtime representatives, and I agreed to do so. Before I could meet with King, however, I needed to meet with Evander. When Evander and I met, I explained that I needed to go to New York to meet with King. Evander asked how much I thought I could get him for a rematch, and I reminded him that the rematch purse was already set at $20 million. Evander said he thought he should get at least $30 million, which is what the press had reported as Tyson's purse. I suggested to Evander that in my opinion Tyson almost surely did not receive that much, given the likely arrangements he had with his managers and King, but Evander said he wanted to make at least $30 million no matter what Tyson got. As usual, Evander asked what his alternatives were. I told him he could either fight for $20 million or retire. He asked how he could retire, and I reminded him that I had specifically and expressly negotiated a clause in the contract with King that allowed Evander to retire at any time with no adverse consequences. Evander thought for a minute and then looked at me.

"Tell him I'm going to retire," he stated.

"Evander, for me to do that, you need to be willing to truly retire," I replied.

We understood each other completely.

"If my alternative is to fight for $20 million, I'll retire."

I went to New York and met with King. King was jovial and told me he had a simple contract all ready because there was nothing to negotiate, and we needed to get the rematch on as soon as possible. I told King we had a bit of a problem, because Evander had decided to retire. King was furious. He yelled at a decibel level only he can reach.

"He can't do that," he boomed.

I calmly told King that one of the few things in life I was absolutely sure of was that Evander could retire whenever he wanted with no obligations to anyone. I told him I was sure of this because we had expressly and specifically negotiated this point and documented it in our contract signed on June 1, 1996, and I knew, being a man of honor, King would honor that agreement. King had a few rather uncomplimentary words to say about me, which I understood, expected, and accepted.

As I prepared to leave, I offhandedly suggested that in my personal opinion, knowing Evander as well as I did, I suspected there was probably some number that would lure him out of retirement. King had a few more observations about me but eventually moved on.

"Bring him on up here, and let's try to figure something out."

King later told me he suspected all along he would not be able to sign Evander for $20 million and would not have respected me if I had let that happen. Although we butted heads many times, we had come to have a grudging but genuine respect for each other's competence.

On December 1, 1996, just over three weeks after the fight, Evander and I met with King, and Showtime's Mark Greenburg, Jay Larkin, and Roy Langbord to try to reach an agreement that would unretire Evander. Everyone at the table knew that everyone else was a veteran at these negotiations so we wasted little time. I showed all of my estimates of sources of income, expenses, and net profits based on various pay-per-view assumptions. King showed me his projections of the same figures, and Showtime gave us their views. Of course my projections showed a huge net profit, and King's numbers showed he would lose his shirt if he paid the fighters a reasonable purse. Little by little we worked toward common ground. After hours of work, I was sure we were on the verge of overlapping our minimum purse demand and King's maximum purse offer. Suddenly, just before 11 p.m., Evander told me he needed to take a break. I whispered to him that we could not break now, because we were on the brink of a breakthrough and we could not afford to lose our momentum. Evander said he just needed a few minutes, but I told him it could cost us millions and could even prevent an agreement if King went backward after a break, which I expected he would. Evander said he understood but needed to take a break.

Evander and I left the room, and after hours of negotiations and seeing victory at hand, I was frustrated. When we got alone, I asked Evander with some edge in my voice what was so important that a break was necessary. He said it was 8 p.m. on the West Coast where his three-year old daughter, Emani, lived, and he needed to call her because it was her bedtime. I could not understand why that couldn't wait, but Evander was insistent, so we found an empty office from which he could make a call. I was standing just outside the open door of the office waiting for Evander.

"Happy Birthday to you," he sang into the receiver. "Happy Birthday to you. Happy Birthday dear Emani, Happy Birthday to you." He then said, "I've got to go now because I'm in an important meeting, but I wanted you to know I'm thinking about you on your birthday. I love you."

I realized once again what a special man I was dealing with. I was very proud to be his lawyer, adviser, and friend.

## HOLYFIELD

*Some things are just more important than money, and one thing for me that can't even compare to money is my children and showing them at all times that I love them.*

When we reconvened, King predictably said he had made some errors in his calculations and we needed to go backward. I expressed my frustration, mostly real, but a little bit put on, and Evander and I almost left. About an hour later, we were very close to a deal. King had $30 million on the table, and we insisted on $35 million. We eventually compromised at a $3 million non-refundable payment that night and $30 million at the time of the fight, plus training expenses, tickets, a Bentley for Evander's car collection, etc. We all shook hands, subject to delivery of a check in the amount of $3 million later that night. True to his word, King had the $3 million check delivered to me within an hour, and we had a deal. To my knowledge, the total package valued at about $34 million was the largest amount ever paid for any single performance by any person in any field anywhere on earth.

The fight was set for May 10, 1997, back at the MGM in Las Vegas. Amazingly, even though Evander had dominated Tyson in November, the oddsmakers made Tyson the favorite in the rematch, and the press agreed. The prevailing sentiment was that Evander had caught Tyson by surprise, and now that Tyson knew that Evander still had some fight left in him, Tyson would blow him away.

A few weeks before the fight, King called me and told me Tyson had suffered a cut that would require a postponement of the rematch. I asked to talk to Dr. Flip Homansky, who was the doctor for the Nevada State Athletic Commission and who confirmed the injury. Even though we had a legal right to an independent medical examination, I waived that right and chose to accept Dr. Homansky's confirmation because I knew him to be a man of honor. I then had to call Evander to break the bad news. When a fighter has been in camp for weeks and has planned when to peak for a fight, a postponement is, at best, a huge disappointment. I called Evander to give him the news. I did not beat around the bush. I told him Tyson had been injured, and the fight needed to be postponed. Evander asked very calmly how long the postponement was likely to be. I told him our best estimate was six weeks. Evander said he understood. I said I was sorry, and he said it was fine; he would handle it. There was no anger, no frustration. Once again, I was greatly impressed by Evander's equanimity.

## HOLYFIELD

*Injuries and postponements are a part of boxing, and I can't let myself get upset about things I can't control. I always remind myself that God has a plan for me and it is not for me to question that plan.*

Because training straight through to the postponed date would cause burnout, Evander had to break camp for two weeks and then come back. During the two-week break, Evander went back to Atlanta to spend time with his children and deal with some personal issues. Unfortunately, Evander was already experiencing problems in his marriage. In fact, there were problems from the outset of the marriage. Evander has explained publicly that he married Janice because he believed it was what God wanted him to do, even though he was not in love with her. He believed that if he did God's will, God would put the love in his heart. Unfortunately for Janice and Evander, it was not happening, and it was sad for both of them.

The fight was rescheduled for June 27, and at the end of May, Evander went back to Houston to resume prefight training camp. Finally, on Sunday, June 20, Team Holyfield assembled in Las Vegas. Once again, our headquarters were in the four-bedroom *Rain Man* suite at Caesar's Palace. With regard to the training regimen, it was another fight like any other. With regard to the media attention, it was unlike any fight in history, and very few sporting events of any kind have received more attention. In terms of media coverage and money, this was the biggest fight of all time.

On June 24, we had the prefight press conference at the MGM Grand. That press conference was very interesting. Horne and Holloway, speaking for Tyson, explained why they thought the outcome of this fight would be the opposite of the last fight, with Tyson punishing Evander. Tyson, himself, said very little. When it was my turn, I said the following in a slow, quiet, and unemotional presentation.

"Mike Tyson is a great fighter, one of the greatest heavyweights of his era. In fact, in my opinion, last November Mike was, and now he still is, the second best heavyweight in the world. I understand and appreciate that John Horne and Rory Holloway think the outcome this time will be different. They should think that. It's their job to think that. But if you look at the facts objectively, why would the outcome be any different?

"Last November, Evander did not beat Mike Tyson; he thoroughly dominated him and finally knocked him out. Tyson was so thoroughly dominated and beaten that after the fight he was humble and respectful for the first time in his career. Now, seven months later, Evander is a much better fighter. He is stronger, faster, has better combinations, and knows he is the superior fighter based upon personal experience.

"Why would the outcome be any different this time? Evander still has superior physical strength, superior inner strength, superior adaptability, superior trainers, superior intelligence, and superior confidence. I expect Tyson to fight just as hard as he did last November, and I'm sure it will be a good fight, but the outcome will be no different. Evander will dominate Tyson once again and eventually knock him out."

Tyson's reaction was very revealing. If Tyson had the appropriate level of confidence, he should have either been angry and defiant or, as Evander would have been, unfazed and mildly amused. Instead, Tyson, who was directly beside me as I spoke, put his head down on his hands on the dais and did not look up. He had the look and aura of a defeated man, certainly not because of what I said, but because of Evander's presence, confidence, and faith, which combined to tell Tyson without the need for words that he could not win. The words just helped it sink in.

There was a prior hint of this defeatist attitude a few weeks earlier when Marc Ratner, the executive director of the Nevada State Athletic Commission, called to tell me Tyson would not fight unless Evander took a steroid test. This did not bother me at all, because I knew with certainty from my many talks with Evander on this topic that he had never used steroids. Evander told me some people had urged him to use steroids, especially when he was moving up to the heavyweight division. Evander always refused for one reason: If he had used steroids and then became heavyweight champion, he would never have known whether he could have done it without the steroids. I wasn't worried about the test, and I knew that a refusal would be taken as evidence of guilt. On the other hand, Tyson had no probable cause to request such a test and absolutely no right to require one as a condition for the fight going forward. I discussed this situation with Evander, who came up with a brilliant solution. He said he would take the test provided that the results would not be revealed to Tyson until after the fight.

## HOLYFIELD

*I laughed when I heard Tyson was demanding that I take a steroid test. I saw Tyson's look when he saw me with my shirt off at the weigh-in for the last fight. He couldn't believe how big and muscular I had become from how hard I had trained. I knew he must have convinced himself that I had won the fight by cheat-*

*ing somehow, because he couldn't face the fact that I was just stronger than him. I was happy to take a steroid test, because I have never used steroids in my life, but I didn't want Tyson to have the comfort of knowing I was not using steroids. I wanted Tyson to continue to think I had an unfair advantage over him so he would give himself an excuse for losing again.*

Finally, fight night arrived. The locker room at the MGM Grand was much less intense than it had been for the first Holyfield versus Tyson bout. There was a very serene, secure sense of confidence in the room. This time when we walked into the arena, Tyson was already in the ring, and the applause for Evander as he walked to the ring was the loudest and wildest I had ever seen and heard before or since. As I stood with Evander and his trainers in the ring, the crowd was going crazy, many hoping to see another triumph of good over evil and some hoping to see the world's favorite "bad guy" get revenge.

In the first round, Evander picked up right where he left off the previous November. He outmuscled and outhustled Tyson. He beat him to the punch, forced him to go backward, demonstrated his superior strength, and most importantly imposed his will on Tyson. The second round was much like the first. As in the first fight, as Tyson tried to jump into his opponent who refused to retreat, there were the inevitable clashes of the two fighters' heads. In one clash, Tyson received a small cut near the corner of his eye. The ring doctor determined it was not dangerous, and Mills Lane, the referee who had been demanded by Tyson, confirmed that it was the result of an unintentional no-fault clash; the fight proceeded.

At the end of the second round, it appeared that Tyson was going to suffer another beating. I turned to talk to Magic Johnson, who was sitting next to me and is a big fan of Evander, and I gave him what for me was a high five and for him was a low five. As the third round began, the crowd had not yet sat down, and I could not see. There was something going on, and I asked Johnson what he saw. He said Tyson forgot his mouthpiece and had to go back to the corner to get it. The round then began, and from the start, Tyson had dramatically picked up his pace and intensity. He was fighting almost frantically, you might even say desperately, and he was landing some good, clean, hard shots. The only problem for Tyson was that he was not hurting Evander. Tyson was not used to landing his best shots and having his opponent appear totally unaffected. Evander just stared back at Tyson and kept going forward, and Tyson was getting frustrated. There was a clinch, and suddenly Evander jumped back and began to jump up and down in obvious pain, holding the side of his head. Instantly everyone in the crowd was on his feet, and I could not see. I asked Johnson what happened.

"I think Tyson bit him," Johnson said.

I could not believe my ears, and I jumped up on my seat, and there was Evander in his corner with blood running down his check from the top of his ear, which had been bitten off and spit out by Tyson.

## HOLYFIELD

*When Tyson bit me, I was shocked by the pain. The worst kind of pain is unexpected pain. If you are ready for pain—like when you see a punch coming, you can deal with the pain. But when you can't see the source of the pain and it is totally unexpected and a kind of pain you have never felt before, it is really intense. The truth is my first reaction was to bite him back, but I had enough control over myself not to react. I just got determined to knock Tyson out. When I had the opportunity to end the fight and be awarded the victory by disqualification, I refused. I really wanted the satisfaction of knocking Tyson out.*

Lane went over to Ratner at the side of the ring.

"He bit him; I'm going to disqualify him," the referee told the executive.

"Is that what you want to do?" Ratner replied.

Lane reconsidered his verdict.

I do not think Ratner was trying to second-guess or overrule Lane at all. I think he was simply surprised by these astonishing events and was making sure Lane did not make a snap judgment he might regret later. Meanwhile, Dr. Homansky was examining Evander's wound. Turner was questioning whether Evander could fairly be asked to continue with so much pain, bleeding, and distraction. Dr. Homansky asked Evander what he wanted to do.

"Put my mouthpiece back in. I'm going to knock him out," Evander stated frankly.

After talking to Ratner, Lane and Dr. Homansky came together, and Lane asked the doctor whether Evander could continue. Honoring and respecting Evander's request to be allowed to knock Tyson out, Dr. Homansky told Lane that Evander could continue. Lane told Ratner that he was going to let the fight continue and take two points from Tyson and disqualify him if there were any further fouls. Lane then went over to Tyson.

"You bit him," Lane stated.

Tyson denied the charge.

"Bullshit!" Lane interjected. "You bit him, and I'm taking two points. If you foul again, I'll disqualify you."

At that point, the third round continued, and soon thereafter Evander and Tyson were in a clinch, and Evander jumped back again and held the other side of his head. Unbelievably, Tyson had bitten Evander's other ear. This time, though, Evander barely stopped, he jumped on Tyson and tried to knock him out. Unfortunately, the time ran out. Lane came over to Evander's corner to find out what happened, saw the teeth marks in Evander's other ear, and immediately disqualified Tyson.

Tyson went crazy, flailing around, trying to get to Evander's corner and inadvertently hitting a security guard. I ran to the ring, got inside, and tried to get at Tyson. Fortunately for me, I didn't get there, because I was intercepted by a security guard and pushed back into the corner with Evander and the trainers. The crowd was outraged that the fight they had paid so much to see was stopped by Tyson's barbaric behavior. Many in the crowd were throwing things at Tyson and screaming at him. Evander stood calmly in his corner. A security guard told us we needed to get into the locker room before a riot broke out in the arena, and he asked us to run to the locker room, which we did.

When we reached the locker room, there was utter chaos. Evander grabbed me and asked me to get everyone to be quiet and gather the team together, and I did so. When order was restored and the room was quieter, Evander told the team he wanted to pray. As usual, the team formed a circle and held hands, and Evander led us in prayer. Evander praised God and declared his forgiveness of Tyson. When Evander was done praying, he was totally calm, and I found my intense anger was gone also. At that point, members of the press began interviewing Evander and some of the rest of us. I was asked why I seemed calm and was not angry about what Tyson had done to my friend. I honestly answered that I had just learned how a man can turn the other cheek under one of the most difficult circumstances imaginable and that I felt no right to be angry when Evander had declared that he had already forgiven Tyson.

In the midst of these interviews, a young man came in the locker room and handed a rubber glove to Hallmark. The glove contained the piece of Evander's ear that had been bitten off. Hallmark put the piece of ear in a small ice chest.

### HOLYFIELD

*When Tyson bit me twice, my faith was put to the test. I could allow hatred to fill my heart or I could be a true Christian and forgive Tyson. I chose the Christian way, and my heart was unburdened.*

Dr. Vaughns made arrangements for Evander to be taken to Valley Hospital for treatment, and the team got into an ambulance.

"The Tyson side will be trying to spin this story," I told Evander before we pulled out. "Somebody better stay behind and protect your interests."

"You're right. You get out and handle it," he told me.

I got out, and the ambulance left for the hospital.

As I looked around, I saw a continuation of the chaos that I had seen in the arena. I later learned that the crowd had entered the casino at the MGM Grand and had overturned gambling tables. There were widespread reports of gunshots. I looked around, and I realized that I was alone and thought about how much Tyson's camp disliked me, and I was concerned. Fortunately, I saw a fighter who trained with Evander under Turner and whom I knew casually. The fighter was Michael Grant, who is six foot seven and 250 pounds, built like a body builder, and at that time had a professional record of 27-0. I called to Grant and asked him to stay with me as I went to the pressroom. When I was done in the pressroom, Grant walked me to the suite available for Evander's use. That was the beginning of a great friendship between Grant and me and eventually led to him hiring me as attorney and co-management adviser, along with Craig Hamilton, who also became a close friend.

From the suite, I could see that, outside the MGM, the chaos continued. After an hour or so, things had calmed down, and I went down to the casino level to get something to eat. I ran into Larkin, Greenburg, and Langbord of Showtime, and we got a bite to eat and had a few glasses of wine. The Showtime guys were appalled, disgusted, embarrassed, and angry about Tyson's latest self-destructive act. They also realized that although Showtime had done absolutely nothing wrong, it was likely to be tied up in lengthy, expensive, time-consuming, and undeserved litigation initiated by irate pay-per-view subscribers. By the time I got back to Caesar's Palace, Evander was asleep.

I got up at about 6:30 a.m. I was sure Evander would still be asleep, but I went to his suite and let myself in so that I would be there when Evander woke up. To my surprise, he was already up. When I asked why he was up, he said he was in so much pain from the bite that he couldn't sleep. He said he had a prescription for pain pills but that he had to wait for a pharmacy to open. I told him I was sure I could find some place open and took the prescription to an all-night pharmacy, got the pills, and returned. Evander took a pill, and 20 minutes later said he felt much better.

"Evander, before anyone else shows up, just between us, how are you doing?"

"I'm doing great!" he responded as he always did.

"I mean about what happened last night."

"Oh, you mean that stuff," he said smiling. "That was yesterday. Today's going to be a great day. I'm the Heavyweight Champion of the World. I just got paid over $33 million, and I only had to fight three rounds. The only bad part is that one ear is a little pointy, but I've thought about that and it's actually a blessing. The marketing people say I'm too nice to be the champ. I think I'll get the other ear done to match this one, and then I'll look like a Doberman Pinscher."

I then told Evander that I learned the night before that a press conference had been scheduled for 11 a.m. Evander said he was leaving for Atlanta and would then be on his way to South Africa representing the Coca-Cola Company. Evander asked me to handle the press conference in his place and to handle all media requests while he was gone. I then told Evander how much I envied him because he would be visiting with President Nelson Mandela. I had always admired Mandela. I had just finished reading his autobiography *Long Walk to Freedom*, and he had become an even greater hero to me as I learned more details of his long struggle for his people and his incredible ability to reject bitterness and forgive his oppressors. It occurred to me that Evander's forgiveness of Tyson showed these two great warriors had this trait in common.

Later that morning I attended the press conference as Evander's representative and answered questions for about an hour. Clips of the press conference appeared frequently on CNN and other networks for the next few days. Throughout the rest of the day, I handled many other interviews, including a telephone appearance on *Larry King Live* while on the plane to Atlanta, a subsequent video appearance on the same show two nights later, and appearances on CNN's *Morning Edition*, CNNSI, and *Burden of Proof*, among other television shows, along with numerous nationwide and foreign radio shows. I must admit I enjoyed the public recognition and praise I received for my demeanor and restraint, but it was easy to look good if I thought about whom I represented and how he would want me to present myself. All I had to do was ask myself what Evander would say and what attitude he would have.

A few days later, Evander called me from South Africa. He told me he had just left President Mandela and that he had something for me from the president. When Evander got back to Atlanta, he gave me a sheet of paper with beautiful handwriting that said:

---

To Jim Thomas,

Best wishes to an
outstanding jurist who
deserves the utmost
admiration and respect.

N. Mandela
7-7-97

---

I was incredibly touched by this gesture from Evander. I framed the gift, and it is displayed prominently as the first thing seen by any visitor to my home.

# CHAPTER 7

## BEGINNING THE QUEST TO REUNIFY THE TITLES

S oon after the Tyson rematch, we began to think about whom Evander's next opponent would be. Evander was the WBA champ. Michael Moorer was the IBF champ. Lennox Lewis was the WBC champ. Evander wanted to unify the titles by winning all three and then retire. Because the WBA had ranked Tyson the No. 1 contender even after his loss to Evander in their first fight in November 1996, the rematch with Tyson satisfied Evander's mandatory obligation and gave him a year until his next WBA mandatory fight was due. We knew the Lewis fight would be extraordinarily difficult to make because Lewis had a contract to fight exclusively on HBO. Because of the way Evander was treated by some people at HBO when he lost to Riddick Bowe in 1992 and because of Evander's friendship with Jay Larkin and how well he was treated at Showtime, Evander preferred to fight on Showtime. Even more importantly, at that time, Don King had a complex business relationship with Showtime that made his promotion of Evander's fights on HBO problematic at best. Because of these anticipated difficulties in working out a fight with Lewis, we focused on getting Moorer's IBF belt first.

Because of the "bite fight" and the way Evander handled it, Evander was enormously popular, and we anticipated great success in selling Evander's next fight on pay-per-view, regardless of who the opponent would be. Furthermore, Moorer had the IBF title and was the only professional fighter other than Bowe to ever beat Evander. On the other hand, it was unlikely that any fight would come anywhere close to the pay-per-view sales of the Tyson rematch, which set a record at just under two million buys. I did believe, however, that the Moorer fight would do at least one million buys.

If I was right, and assuming the fight sold for $49.95, the gross pay-per-view revenues would be approximately $50 million, and the net to the boxing promotion after the cable operators were paid their 50 percent would be $25 million. Add in an estimate of $5 million from the gate, and $5million from international sales, merchandise, closed circuit, and the other minor miscellaneous revenue sources, and I was projecting total revenues at approximately $35 million. With marketing, undercard, and other costs estimated at $5 million, I projected the net revenues over costs to be about $30 million, subject, of course, to my pay-per-view estimate. If, as I assumed and had ferreted out, Moorer and his promoter, Main Events, insisted on receiving about $10 million, there would be about $20 million left to cover the total of Evander's purse and a reasonable profit for DKP and Showtime.

I shared all of my thoughts and calculations with Evander and told him I thought Showtime and DKP would probably not be willing to assume a million pay-per-view buys in calculating a guaranteed purse, but I thought with some work and patience I could eventually get Evander a guaranteed purse of $15 million.

"I won't fight for less than $20 million," he said after some thought.

I explained that if Evander got paid $20 million, even if we hit the million pay-per-view target, there would be no profit left for DKP and Showtime, and King had told me many times, "I don't work for free." Evander just smiled.

"I know you can do it," he said.

I told him that, as always, I would do my best.

## HOLYFIELD

*I knew that a guarantee of $20 million was a stretch for the Moorer fight, but after the two Tyson fights, my thinking was that I was considered the true Heavyweight Champion of the World* *and was extremely popular, so I felt I deserved $20 million. Of course I could have taken a guarantee of $15 million with an upside on pay-per-view sales, but I had never seen one dollar from a pay-per-view upside, so I decided to press for a guarantee of $20 million. Jim is a creative guy and a guy who can handle pressure, so I knew my best chance to get what I wanted was to put the pressure on Jim to figure out how to get there. I knew Jim would either get it for me or at least do everything in his power to get it.*

The negotiations with King and Showtime went about as expected, and because we knew each other well, it did not take too long to get to the point of a $15 million guarantee for Evander, but we were stuck at that level. I reported to Evander where we were, and he insisted he wanted $20 million. Larkin and I then met to brainstorm how to bridge the gap. Larkin explained that he thought Showtime might be willing to risk a loss of money on the Moorer fight if they could be assured that they would have a chance to make up the loss on a fight later, but if Showtime took a foreseeable loss and King then took Evander to HBO for the next fight, the jobs of Evander's and my friends' at Showtime might be in jeopardy. Furthermore, it was not only possible but likely that our next fight would be Lewis, which would have to be on HBO. Together Larkin and I developed a creative way to meet Evander's demand, avoid the disaster scenario feared by Showtime, and increase the chances of Showtime making up any loss suffered in the Moorer fight on Evander's next fight. Larkin agreed to propose this compromise to his colleagues, and I agreed to take it to Evander with my recommendation to accept it. When I explained the deal to Evander, he was impressed and delighted. He kidded me, saying I needed to be more confident because he always knew I would find a way to get the extra $5 million he wanted. Ultimately, with a few minor adjustments, Showtime agreed, and after some negotiations between Showtime and King in which King initially refused to take any financial risk, King agreed. We had a deal on our part of the transaction, now King needed to make a deal with Dino Duva of Main Events for Moorer to accept the fight.

I offered to join King and support him in his negotiations with Main Events, but he declined my offer. I feared that I knew why. King had several discussions with Duva, but no agreement was reached. King reported that

Duva was being difficult and he did not believe Duva really wanted to make the fight, but he would keep trying. When no progress seemed to be imminent, I called Main Events' attorney, Pat English, to see if I could figure out what the problem was. English said the problem was very simple. The money, although not finally agreed upon, would not be a problem. The problem was that King was insisting on getting future promotional rights on Moorer if Moorer won. English assured me that there was absolutely no possibility whatsoever that Main Events would concede any part of their promotional rights to Moorer's future fights. I immediately directed an associate to do some specific research on the implied contractual covenant of good faith and fair dealing under New York law, with which I was already fairly familiar from the many banking litigation cases I had handled. I also began work on a formal complaint to be filed, if necessary, in U.S. District Court for the Southern District of New York. This practice of promoters insisting on the futures on opponents was common, and many promoters did it at least occasionally, but I was convinced it would not be condoned by the courts if properly and effectively challenged under the right set of facts.

That night my associate confirmed that the applicable law was as I remembered it, and very early the next morning I flew to New York to meet with King. When I arrived in New York, I called King at his apartment and told him we needed to meet. He said he would be busy all day in a deposition and then had a dinner engagement. I told him that it was urgent, that we needed to meet as soon as possible, and that I would wait for him in my hotel room at the Marriott Marquis. King said it might be late, but he would be there. Obviously, I could have spoken to King over the telephone, but I felt sure that what I planned to say needed to be said face to face so that King would be sure I was not bluffing. I called Evander, explained what I was doing, and asked for his support, which he gave me.

**HOLYFIELD**

*I had no desire to have a legal battle with Don King, but I felt it was wrong for my fight with Michael Moorer to be held up because King wanted promotional rights over Moorer if I lost. I authorized Jim to do what was necessary to get me the opportunity to fight Moorer and win the IBF title. If it required a legal battle, that would be on King for not believing in me enough to make the fight without a backup plan.*

████████████████████████████

At about 11 p.m., King knocked on my door. I let him in, we sat down, and I offered him a drink, which he declined. Just then I realized I had not called my home or office and that no one knew where I was staying. I apologized and told King I needed to make one quick phone call before we started. I turned my back to King, called my wife, and as quietly as possible, so that King would not hear, told my wife I was in room 2227 at the Marriott Marquis and that she should call me there in an hour, and that if I didn't answer, she should send someone to check on me. When I turned around, King, who had apparently heard me, was laughing.

"I ain't gonna kill ya, man," he chuckled.

"Don, when I tell you what I'm about to do, you may change your mind."

king became instantly serious, but at least the ice had been broken with a little humor. I told him that Evander's mission was to unify the heavyweight titles, that he was almost 35 years old and had no time to waste, and that he needed the Moorer fight to happen. I told King that it was my job to do everything within my power and within the law to get him what he wanted and that by holding up the fight in an effort to get the futures on Moorer, he was leaving me no choice but to take drastic action. Looking King in the eyes, I explained my view of the law and the facts. I was prepared to file a complaint in the United States District Court for the Southern District of New York, where criminal fraud charges were then pending against King and that I was confident Evander would be successful in having his contract with DKP declared terminated. King was clearly and visibly very angry, but he kept his composure.

"What do you want me to do?" he asked after a few moments of silence.

"I simply want you to give up the futures and close the deal."

To my surprise, King got up, walked over to the telephone, and called Duva at home. He quickly and directly told Duva he was giving up his demand for the futures and that he and Duva should meet the next day to close the deal on the Holyfield versus Moorer fight.

"Are you happy?" he said as he turned around.

I said I was and that I really appreciated what he had just done, and I meant it. We shook hands and as King was leaving, he stopped.

"You fight hard for Evander, and you didn't go behind my back. I respect that."

Within days, the deal was done between DKP and Main Events, but there was yet one more problem. A promoter named Butch Lewis had somehow managed to have a heavyweight fighter he promoted named Vaughn Bean ranked as the No. 1 contender by the IBF. Butch Lewis had petitioned the IBF to force Moorer to fight Bean next in his mandatory bout or be stripped of his title, and it appeared that the IBF was going to support Lewis's claim. Without the IBF sanction of the Holyfield versus Moorer bout as a title bout, we had no fight. English spoke to the IBF's lawyer, Walter Stone, to explore possible solutions to this problem. After some further discussions, it appeared that the IBF would sanction our fight if we paid Butch Lewis and Bean $400,000 as a "step aside" fee. Everyone involved in our fight was outraged, because there was not one credible, unbiased boxing expert who thought Bean deserved to be the mandatory challenger. Nevertheless, as a practical matter, we were forced to consider this payment. I took the initial position that this was Moorer's problem and that he needed to resolve his mandatory requirement issue. John Davimos, one of the best people I have met in boxing, was Moorer's manager and took the position that this was a promotional cost and needed to be paid by the lead promoter, DKP. King was already concerned that he had no way to make a profit and had no intention whatsoever of making this payment, especially not to Butch Lewis, with whom King had a history of disputes. English helped arrange negotiations directly between Davimos and me, and we eventually agreed on a formula to share the payment with the winner of the fight paying more than the loser. In unrelated legal proceedings later against the IBF and its president, Bob Lee, there were accusations and admissions of bribes having been paid for rankings. I have never had any firsthand knowledge of any such bribes, and this step aside payment was openly agreed upon and not a bribe, but it made me sick to be forced to pay it.

**HOLYFIELD**

*Of course I didn't like the idea of paying a step aside fee to Butch Lewis and Vaughn Bean, but the simple fact of the matter is that, under the rules, Moorer was obligated to fight the mandatory challenger, and I have consistently been in favor of following the rules, even when I didn't agree with the rankings. Whether or not Bean should have been ranked No. 1, the fact is he was No. 1 and he had the right under the rules to fight Moorer or have Moorer stripped or agree to step aside for a fee. Paying a step aside fee was the best alternative for me and was consistent with the rules, so I went along with it.*

Holyfield versus Moorer was scheduled for November 8, 1997, to be held at the Thomas & Mack Center on the campus of UNLV, with the Mirage Hotel, owned by Steve Wynn, as the host hotel. Team Holyfield arrived in Las Vegas on Sunday, November 2. Fight week went by with no significant problems, and on Saturday, November 8, it was time to try to unify the WBA and IBT championships.

The Moorer fight was a great fight. The first round was essentially even, with Moorer holding Evander off very well with his great right jab (Moorer is a southpaw). Early in the fight Evander suffered a cut from a head clash. Although the cut was serious, Evander didn't panic because he had been cut several times before. Evander went about studying Moorer's tendencies and patterns. Because Evander had prepared so well for Moorer, he was able to make adjustments to counter what Moorer was doing. In the early rounds, Moorer was staying outside and fighting defensively behind his quick jab. Evander was very aggressive and active, which caused Moorer to move and jab even more. Then Evander made a brilliant and inspired adjustment.

During the prefight buildup, in addition to talk about Evander wearing himself out, there was the usual talk about how fighters seem to "get old in the ring," meaning that, from one fight to the next, the fighter becomes old and slow. Moorer was no doubt hoping that if he could get by the early rounds, Evander would tire. Evander played right into this misconception. He slowed his pace, stopped going forward, and then dropped his left hand as if he were tiring, which must have reminded Moorer of the first fight with Evander in which Evander could not hold his left arm up because his shoulder was injured. Moorer saw what he wanted to see and jumped in, and Evander caught him with a solid uppercut that dropped Moorer. Moorer got up and was clearly discouraged and angry with himself. When the fight resumed, Evander again demonstrated his tactical superiority and maturity. Most fighters, when they hurt an opponent, desperately try to take the opponent out before he recovers, but Evander stayed patient.

*When I was younger, I was not as much of a student of the game. I didn't watch videotapes of my opponents, because I didn't know what to look for or how to make adjustments even if I saw something. As I matured, I became a true student of the game. I now watch a lot of videotape and become aware of my opponent's tendencies and reactions in different circumstances. When you start to get a little older, it's hard to get a lot better physically, but you can get much better mentally, and in that sense I was better in 1997 than ever before. I knew how to set a trap for Moorer, and it worked. When I hurt him, I didn't get desperate like a lot of guys do. When you get somebody in trouble, the tendency is to throw everything you have to make sure you take him out before he recovers. Behind that thinking, though, is a lack of confidence that you can't do again what you did to get the opponent in trouble. I stayed patient when I knocked Moorer down because I knew exactly how I did it, and I knew I could do it again.*

If Evander had jumped on Moorer with a furious flurry, an experienced and skillful fighter like Moorer would have just covered up and let Evander waste energy. Instead, Evander stayed patient, backed off, and methodically set Moorer up again. By the eighth round, Evander had knocked Moorer down four times, each time patiently setting Moorer up and then springing the trap. With the exception of the first Tyson fight, I think the Moorer fight was the most intelligent of Evander's career. For Moorer's part, he displayed amazing courage. If a warrior is someone who never quits, Michael Moorer was a warrior on that night. Near the end of the eighth round, Evander knocked Moorer down for the fifth time and Moorer was unable to continue. Ironically, due to his courageous performance, Moorer gained more respect in defeat than he had ever received in victory. Maybe that is why Moorer hung up his gloves after that fight. He had finally gained the respect he was fighting for. Moorer had always been either distant from me or antagonistic to me, but after the fight when I told him how much I respected his performance, he gave me a big sweaty hug and I was happy for him.

For Evander's part, he firmly established himself as the consensus best heavyweight in the world, although Lennox Lewis still held the WBC belt. Evander had achieved two-thirds of his goal and had one belt to go. After the customary post-fight interviews and press conference, Evander, Janice, and I got in a limo for the ride back to the Mirage, and we had a bit of a scare. Evander was experiencing severe chest pains. When we got back to the hotel, Dr. Vaughns examined Evander and determined that he had a bruised sternum and was experiencing some associated cramping. Apparently, Evander had received a shot to the sternum that would have stopped a lot of fighters, but Evander simply fought through the pain.

## HOLYFIELD

*In the limo on the way back to the hotel after the Moorer fight, I had severe chest pains, and I must admit it hurt so bad that the thought occurred to me that there might be something wrong with my heart. I could hardly get out of the car. I was relieved when Dr. Vaughns determined that I had a badly bruised sternum, and the muscles in the sternum area were cramping.*

Soon after the Moorer fight, Evander and I met to discuss what he wanted to do next. Evander left no doubt that he wanted to fight Lennox Lewis next and as soon as possible. I then met with King to discuss Evander's desire for the Lewis fight and how we could make it happen. King said he would work on the Lewis fight but noted that we would need permission from the WBA, because Evander's WBA mandatory bout was coming up. The No. 1 ranked heavyweight in the WBA's ratings was Henry Akinwande, a King fighter. I pointed out that the second Tyson fight had been sanctioned by the WBA as a mandatory bout, so the WBA mandatory was not due until the end of June and we could schedule the Lewis fight for March or April. King said he would explore the Lewis fight, but I did not sense a lot of enthusiasm.

While Evander was occupied with trying to unify the three major heavyweight titles, his marriage was falling apart. Evander was waiting and waiting for God to put the love for Janice in his heart, but it was not happening. A few days after the Moorer fight, on November 14, 1997, Evander and I went to Los Angeles for some personal appearances. We often used trips like this to catch up on the accumulated business issues we needed to discuss as well as what was happening in our personal lives, and long plane rides were the best opportunity we had to spend a lot of time together without much interruption. On this trip we talked at length about the state of Evander's marriage, and Evander indicated that he was about ready to accept the fact that he had made a mistake in marrying Janice. The problem was not anything Janice had done, but instead the simple fact that Evander was not in love with her.

When we got to Los Angeles, Evander and I did an interview together on Jim Rome's radio show, and Evander made one of his frequent appearances on *The Tonight Show with Jay Leno*. We went to a few more interviews and then met Evander's daughter, Emani, who lives in Los Angeles, for lunch. Emani was two weeks short of five years old and as cute as she could be. Evander tries to see Emani whenever he is in Los Angeles and has her visit him in Atlanta frequently, and it was touching to see the two of them together and watch Evander's concern and guidance.

About three weeks later, Evander and I went to Las Vegas for the Billboard Music Awards, where Evander was to present one of the awards. When we arrived in Las Vegas, we checked into the MGM Grand, where the awards show was being held and then went down to the MGM Garden Arena for the show. After the show, Evander and I ran into Evander's friend, LL Cool J, one of the most successful rap artists of all time, who was with his wife. We decided to forego the post-show party and go up to Evander's suite and order dinner. I had never met LL before, and I was surprised that Evander had a close friend who was a rapper. As we all sat around the dining room table and talked about a wide array of topics, I could understand why Evander and LL were friends. LL, whose real name is James Todd Smith, turned out to be a remarkably warm, friendly, intelligent, and thoughtful man, who was clearly devoted to his wife. Since that first meeting, I have had the privilege of spending time with LL on several occasions, and it is always a great pleasure.

Soon after we began our little dinner party, we had an unexpected and pleasant surprise. We had a knock on the door, and it was Toni Braxton and her sister. Toni said she heard Evander was in the hotel and came by to say hello. She and her sister joined the party. It was a great opportunity for me to watch these celebrities out of the public view, so unpretentious and real. I was accustomed to this phenomenon with Evander, but it was a revelation to see it in other stars. Over the years, I have been fortunate enough to spend time with many of Evander's celebrity friends, and almost without exception I have been pleasantly surprised by their warmth and sincerity. I assume not all celebrities are so genuine, but the ones who are Evander's friends truly are.

When we returned to Atlanta on December 10, I went back to work on Holyfield versus Lewis. I met with Larkin of Showtime to discuss Evander's desire to fight Lewis. Larkin and I were painfully aware that Lewis had a long-term contract with HBO that restricted him to fighting only on HBO and its pay-per-view arm, TVKO. Although we did not have a similar contractual restriction with Showtime, Evander and I did feel a sense of loyalty and gratitude for the treatment we had received from Showtime. When Evander lost to Riddick Bowe and immediately got the cold shoulder by some of the top people at HBO, one of the HBO executives explained, "It's just business." Showtime, on the other hand, proved that the relationship between Showtime and Evander was more than just business. Although they could have caused problems in making the Lewis fight due to their contractual relationship with Don King Productions, Matt Blank, Mark Greenburg, and Larkin agreed to support Evander's effort to fight Lewis to unify the titles even though the fight would need to be on HBO. In return, Evander and I made a gentleman's agreement with Showtime that if the Lewis fight occurred on HBO, Evander would come back to Showtime as soon as possible.

Next, I had several discussions with HBO's president, Seth Abraham, who said he very much wanted the Holyfield versus Lewis fight to happen. Because only King could make commitments concerning the fight, my discussions with Abraham were merely informal talks. Abraham wanted to know whether Evander's demands would make the fight impossible to fund. I told Abraham that I would not and could not negotiate Evander's purse with him, but that I would tell him one thing I was sure of: Evander would not take less for the Lewis fight on HBO than the $20 million he got for the Moorer fight on Showtime. Abraham said that he felt sure that Lewis's side would take the fight for $10 million. Abraham said that he was sure a good site deal could be made with Madison Square Garden and that if Evander would take the fight for $20 million, HBO would be willing and able to guarantee enough money from pay-per-view sales to pay the fighters their purses, pay all other expenses, and leave a reasonable profit for King. Abraham said the only thing that would prevent the fight would be King insisting on a huge guaranteed profit. I then met with Evander and explained where we were in the negotiations. Evander said he wanted to make more for the Lewis fight than he got for the Moorer fight and asked me to try to get him $25 million. Evander did, however, give me authority to make the deal at $20 million if necessary, because he wanted the Lewis fight so badly so that he could unify all of the major heavyweight titles. Meanwhile, King had been talking with Abraham and with Lewis's primary promoter, Panos Eliades.

After meeting with Evander, I met again with King. I told King about my discussions with Abraham, which set King off, because he said that nobody was going to put any limits on what he could make and that I should not have been talking to Abraham. King insisted that he didn't work for free, and that if he wasn't assured of making at least $5 million, he was not going to make the fight. I argued that King's demand was unreasonable and breached his obligations to Evander and that it was reasonable for King to make a profit for his efforts, but not a guaranteed minimum of $5 million. I pointed out that years ago promoters were the parties who took the financial risk in fights, but today it is the television companies who take the risk and consequently, there is no justification for a promoter making a huge profit. I argued firmly that it is the fighters—not the promoters—people pay to see, so the fighters ought to get the bulk of the money.

My discussion with King turned to what Evander wanted to make for the fight, and I told him the number was $25 million. King said that was way too high and that he could not possibly guarantee Evander a purse that large. We ran projections of revenues and costs and ultimately agreed that King might need to come off his guaranteed minimum number and Evander might need to come off his. We agreed in principle that King and Evander might need to take some of their desired compensation on an *upside basis*, meaning if the fight did well enough in terms of pay-per-view sales, they could make some upside money over their guaranteed amounts. With that understanding, King and I set up a meeting with Abraham, Ross Greenburg, and Mark Taffett of HBO on December 22, 1997.

In the meeting with the HBO executives, we exchanged pleasantries and all generally agreed how great it would be to have this fight happen. Then we got down to business. Abraham confirmed that the Lewis side would take $10 million and asked what Evander wanted to make. I told him Evander wanted a guarantee of $25 million. Abraham predictably said that would not work, and I said there was some flexibility in that number, which Abraham correctly interpreted as a signal that in the end we would take a guarantee of about $20 million. Eventually we received HBO's offer. In essence, HBO was offering to put up a guarantee that, along with other anticipated revenue sources, would be enough to pay the two fighters a total of $30 million. Depending on what numbers were plugged in for things like international television sales, however, not all of the costs of the fight would be covered, and there was no money on the table for King to make anything.

I was not too disturbed about this offer because, although it was clearly inadequate, it was after all, just an opening offer. An hour later, however, I was becoming very discouraged, because HBO had not moved one dollar. King explained that he would have the financial responsibility for the costs of the promotion, would have numerous people from DKP working for months, would have no assurance of receiving any revenue from the fight, and could lose a lot of money. Taffett explained that HBO simply could not increase its offer. I told Abraham I was very disappointed, because I understood from my prior discussions with him that if Evander would fight for $20 million, HBO's guarantee would cover the purses, costs, and a reasonable profit for DKP. Abraham said that he had to defer to others on estimating the revenues from the fight, especially the international sales, and that based on HBO's calculations, the offer made by HBO would allow King to make some money. When King and I tried to continue the negotiations, we were told that we were all wasting time and effort because the decision as to the amount of HBO's guaranty was made at the highest levels of the Time Warner organization. The meeting ended, as did any chance of Evander fighting Lewis any time soon.

# CHAPTER 8

# 1998: THE YEAR OF WAITING

During January 1998, Evander and I turned our attention to lining up Evander's next opponent now that Lewis was not a possibility in the immediate future. Don King was pushing a fight against a white South African fighter named Frans Botha (a.k.a. the "White Buffalo") to be held in South Africa as part of a celebration of President Nelson Mandela's 80th birthday. Evander knew President Mandela from his trip to South Africa and had great respect for him, and I was a great admirer of President Mandela, so we liked the idea of the fight in South Africa. King was insisting that he could and would put together this fight and that the South African government would support the fight financially. Ambassador Andrew Young's partner in a company named Good Works, Inc., Carl Masters, however, told me that it was very unlikely that the South African government would put a substantial amount of money into the fight. Masters was very well connected in South Africa and had recently hosted President-elect Imbeke at his home in Jamaica, so I gave Masters's information great weight. I was very skeptical about the South Africa fight ever happening, and I was worried about losing time while we chased this ghost.

By early February, there was a lot of buzz about the South Africa fight, and I was receiving calls from all of the reporters. Although I hoped the South Africa fight would materialize, I remained very skeptical, and I sent a series of letters to King designed to preserve Evander's legal options if the fight did not occur. By contract, DKP owed Evander a fight no later than May 9. I did not believe King could pull off the events he was planning in South Africa in the 90-day period remaining, and I did not want DKP to have an argument that Evander had waived the deadline by supporting the efforts to make the Botha fight. Consequently, while Evander and I were publicly supporting King's efforts to make the Botha fight, I was privately protecting Evander's legal rights to the great annoyance of King.

While the Botha fight was being discussed in the newspapers, Butch Lewis, who promoted Vaughn Bean, and whom we were forced to pay in order to do the Moorer fight, called me to ask what Evander was planning to do. Lewis said he would allow the South Africa fight to proceed because of the worthy cause it served, but he wanted assurances that Evander would fulfill his IBF mandatory bout with Bean immediately afterward. I told Lewis that Evander would definitely fulfill his IBF requirement but needed to worry about his WBA mandatory also, which was due in June 1998. Lewis insisted that the Bean fight go before the WBA mandatory, and he and I agreed to disagree for the time being and wait to see what happened. I also discussed the conflicting mandatory requirements with the IBF's general counsel, Walter Stone, who promised to work with me and be reasonable in developing a schedule for Evander to keep both the WBA and IBF belts.

While all of this was happening on the boxing front, I learned from Evander some startling and disturbing news. While Evander's marriage was crumbling in 1997 and he was trying to decide what to do about it, he had spent time with two women, both of whom became pregnant in late 1997 after Evander had decided to divorce Janice. I was deeply saddened by seeing how embarrassed and repentant Evander was about these self-proclaimed mistakes, and he and I knew in our hearts, especially because of Evander's refusal to lie, it was just a matter of time before the news got out.

Then, on February 9, 1998, Evander and I went to New York for the ESPY Awards, where Evander won the award for best boxer of 1997. It was on this trip that Evander told me that Janice was about two months pregnant. When I called Janice and congratulated her, it was obvious that she was thrilled to be pregnant. I advised Evander that I fully realized and respected the fact that he needed to make his own decisions about his marriage, but that from a public relations perspective, it would be a big mistake to leave Janice while she was pregnant. Evander said he had already decided he needed to stay until the baby was born.

Soon thereafter, Evander and I were asked by Senator John McCain and his chief of staff, Paul Feeney, to meet with the senator in his office in Washington. Senator McCain was, and continues to be, a champion of boxing reform, and we were honored to be asked to help. We met with Feeney and Senator McCain on February 2, 1998, for about 45 minutes, during which the senator asked for our thoughts on what measures could be taken to improve boxing and better protect fighters against economic exploitation. Evander and I shared a number of thoughts and observations. One of the things Evander emphasized was that fighters needed to have a competent, committed lawyer to fight solely for the fighter.

## HOLYFIELD

*I've seen a lot of fighters get taken advantage of in this game. The promoters say they're for the fighters, but they're really trying to take care of themselves. The managers are supposed to take care of the fighters, but too often they are concerned about their long-term relationships with the promoters and television companies. A lawyer has a duty to put his client first. I decided to have my representative be a lawyer in a top-notch law firm, and it was one of the best decisions I've ever made. I would like to see all boxers have a lawyer who is responsible for taking care of their interests.*

In late February, with the issues regarding Evander's next fight still unsettled, I got a call from Greg Fritz, who was a friend and adviser to the great light heavyweight (175-pound limit) fighter, Roy Jones Jr. Fritz said he and Jones wanted to come to Atlanta and have dinner with Evander and me and pick our brains on what Jones should do next with his career. I talked to Evander, who readily agreed, and we all met in a private dining room at my favorite Atlanta restaurant, Pricci.

After all the pleasantries, Jones expressed his frustration about not having enough viable opponents who would justify big purses. Jones had thoroughly dominated his weight division and was looking for a challenge. He asked whether Evander had any interest in fighting him. Jones was then fighting at 175 pounds and had moved up from middleweight (160) to super-middleweight (168). Evander very politely and respectfully told Jones that he would not participate in a bout with anyone Jones's size because Evander had nothing to gain. If Evander won, people would say he merely beat a guy who was too small to fight as a heavyweight. Evander did tell Jones, however, that if Jones beat another top heavyweight, Evander would fight him.

By March, it had become clear that the South Africa fight could not be held soon enough to be Evander's next bout, if ever. Evander had two mandatory bouts due. The WBA mandatory contender was a Nigerian named Henry Akinwande, who was promoted by King. The IBF mandatory challenger was Bean, promoted by Lewis. It was apparent that King wanted Evander's next opponent to be Akinwande. The problems I could foresee with a fight against Akinwande were several. First, Evander's IBF mandatory bout with Bean was due immediately. We assumed the IBF would have allowed a unification fight with Lennox Lewis before Evander fought the IBF mandatory bout, but I had much less confidence that the IBF would grant an extension for Evander to fight his WBA mandatory first. Second, Akinwande had been embarrassed in a bout with Lennox Lewis only six months earlier, in which Akinwande was disqualified for excessive holding after several warnings. Consequently, most boxing writers and commentators did not consider Akinwande to be a worthy opponent. Third, there were questions about how Akinwande became the mandatory challenger under the WBA rules. A fighter named Orlin Norris had initiated legal proceedings in a federal district court in Philadelphia claiming he should be the WBA mandatory challenger. Fourth, Don Turner trained Akinwande, and although it was clear that if forced to choose, Turner would choose to train Evander, we preferred to avoid putting Turner in that position if we could. King and I engaged in a series of telephone calls, meetings, and correspondence as we negotiated for Evander's next fight, and I kept Evander informed daily on the status of the negotiations. Unfortunately, Bean was held in even lower regard by the boxing press than Akinwande, and there was widespread criticism of Bean being ranked No. 1 by the IBF. Many writers opined that Bean did not belong in the top 10. This was not an easy choice, but between the two, Akinwande was a more attractive and marketable opponent.

For the Moorer fight, Evander declared that he would not fight a major title fight for less than $20 million. This was not a matter of greed, but a belief that if properly promoted, a major title fight ought to generate a huge profit. In the case of Holyfield versus Moorer, however, for whatever reasons, the fight did not attract a large pay-per-view audience, and Showtime lost a lot of money. Knowing this, Evander and I knew that he could not receive anywhere near $20 million for a fight against Akinwande. Evander's master contract with DKP at that time guaranteed Evander at least $10 million per fight, and Evander authorized me to close a deal for the Akinwande fight for that amount, but I wanted to do better. I spent almost all of March in negotiations with King and Showtime trying to increase the value of the fight to Evander in ways that the other side could tolerate and justify. Through these negotiations we developed a unique and mutually beneficial deal that added several million dollars of value for Evander while costing the other side very little.

Our deal for the Akinwande fight, scheduled to take place at Madison Square Garden on June 6, was concluded on March 21, 1998, and immediately thereafter I went to Rome, Italy, for a week for a long-overdue vacation. While I was in Rome, a reporter with whom I had always had a good relationship, Wally Mathews of the *New York Post*, wrote an article sharply criticizing the choice of Akinwande as an opponent for Evander. Then when Mathews was preparing that article, he called me and I did not return the call because I was in Rome, so he wrote that I appeared to be on my way to becoming "a Don King pawn." I was outraged and hurt because I knew that I had fought as hard for Evander as anyone had ever fought for a fighter. I was so upset that I cut my vacation in Rome short and flew to New York to discuss the article with Mathews and attend the press conference for Holyfield versus Akinwande, which Evander and I had previously agreed I would miss so I could take a vacation. To Mathews's credit, when I explained the facts to him regarding Evander's options for an opponent, he sincerely apologized. I spent most of my speech at the press conference asking the many reporters assembled there to be more careful about the negative things they write about the sport of boxing and the people in it.

Ironically, four days later, on April 3, Evander and I attended the Boxing Writers Association Annual Awards Banquet, where Evander predictably was named Fighter of the Year, but where I surprisingly received a number of votes for Manager of the Year even though I was not technically a manager.

On May 29, I flew to Houston to meet with Evander, and we then flew to Los Angeles for a press conference for the Akinwande fight. Evander then gave a series of interviews, and that evening we attended the L.A. Sports Spectacular, a charity event featuring many of the world's best and most famous athletes. Of all the great athletes I talked to that night, no one was more impressive than Scott Hamilton, who had overcome childhood illness to become a world champion skater, then conquered cancer, and still had such an amazingly positive spirit. The highlight of the evening for me was that I had arranged for Evander to present an award to his friend Barry Bonds, the great San Francisco Giant outfielder, and I had the honor of introducing Evander to present the award to Bonds. The next day, Sunday, May 31, we flew to New York for fight week.

Fight week was occupied with the usual tasks and activities, including countless interviews—especially at Evander's daily workouts—preparation for and attendance at the final press conference, production meetings, rules meeting, and weigh-in. Finally, on June 5, we went to Madison Square Garden for Evander's final workout before the fight. Evander and all of the rest of the team were eagerly anticipating reaping the rewards of a long and hard training camp. Then we received a shock.

Soon after Evander began his workout, I was informed that Akinwande's blood test from his routine physical exam had just come back and showed that he had hepatitis B, a serious, difficult to cure, and contagious disease that Akinwande might have contracted on his trip to Africa a few months earlier. My heart sank with disappointment, and I dreaded having to disappoint Evander with the news that the fight had to be postponed, if not canceled. First, I told Turner, Hallmark, and Brooks, and we pulled Evander aside so that I could give him the news before a reporter did. When I told Evander what had happened, he took it as I should have expected.

## HOLYFIELD

*When I found out Henry Akinwande had hepatitis the day before the fight, I was obviously disappointed, but, once again this was something in God's hands and out of my control. I had no choice but to accept it. Getting angry and frustrated wouldn't have changed anything. Fighting Henry at that time was just not part*

*of the plan, so I calmly answered all of the reporters' questions and*
*flew back to Atlanta.*

I immediately began gathering information so that I could try to determine whether there was any action that could or should be taken. I talked to the members of the New York Boxing Commission and the doctor who had examined the lab reports on Akinwande's blood sample. Mostly, I wanted to know how this information could possibly not have been known prior to the day before the fight. I have never discovered any deliberate wrongdoing by anyone, but I have also never received any satisfactory explanation of how this could have happened. That night I met with Larkin and Greenburg of Showtime and King and Charlie Lomax of DKP to discuss what to do next. The best idea we would come up with was to get a drink, which helped us come up with the idea of possibly putting Evander's next fight in Atlanta. The next day, Evander and I returned to Atlanta without having satisfied Evander's WBA mandatory obligation, without a victory for Evander, and without Evander's purse of more than $10 million.

On June 8, there was a whirlwind of activity. I received scores of calls from reporters; Butch Lewis (about Evander's IBF mandatory obligation); Bob Halloran of the Mirage in Las Vegas (about what we would do next); King and Larkin (about options for Evander's next bout and Akinwande's medical prognosis); Dr. Vaughns (to give me a crash course on hepatitis B); representatives of Lennox Lewis (to ask what we planned to do next); Charlie Shaffer, the president of the Atlanta Sports Council (to ask about a leak from a reporter about the possibility of a fight in Atlanta); and many more. For the remainder of that first week after the Akinwande fight was postponed, I worked with Evander, Showtime, and DKP to explore ideas for a fight for Evander as soon as possible, because (a) he had received no boxing revenue in 1998 and (b) Evander had to deal with his IBF mandatory obligation.

On June 16 we met in New York and began to explore seriously the requirement of fighting Bean to satisfy Evander's IBF mandatory obligation. It appeared that Akinwande would be unavailable indefinitely. One of the major problems was that we would be going from a fight the boxing commentators generally disliked to a fight the boxing commentators universally hated. Nevertheless, we faced the very real possibility of Evander being stripped by the

IBF if he did not fight Bean next, which would make his goal of unifying the three major titles much more difficult. Another major problem was that there was no way to generate enough revenue from a Bean fight to pay Evander his guaranteed minimum of $10 million per fight. The question posed to Evander was whether he would be willing to take a substantial cut in pay to keep his IBF belt if the fight could be made in Atlanta.

**HOLYFIELD**

*I knew I had the right to demand a minimum of $10 million, which would have meant the fight would be in Las Vegas or New York, but when I found out there was a chance to fight in Atlanta, I was willing to take a huge pay cut so that all my friends, neighbors, and fans in Atlanta could get to see me in a heavyweight title fight. One thing I did insist on, though, was that most of the tickets be low enough in cost so that anyone and everyone could come. We could have fought in a 15,000-seat arena with high prices, but I wanted to fight in the Georgia Dome where we could sell tickets at very low prices because the dome would hold 40,000 people for a boxing event.*

With the help of Shaffer, I began to explore dates and costs with regard to a fight at the Georgia Dome. The only way to generate enough revenue to make the fight possible and make a large number of low-cost tickets available was to put the fight in a huge arena. We determined that the Georgia Dome could be configured for a boxing event with approximately 40,000 seats, but selling 40,000 seats for a fight was a daunting challenge. While I was working on venue issues, I was also working on satisfying the IBF and Lewis and Bean. Slowly, the off-the-wall idea of a heavyweight title fight in Atlanta was becoming a reality.

It was difficult to get much of King's attention at this point in time because he was fighting a battle that was much more important to him: a battle to stay out of prison. King had been indicted on insurance fraud allegations in U.S. District Court for the Southern District of New York, and his case was scheduled for trial in June 1998. While the King criminal trial was ongoing, Greenburg, Larkin, and I were trying to put together the Bean–Holyfield fight in Atlanta, conferring with King from time to time when we could get his attention—at night and on weekends. I even went to the courthouse in New York a few times to get a chance to talk with King and make my own assessment of how the trial was going. Although there were some difficult facts for the defense to deal with, I was impressed with King's defense counsel, Peter Fleming and Billy Murphy, and I got the sense the trial was going King's way.

Throughout the next three weeks, July 20 through August 10, I worked every day on trying to conclude the various deals for the Bean fight at the Georgia Dome. Finally, when Evander agreed to give up millions of dollars so that he could give this gift to his fans and neighbors in Atlanta, we had the deal done. Once the deal was done and the fight was announced for September 19, 1998, the real work began, because we had only six weeks to promote the fight. Normally, fight promotions are handled primarily by the television distributor and the promoter, but in this case, because it was our hometown, Evander and I were expected to do much more promotional work. I considered it my responsibility to do as much of the work myself as possible so that Evander could concentrate on training. I proposed a plan by which Evander would do no more than one hour of promotional work each day, and I would do the rest, and Evander approved the plan. With a few exceptions, any project that took more time than one hour would either not be possible or would have to accept me as a poor substitute for Evander. For example, Evander was asked by the Atlanta Sports Council to sit on a panel at a meeting of several hundred people along with legendary University of Georgia football coach Vince Dooley and the Atlanta Braves' stellar and ultra-successful general manager John Schuerholz. Because Evander was unable to attend due to his training schedule, I was asked to take his place to talk about the fight. As I said to the audience, sitting between these two sports giants, I felt like a Little Leaguer sitting between Hank Aaron and Babe Ruth. I also noted that even I was disappointed to be hearing me instead of Evander, so I could imagine what the audience thought. The audience was very kind.

During training camp for the Bean fight, Evander had another distraction in addition to helping with the promotion of the fight. Janice was due to deliver her baby in mid-September, and the fight was scheduled for September 19. Consequently, Evander moved his camp from Houston to his own gym on his estate south of Atlanta for the last few weeks before the fight. Janice was expecting soon, and that meant Evander took a lot of responsibility for his children while he was training for the fight. Evander would start his morning workouts at 5 a.m. so that he could finish in time to join his children at the breakfast table and then take them to school. It was touching to watch the warrior make the transition in a matter of minutes from throwing punches to making sure the kids had everything they needed for school.

### HOLYFIELD

*Some people made a big deal out of the fact that I was taking care of my kids while Janice was about to deliver our baby and I was training, but to me it was simple. Being a father and boxing were my two most important jobs, in that order, so I had to do what was necessary to get both jobs done.*

By the time fight week arrived, we were all tired but excited and relieved to know that the fight would be a huge success because it was becoming increasingly apparent that we would sell out the Georgia Dome. Everything seemed to be going so well, and we could not wait for the fight. Then the biggest distraction of all for Evander occurred.

Early in the morning on September 12, just seven days before the fight, Janice's and Evander's son, Elijah Jedidiah Holyfield was born, but that was not the major distraction. When Elijah was born, the public knew that Elijah became Evander's seventh child. Later on the same day, someone placed an anonymous telephone call to Jeff Shultz, the primary boxing writer for *The Atlanta Journal-Constitution*, and told him that Evander had had two more children within the last year. Shultz, who had become a friend over the years we were both in boxing, came to see me and privately asked me how many children Evander now had after Elijah's birth. I told Shultz I did not want to talk about this issue. Shultz said he already knew that Elijah was Evander's ninth child and that he knew about the two undisclosed babies. I told Shultz I could not respond.

"Jim, I already know the truth, and you know and I know that when I ask Evander, he won't lie and he won't disavow any of his children, so I have to write the story," he said plainly.

Shultz, who liked both Evander and me, obviously hated the position he was in and explained that he had no choice but to write the story and had come as a courtesy to give Evander and me the opportunity to tell Evander's side of the story. I made the best arguments I could for why this was not sports news, and Shultz explained that the story would certainly come out soon and when it did and it was discovered that Shultz had sat on it, he would be fired, and he and his family could not accept that risk. I asked for some time to talk the situation over with Evander and decide what to do, and Shultz said we could have the weekend to decide what to do, provided I promised to call him immediately if I had any reason to suspect that someone else might break the story. I agreed. I went immediately to Evander's house and explained the situation. I recommended to Evander that I try to get the newspaper to hold the story until after the fight and that we then sit down with Shultz and explain the facts from Evander's perspective. My feeling was that, if the story had to come out, at least we could try to make it as accurate as possible, and Evander agreed.

**HOLYFIELD**

*I have made many mistakes in my life, but this was one of my worst. While my marriage was falling apart, I did some foolish things. I had my reasons, but I make no excuses. What I did in having sex with other women while I was still married was wrong and I take full responsibility. Some people said the problem was that I didn't use birth control, and I understand what they mean, but to me, they are missing the point. If I had used birth control, maybe the babies wouldn't have been born, but what I did would have been just as wrong. Once it had been done, however, there was nothing to do but make the best of it and try to learn from it and hope I could teach my kids not to make the same mistake. One thing I will never do is turn my back on any child of mine, so when asked, I freely admitted these were my children, and I would care for them and love them all their lives.*

On September 15, I called the paper's business manager, who told me he could not discuss content in the paper due to an absolute "Chinese Wall" between the business side and the editorial side of the paper. I then called Don Boykin, the editor of the sports section, and made my arguments on why the story should not be reported. He listened sympathetically, but respectfully and firmly disagreed. When it became clear that this was not a case I could win, I moved to my next request, which was to hold the story until after the fight, not only for Evander's sake but also for the benefit of everyone who had worked so hard on this event. We eventually agreed that the story would be held until after the fight on two conditions: (1) Evander would sit down with Shultz immediately after the fight and tell his side of the story, and (2) if I got any indication that anyone else might break the story, I would call Shultz immediately.

Evander has amazing powers of focus and concentration when it comes to training and fighting. He had beaten Buster Douglas just days after being surprised with divorce papers from his first wife, Paulette. But the fact that he was about to be ridiculed around the country, and to some extent the world, within one week and that he would widely be called a hypocrite had to take a toll on him. I know it did on me.

## HOLYFIELD

*Of course it was difficult knowing that the newspaper would soon report that I had had two children out of wedlock, but I had to live with the consequences of what I had done. If I had let myself get down and feel sorry for myself, that would have just been another way of quitting. The issue of my mistakes was a matter between me and God, and other people could think what they wanted. I could not control or worry about that. I had a job to do, and I needed to focus on it, and defeat Vaughn Bean, but it would be dishonest to say it was not difficult to concentrate totally when I knew my children and my whole family would need to deal with this news. All I could do is pray, learn from my mistakes, and live the best life I could live going forward.*

Finally, it was fight night, and Team Holyfield was to arrive at the Georgia Dome by 9 p.m. I arrived separately at 7 p.m. to see if there was anything I could do to help. As the preliminary matches were fought, it was exciting to see the dome begin to fill up. Very few fights in the history of the United States have had as many as 20,000 fans, and only one had ever had more than 40,000. By 9:15 p.m. when the team's limo had not arrived, I was becoming very nervous. I called Evander on the cell phone and got good news and bad news. The good news was that the streets were jammed with people going to the fight. The bad news was that the team limo was stuck in traffic. Finally, a little after 9:30 p.m., the team arrived and I breathed a sigh of relief. After the usual prayer, gospel music, and warmup, we left the locker room for the ring. The sound of 40,000 hometown fans screaming for Evander was beautiful, and the view of such a huge crowd from the ring was awesome. Finally, the fight was on.

Evander fought well and with energy in the first few rounds, clearly winning but not doing much damage. Bean was fighting defensively, holding repeatedly and covering up whenever Evander attacked and then holding again. It became apparent that Bean was not really trying to win, at least not early, but instead was trying to survive, possibly thinking Evander's age would slow him down in the final rounds if he could just last until then. Bean had the kind of defensive style that gives Evander trouble and sometimes frustrates him. Evander believes fighters have an obligation to try to win regardless of the odds, and Bean did not seem to be doing that. In the middle rounds, Evander didn't do much.

After the fourth round Turner told him, "You took that round off."

I believed I was seeing the same kind of frustration in Evander I saw in the Bobby Czyz fight. Evander was fighting a guy who could not hurt him, could not win because he would not take a risk, and was merely trying to go the distance and win a moral victory. Evander told me later he wondered what he was doing in the ring with a guy like this.

In the closing rounds, Evander seemed to get over his frustration and started to attack again. In the 10th round, Evander knocked Bean into the ropes and then dropped him hard as he bounced off the ropes. It looked like Bean was out, but he somehow got to his feet before the count of 10 and was then saved by the bell. When Evander dropped Bean, Butch Lewis jumped up on the apron of the ring and was screaming at the referee, claiming there was some kind of foul. Then Lewis started screaming at and taunting Evander. In my opinion, Lewis was probably trying to steal the fight for Bean in the only way Bean could win—by disqualification.

## HOLYFIELD

*Vaughn Bean was a very frustrating guy to fight because he was awkward and didn't seem to be trying to win, but instead seemed to be trying to survive. When I finally caught him and his promoter broke the rules and jumped up on the apron and started*

*yelling at me, he was very lucky he jumped down in time, because*
*I was about to airmail him back to his seat.*

The last two rounds were uneventful, and Evander won the fight on a unanimous decision. Immediately after the fight, however, Lewis was in the ring screaming and yelling at the referee. At the press conference after the fight, Lewis continued his tirade and promised to protest the bout. Later, when the Georgia Boxing Commission threatened its own sanctions against Lewis, and maybe after he saw the video replay, he decided not to proceed with any protests.

The Atlanta fight was over. Evander had won, and the promotion was a success, but Evander had not won impressively against an opponent considered second rate. The situation was similar to the aftermath of the Czyz fight, and the consequences may also have been similar, because suddenly the Lennox Lewis camp, seeing Evander look so vulnerable, seemed to actually want to put together Holyfield versus Lewis. But first we had to deal with the unpleasant task of fulfilling our promise to *The Atlanta Journal-Constitution*.

On the day after the fight, Evander and I and one of Evander's ministers, Rev. Chris Halverson, met at Evander's house with Shultz. Evander was extremely forthcoming and candid with Shultz, and when the interview was over, Shultz sincerely thanked us and was clearly relieved to be done with this unsavory obligation. The next day, an article appeared in *The Atlanta Journal-Constitution* criticizing Evander severely, and then there was a torrent of press attention, criticism, and sick jokes about Evander.

It was very painful for me. I was defensive about my friend and angry that people seemed to be so willing to write off all of Evander's good deeds and behavior because he had made some serious errors in judgment. I saw tremendous hypocrisy in the accusers of hypocrisy. Evander took it much better than I did, caring much more about the judgment of the merciful and forgiving God he prayed to than the judgments of people who knew only a small portion of the facts. Nevertheless, at times the criticism did hurt Evander deeply, not because of what people thought, but because he knew he had made mistakes that warranted the criticism and because he had subjected his family to the embarrassment of this situation.

A few days later, another sportswriter for the Atlanta paper, and another generally good guy, Steve Hummer, wrote a scathing attack on Evander. I wrote, and the paper published, the following letter to the editor in response to Hummer's editorial, which expressed and reduced somewhat my anger and frustration.

---

I am writing in response to Steve Hummer's gratuitous, self-righteous, and misleading condemnation of Evander Holyfield and tacit dismissal of the many generous contributions Evander has made to our community during the past 14 years. Although I am Evander's attorney, advisor, and friend and obviously cannot be completely unbiased, I will attempt to be as objective as possible and point out certain facts about, and inconsistencies in, the opinions expressed by Mr. Hummer.

There is absolutely no "news" in Mr. Hummer's column. Instead Mr. Hummer has deemed himself invited and qualified to sit in judgment of Evander, and Mr. Hummer's conclusion is that mistakes made by Evander in his private life render his many years of voluntary public service meaningless. One wonders upon what basis this sportswriter deems himself qualified to render moral and philosophical judgments on others. If Mr. Hummer's opinions were not so unfair and misleading, they could simply be dismissed, but several points demand a response.

First, Mr. Hummer responds to the contention by many that Evander's personal problems are none of Mr. Hummer's business by stating "it was Holyfield who came clean," implying that Evander volunteered to have painful and embarrassing information publicly disseminated. Mr. Hummer knows that Evander provided information only when it was made clear to him that an article would be published with or without his participation.

Second, Mr. Hummer calls Evander a "champion who had constructed a shining image." Mr. Hummer knows perfectly well that Evander is one of the few celebrities of his stature who does not have a publicist or public relations agent.

Evander was content to be himself and allow others to draw their own conclusions, and he has never tried to construct any image.

Third, Mr. Hummer declares last week's *AJC* article to be "the first undressing of [the Holyfield] myth" and refers to Evander as "this publicly pious fighter." Mr. Hummer knows that Evander has always admitted he has fathered children out of wedlock and has never purported to be anything other than a man who has flaws and makes mistakes like any other man. If Mr. Hummer is disappointed to know Evander is not perfect, that disappointment is the result of Mr. Hummer's own unrealistic expectations.

Fourth, and most significant, Mr. Hummer declares that, because Evander made mistakes in his personal life, there is nothing about Evander that is worthy of respect or appreciation other than his performances in the ring. According to Mr. Hummer, Evander's life outside the ring should be judged solely upon recent personal problems, and we should forget or disregard:

a. the thousands of hours Evander has dedicated over many years to charitable endeavors in our community;

b. the millions of dollars contributed by Evander over many years to numerous community organizations to help the less fortunate;

c. the projects initiated by Evander to feed the hungry and provide disaster relief;

d. the fact that Evander has always made himself available to everyone in our community (including sportswriters who have often underestimated and criticized him);

e. the fact that Evander has always been open and honest about his mistakes and that the *AJC* was able to break this story only because Evander refused to lie or respond "no comment" when asked how many children he now has, because he will never disavow or fail to care for his children; and

f. the hundreds of speeches to children in which Evander tried to teach them his formula for success in his career: listen carefully, follow directions, and never quit.

These are some of the reasons why so many people have come to respect and admire Evander both in and out of the ring, not assumptions about marital fidelity or birth control practices. Evander has freely admitted to making mistakes in his personal life. Those mistakes are not insignificant, but they certainly should not overshadow the years of community service and good deeds by Evander. Life is not as simple as Mr. Hummer would have us believe. Even the best people have flaws, but that does not negate their better qualities. Evander is a kind, generous, honest, hard working, and yes, Mr. Hummer, admirable and inspiring man, who like all of us here on earth has made mistakes. Let those who have done more good for our community and have no flaws judge him harshly. Let the rest of us appreciate his contributions, and forgive his failures.

James J. Thomas II, Esq.

---

I received a great deal of support for my defense of Evander, and also some criticism, but from that point on, Evander and I agreed that we would no longer comment on this issue but would instead refer anyone inquiring about it to Shultz's article and my letter to the editor. Slowly and agonizingly, the references to this topic on television and radio talk shows and other media outlets began to subside.

Beginning immediately after the Bean fight and throughout the next three weeks, there was a frenzy of activity in an effort to put together a fight between Evander and Lennox Lewis. During this period, I was engaged in meetings or telephone conferences every day with Evander; King; Greenburg, and Larkin of Showtime; Abraham and Lou DiBella of HBO; English, the attorney for Main Events; and Milt Chwasky, the attorney for Lennox Lewis, with less frequent telephone discussions with Panos Eliades, whose company, Pannix Productions, was Lewis's European-based promoter. My main focus was on making sure King knew how badly Evander wanted this fight, with continuing subtle and at times not so subtle references to our alternatives if the fight could not be made due to any overreaching by King for his own benefit. Behind the scenes, I had my firm's litigation department evaluating and developing litigation strategies in the event they became necessary. I was also in frequent contact with King's in-house lawyers, Charlie Lomax and John Wirt, making sure they knew what our legal positions were, and I followed these conversations with correspondence preserving our legal options in the event things did not develop favorably. This was an extremely delicate task, because I very much wanted and needed King's cooperation, but I also needed to be ready to go to war if necessary, and this created a great deal of tension between King and me throughout this process. Adding to this tension was the fact that King and his lawyers disputed my right to be talking to any other parties and regularly threatened me with claims of improper interference with King's contractual rights.

I was especially careful during this potentially explosive period about my tone of voice and spoken and written word selection. Although I was obligated to Evander to protect his options to the maximum extent possible, I was well aware from firsthand experience that King does not respond well to threats or perceived threats. I was careful to call King and his lawyers before I sent a provocative letter and tell them it was coming and why I felt it was necessary, and I was extremely careful never to undercut King's bargaining positions publicly or disclose any confidential information he confided in me. Even though I was a constant thorn in King's side, we were able to work together because he respected the fact that I was honest and direct with him, and he knew that if we were forced to go to war it would not be because I did something behind his back. Although I made it harder for King to maximize his share of the pot at Evander's expense, he told me on several occasions he respected my commitment to Evander and my tenacity on his behalf.

Inevitably, there came a time when the negotiations between King and HBO hit the wall. In a nutshell, King wanted a higher guarantee from HBO, and HBO was not prepared to raise its offer any further. By my calculations, King was assured of at least a reasonable profit and had a good chance of making a huge profit. I shared my calculations with King, and as always, his numbers led to a different conclusion. I believed that King was holding out for a guaranteed huge profit for himself, and it was my position that killing the fight in this manner was a breach of King's implied covenant of good faith and fair dealing under New York law, which governed the contract between DKP and Evander. On the other hand, I felt that HBO and its parent company, Time Warner, had much to gain from the Holyfield versus Lewis fight and could afford to pay more for the distribution rights. In addition to other benefits,

After Don King and I (center) negotiated the Holyfield versus Tyson fight, Evander (far right) was able to defeat Mike Tyson to become the WBA heavyweight champion. *AP/WWP*

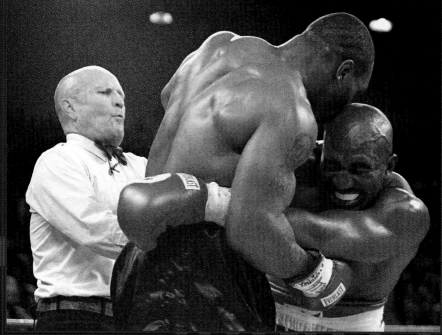

In the Holyfield versus Tyson rematch, Tyson shocked everyone when he bit Evander's ear twice resulting in his disqualification by referee Mills Lane. *Jeff Haynes/AFP/Getty Images*

Team Holyfield helped Evander prepare for every aspect of a bout—(back row from left to right) Tim Hallmark, Eddie Gilbert, me, Evander, Sharon Steuart, Gary Bell, Don Turner, (front row from left to right) Tommy Brooks, and Mike Weaver. *Photo courtesy of Jim Thomas*

Evander loves to dance. In fact while I was finishing up negotiations for the first Holyfield versus Tyson bout with Don King in Toronto, Evander was at a nightclub called the White Dove. Here he is dancing at a club we went to in Hamburg named Trax. *Photo courtesy of Jim Thomas*

As a fellow competitive athlete and someone who had served the interests of sportsmen, I was a natural fit when Evander needed litigation counsel after becoming the undisputed Heavyweight Champion of the World in 1990. *Photo courtesy of Jim Thomas*

In 2000 Evander and I attended the Olympics in Sydney, Australia, while we struggled to put together a rematch between Evander and John Ruiz. *Photo courtesy of Jim Thomas*

Evander and I were able to do a little bit of sightseeing before the third Holyfield versus Ruiz fight, which was scheduled for August 4, 2001. Unfortunately, Ruiz injured his neck and the fight was postponed and relocated to the United States because HBO was concerned about the safety of its crew internationally following the September 11 attacks. *Photo courtesy of Jim Thomas*

Evander battled John Ruiz in a rematch in March 2001, where Ruiz won a unanimous decision after 12 rounds of close fighting, becoming the first Latino Heavyweight Champion of the World. In my opinoin, Evander knocked out Ruiz in the 10th round, but the referee mistakenly called the knockout punch a low blow, penalized Evander, and allowed Ruiz to recover. *John Gurzinski/AFP/Getty Images*

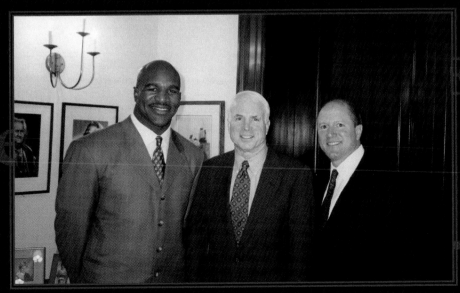

Evander and I met with Senator John McCain to help protect boxers and continue to improve the sport of boxing in the United States.
*Photo courtesy of Jim Thomas*

Shortly after Evander attended the Miss Universe Pageant, *Sports Illustrated* asked him to appear in their annual *Swimsuit Issue*. They asked with whom Evander wanted to pose, and Evander allowed me to choose his compatriot. For me there was only one option: Heidi Klum. I got to spend the day with her at the photo shoot, and Evander took this picture at the magazine release party.
*Photo courtesy of Jim Thomas*

Evander chats with some of his fellow judges at the Miss Universe Pageant, including Melania Knauss (second from left), who is now Donald Trump's wife.
*Photo courtesy of Jim Thomas*

In representing Evander I have been very fortunate to meet many celebrities at the various events Evander attends. Here I was able to hang out with Steven Seagal at a fundraiser for Muhammad Ali. *Photo courtesy of Jim Thomas*

Evander and Ali are the only two three-time Heavyweight Champions of the World. *Photo courtesy of Jim Thomas*

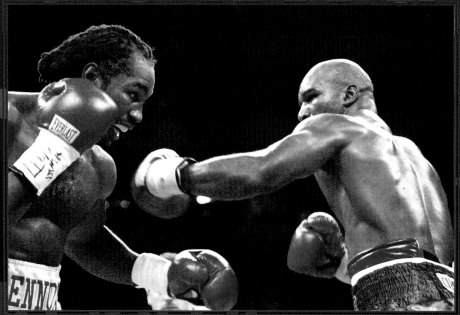

On November 13, 1999, Evander fought Lennox Lewis for the undisputed Heavyweight Championship of the World. I, along with many others, thought Evander won the fight, but the judges gave the decision to Lennox, depriving Evander of his goal of retiring as the undisputed champion. *Jeff Haynes/AFP/Getty Images*

Lewis was still relatively unknown, and if he were to defeat Evander, HBO would have a hot property—the undisputed Heavyweight Champion of the World. I wanted HBO to put more into the pot, but HBO was digging in its corporate heels and would not budge. Under these circumstances, I was publicly and officially pushing HBO to satisfy King's demands while privately attempting to pressure King into lowering his demands. By talking with Evander every day, I kept him fully informed of all developments, and he always had the ability to dictate another direction, but we were fully in accord.

## HOLYFIELD

*I wanted to fight Lennox Lewis because he had the belt I needed to become once again the undisputed Heavyweight Champion of the World, and I understood that I could get the fight by agreeing to an unfairly low purse, but, as a matter of principal, I was not willing to do that. Jim and I knew the amount of revenue the fight was likely to generate, and I wanted my fair share. I did not think it was fair for the people who sat safely outside the ring to make the money.*

With the negotiations between King and HBO stalled, I went to New York on October 15 for meetings scheduled to be held throughout the day between King and Abraham, while I kept Evander informed with telephone calls throughout the day. It became clear that HBO was interested in doing the deal only if the fight were held at Madison Square Garden, and in our discussions, we assumed the fight would be at MSG. I felt this was a pivotal day and I began to fear it would end like the meeting in New York almost a year earlier when we all shook hands and accepted that the deal could not be made. Toward the end of the day, little progress had been made. Apparently, hoping that a change of atmosphere might help, Abraham invited King and me to his apartment that evening for dinner and drinks and a continuation of our negotiations. When we arrived at his apartment, we met his wife and daughter, sat in the living room of his apartment, and exchanged small talk. Eventually, we started to get down to business. Soon thereafter Chwasky and DiBella arrived. I was surprised they had been invited and felt that King and Abraham would have had a better chance of making a deal without their presence. King explored ways to sweeten the pot, and Abraham tried hard to convince King that it was as sweet as it was going to get. Finally, late that night after hours of discussion and a very nice meal, Abraham made a very significant concession on the condition that it would end the negotiations and King would not ask for more.

At that point, I asked to take a break and talk to King. We went outside the apartment to the hall, and I made a decision on what to do. One option was to tell King that his failure to accept the financial terms now on the table would be a clear breach of his contract with Evander and would give us grounds to terminate it. Instead, I took a different route. I told him I had two points I wanted to make. First, I asked him to please accept this deal for Evander's sake. Second, I told him that if he did so, I would waive all of the potential breaches of the contract in the past, which I had been holding over his head, and would never raise them again. We looked at each other for a while.

"I'm going to do it for Evander," he said finally, "and I'm going to hold you to what you just said. This deal will not get held up over money, but let me do it my own way."

I thanked him, we shook hands and rejoined the others, and I trusted him to keep his word. It might surprise some people that I trusted King to keep his promise, but although I had often had great difficulty getting King to agree to what I considered reasonable positions, in my personal experience he had never broken a direct man-to-man promise to me once he had made it.

King told Abraham that he appreciated this revised offer, and it just might be enough to get the deal done depending on a lot of other smaller issues that needed to be worked out between DKP and HBO, such as rooms and tickets for the fight and who paid for the necessary press tour, etc. King and Abraham agreed to work together on those issues as soon as possible, and both agreed that they should be able to reach agreement and would have their respective lawyers begin work on the necessary contracts. At that, we all shook hands, and King and I left.

Once we were outside, I thanked King, but he reminded me that he still needed to reach agreement with Eliades and that he was going to need to get some type of rights to Lewis's future fights to do the deal. I decided not to argue that point at that time and just let it pass, knowing King knew very well my position on extracting futures on an opponent as a condition to a fight. King also noted that there were open issues with HBO and he did not yet have a site deal with Madison Square Garden. He said we needed to sign a bout agreement for Holyfield versus Lewis as soon as possible, and we agreed to meet at his New York apartment on the following day to work out the agreement. I was very excited, and I called Evander to tell him about the progress we had made.

The next day I went to King's apartment to work on a bout agreement with King and Wirt. While I was there, King was on the telephone with Eliades in London negotiating the deal between DKP, as the lead promoter of the fight, and Pannix Productions and Main Events as promoters for Lewis. As expected, King was insisting on the futures on Lewis, and Eliades was steadfastly refusing any futures, except to agree to a rematch if Lewis won. King and Eliades were also negotiating the terms of the potential rematch. Eliades wanted to talk with Chwasky and English, and King and Eliades took a break from their negotiations.

King and I then met. King began by accusing Eliades of having reneged on his deal with King on the futures, but I already knew from English and Chwasky that whether or not Eliades had made such a deal, Main Events and Lewis were never going to agree to give DKP the futures on Lewis, and Main Events and Lewis needed to sign off on any such deal. I told King that I did not believe there was any chance he would get the futures on Lewis, and he suggested that there would be no deal without them, which caused me to remind him that such a position was, in my view, a breach of his duties to Evander. King said he would give up his demand for the futures, but only if Evander agreed to stay under contract with him even if he lost. King's position was that he could not afford to have no piece of Lewis, lose Holyfield, and be shut out of the top of the heavyweight division, something that had happened to him in the early 1990s and that he vowed would never happen again. It was very hard to tell whether King would have killed the fight over this issue. Throughout the years he had prospered precisely because he has always hedged his bets, and there was no assurance he would go forward without a guarantee that he would have either Evander or Lewis when this fight ended. On the other hand, if I could have proven that this fight did not happen because of this issue, I would have the strongest ground yet for terminating Evander's contract with King, but not without an intense legal battle and very likely losing the chance for Evander to consolidate the titles. It was a tough decision.

I told King I needed to discuss this issue with Evander, and I left the apartment to call Evander, whom I had asked to stay by the telephone. I explained the entire situation to Evander. I told him King might be bluffing and that one strategy was to call his bluff, refuse to give future promotional rights if Evander lost, and hope if we had guessed wrong, we would have the opportunity to cave in later. Evander did not like this strategy. He astutely noted that these negotiations could fall apart at any time, and he didn't want to take that risk, especially when Lewis's side would be able to truthfully blame the inability to do the fight on King's insistence on the futures. Above all, however, Evander said to give King what he wanted, because there was absolutely no chance Evander would ever lose again, so the issue was moot. This was Evander's call, and he made it with the awareness of all of the issues and consequences, and, as always, I implemented his decision. I went back to King's apartment, and we worked out the bout agreement with no further problems. Evander was to receive a guaranteed payment in excess of $20 million, plus a potential upside on the pay-per-view buys. The following day, Evander and I went over the bout agreement, he signed it, I sent it back to King, and our part of the deal was done, but King still had issues outstanding with HBO, MSG, and Pannix/Main Events. He did, however, honor his promise to give up his demands for the futures, and he did keep his promise not to kill the deal by seeking more money from HBO.

### HOLYFIELD

*I was willing to agree to stay with Don King if I lost for three reasons. First, I did not see any way I would lose. Second, I would need to be promoted by somebody, and King would probably have the power to give me the best chance to get another shot at the titles. Third, I did not want to go through an extended legal battle at this stage of my career.*

For the next month, from October 15 until November 15, the negotiations between King and HBO, between King and the Lewis camp, and between King and Madison Square Garden dragged on. One of the big issues between King and Lewis was that King had obtained tentative approval from the WBA to sanction the bout as a WBA heavyweight title bout despite the fact that Evander's WBA mandatory bout had been overdue since June 1998. The WBA's sanction was given on the condition that both Evander and Lewis would commit to fight the WBA mandatory challenger in the winner's next bout or voluntarily surrender the WBA title. Evander had readily agreed to this provision in his bout agreement, but Lewis and his advisers were balking. The lawyers on the Lewis side were attempting to alter this provision, and King's lawyers were not agreeing to the alterations, contending that the WBA would not agree to the changes. Ultimately, Lewis did sign the provision insisted upon by King.

As King's negotiations with HBO dragged on and once again reached an impasse, King again turned to Evander and me for help in making the deal. He claimed the numbers did not work for him due to cash flow considerations. King had been obligated to give us a letter of credit for Evander's purse 21 days before the fight. King was asking Evander to reduce the amount of the letter of credit by $2 million and accept a check for that amount immediately after the fight. I had always made absolutely sure Evander was guaranteed payment of his purse, and this would be an exception, but Evander agreed to do what King asked. His reasoning was "I'll trust the man this one time, and if he doesn't pay me, I'll be done with him."

The HBO deal was still not done by early November, and I was scheduled to travel to Ottawa for several days to visit my friend and former partner, Gordon Giffin, who was then serving as the U.S. ambassador to Canada. Before leaving, I wrote a restrained and carefully worded, but strong, letter to King, with a copy to Lomax, insisting that the deal would have to be closed immediately or Evander would need to explore his other options, including termination of the promotional contract with DKP. I was careful to emphasize that was not the result we wanted and would greatly appreciate King doing whatever was necessary to get the deal closed immediately. I sent the letter by fax and left immediately for Ottawa.

That evening Ambassador Giffin and his wife, Patti, hosted a formal dinner at their residence with some of the most powerful and influential ministers, members of Parliament, and business leaders in Canada and their wives. I was nervous and very much wanted to make a good impression and at least not embarrass the Giffins. After we discussed Canadian political matters for a while, Ambassader Giffin turned the conversation to boxing, and it led to the status of our negotiations for the Lewis fight, which was of some special interest to Canadians because Lewis had lived in Canada and had fought for the Canadian Olympic team in 1988. While we were talking, the ambassador's butler, Gianni, came in and whispered to the ambassador.

Ambassader Giffin turned to me and said, "Jim, you have a telephone call."

I was very embarrassed and told Gianni to take a number and explain that I was with the ambassador and his guests and could not be interrupted for anyone.

"I have already done so, sir," Gianni replied, "but the gentleman simply will not take no for an answer. It's a Mr. Don King."

Everyone at the table laughed and asked me to please take the call.

I stepped into the next room and said hello to King and Lomax, who said they had just received my letter. Lomax and King were in an unusually good mood, especially in light of having received my letter.

"What does Holyfield have over you? We've never seen anyone fight so hard for a fighter," they kidded me.

I said I was just doing my job, and Lomax asked if I would mind taking a little vacation and giving them a break.

"Jim, tell Holyfield I'm gonna do the deal," King said. "It might take a few days, but it will get done, so just be patient a little longer. You have my word."

I returned to the dining room to apologize for the interruption but was greeted with congratulations from everyone. I asked how they knew what had happened, and they said they could hear every word King said and wondered if I could still hear after having my ear so close to the phone.

Finally, two months after the negotiations for Holyfield versus Lewis had begun, we had a deal just in time for Thanksgiving. The first thing Evander and I did was fly to New York to meet with the Showtime executives for dinner and thank them for allowing the fight to proceed. Then we spent Thanksgiving in Atlanta and went back to New York to start the press tour for the fight.

We began with two days of videotaping and still photography for the marketing of the fight and then held a press conference in New York at Madison Square Garden, followed by press conferences across the United States on four consecutive days. The fighters and their representatives, the HBO executives, King and his group, and Madison Square Garden representatives all traveled together on the venue's Boeing 727, which was used to transport the New York Knicks and the New York Rangers. The plane was extremely comfortable, and the food was great. Lewis and his team took the back portion of the plane, Evander and our team took the front portion, and the purportedly neutral parties took the center section. Although the press conferences became monotonous, the travel and camaraderie were enjoyable, and we all got along surprisingly well. Evander and Lewis did not avoid each other but did not spend any time together either. The rest of us interacted as either friends or friendly foes.

After the press tour, it was time to go to work. Evander went to Houston to train, and I went to Atlanta to work on a number of matters for Evander. I was working hard to line up endorsements in time for the big fight. Also, I was taking a large role in acting as Evander's representative with respect to a documentary Evander had agreed to fund about boxing and his career and life. The film was to be directed and produced by three-time Academy Award winner, Jana Sue Memel, and I would act as executive producer along with her. Memel turned out to be a great talent and a tireless worker, and I thoroughly enjoyed working with her and her staff for the next two years.

At the same time, Evander also began investing his money in projects outside of the boxing world, specifically in the restaurant and music industries. With few exceptions, it was my philosophy that Evander should concentrate on boxing and boxing-related endorsements and appearances until his career was done. I was also strongly opposed to any deals in which Evander had to invest his own money. I thought we should do only deals that involved Evander being paid for his endorsement of products or in which Evander had no financial exposure or liability. Evander, however, had other ideas. First, although my strategy allowed Evander to keep the money he earned and add to it marginally, Evander wanted to be a billionaire and use his wealth to help people all over the world. Evander, therefore, was not in favor of my conservative approach. He wanted to go for great wealth and realized that to do so, he needed to take financial risks. Second, Evander wanted to own his own businesses so that his children would have businesses to run when they grew up. Third, it was clear that Evander felt the time had come to begin launching his own businesses because he expected his boxing career to be finished in the immediate future. Evander was certain he would defeat Lewis and be declared the undisputed Heavyweight Champion of the World. At that point, there would be nothing left for Evander to accomplish in boxing, and it would be time for him to retire.

# CHAPTER 9

# 1999: THE YEAR OF LENNOX LEWIS, GREAT FUN, AND TERRIBLE DISAPPOINTMENTS

The Lewis fight was scheduled for March 13, 1999, at Madison Square Garden, and on March 7, Team Holyfield arrived in New York. We stayed at the beautiful Trump International Hotel at Columbus Circle and trained at the Church Street Gym downtown, which meant we spent more than an hour a day in New York traffic. On the whole, though, our team was upbeat and extremely confident, and we looked forward to Saturday, when Evander would finally reach the goal he had been seeking since his comeback from his forced retirement in 1995. I had one concern, however. During the media frenzy leading up to the fight, Evander had publicly guaranteed he would knock Lewis out in the third round. This troubled me greatly for two reasons. First, it was completely out of character for Evander, who was always confident but always respectful and humble. Evander had followed the same approach for 15 years of professional boxing with great success, and I worried about what might have caused him to change so drastically. Second, as a practical matter, it was going to be extremely difficult to fulfill his prediction. A fighter as big, skilled, and cautious as Lennox Lewis could almost always avoid a knockout in any given round, and I wondered what the psychological effect on both fighters might be if Lewis avoided a knockout in the third round.

**HOLYFIELD**

*My guarantee of a knockout of Lennox Lewis in the third round was a mistake. I was on a conference call with dozens of boxing reporters, and they started telling me that Lennox was calling me a hypocrite for calling myself a Christian and having children out of wedlock. They asked for my reaction, and I said I was going to knock Lennox out, and for emphasis I said I would do it in the third round. Once I said it, the reporters tried to get me to back down, and I dug in my heels. I never even hinted God had said anything about a third-round knockout, but that is how the stories came out. This statement was not like me, and, in the end, it turned out to be a mistake I would learn from and not make again.*

Finally, the night on which we expected Evander to leave the ring as the undisputed Heavyweight Champion of the World arrived. We arrived at Madison Square Garden at about 9 p.m., with everyone on our team upbeat and confident, except that Evander was quieter than usual. After the obligatory locker room interviews, at about 10 p.m., Evander had his hands wrapped, put on his trunks, and went through his unvarying 20-minute stretching routine with Tim Hallmark. It was during the stretching that I first became concerned, because Evander was sweating profusely, even though the routine was slow, relatively easy, and normally did not cause Evander to sweat. I had done the warmup along with Evander many times and did not sweat much. Then, when Evander began to shadow-box and hit the hand pads, I became extremely concerned. Evander typically looked almost happy as he hit the pads and prepared to walk out to the ring, but this time he had a look of pain on his face, and he did not seem to be able to get comfortable in his stance. Hallmark asked what was wrong, and Evander said his legs and stomach were cramping and he couldn't stay down in his stance. Evander even tried to throw up to make himself feel better, but nothing helped release the cramping and pain.

## HOLYFIELD

*I felt terrible and considered not going forward with the fight, but I had convinced myself I would knock Lewis out in the third round, and I was sure I could make it through three rounds.*

Later, as we walked out of the locker room through the tunnel and into the arena, the crowd was going crazy. Lewis was already in the ring, and thousands of people from England, who had traveled to New York for the fight, had been cheering wildly for Lewis. Then, when Evander began to walk in to his gospel music, the Americans went wild. The atmosphere was electric. After the typical announcements, I left the ring to go to my seat next to Dr. Vaughns, and the fight began.

In the first two rounds, Lewis moved and jabbed and moved and jabbed, doing no significant damage and not committing himself. The problem was that although Lewis wasn't doing much, Evander was doing less, and I felt sure the judges would give the first two rounds to Lewis. Then the all-important third round began, and Evander looked completely different. He was quick and aggressive and was stalking Lewis, who was moving away trying to avoid the predicted knockout. It was obvious to me that because Evander felt so bad, he had given the first two rounds to Lewis so as to save his strength and surprise Lewis in the third, and it was working. Evander got to Lewis with some hard shots, and then he had Lewis in real trouble. But Lewis fought out of trouble and survived the assault, and Evander took a short break. Then Evander had Lewis in trouble again, and I think everyone in the arena was wondering whether Evander was actually going to deliver on his bold prediction. But then Lewis covered up and was content to simply survive the round, which was dominated by Evander.

At the end of the third round, even though he had been hammered, Lewis had a triumphant smile of relief on his face, which told me he had truly been worried about the prediction. Evander, on the other hand, slowly walked back to his corner, clearly very disappointed. Evander told Hallmark to work on his legs, which were cramping.

HOLYFIELD

*After the third round, I was discouraged because of how bad my legs and stomach felt. I knew I was in for a long, hard battle, and I felt terrible. I just prayed to God to give me enough strength not to quit and to help me make it to the end of the fight no matter how it came out.*

After seeing the third round, one would have expected to see a continuation of Evander's onslaught, and Lewis did appear to be very cautious. But Evander just didn't have his typically quick feet and couldn't get to Lewis as he did in the third round. Initially Lewis did very little but then seemed to sense that he was no longer in danger and threw some punches. The round was very close, too close for me to call for sure. Two of the three judges scored the round for Lewis, and one thought Evander won the round. Later, when I studied the videotape repeatedly frame by frame, I still thought the round was very close, but I thought Evander had a slight edge.

When the fifth round began, the fight was fairly even. Lewis had won two rounds but with no damage. Evander had one big round in which he hurt Lewis, and one round was very close. In the fifth round, however, Lewis turned Evander clockwise with his left hand on Evander's right shoulder and hit him with a hard right directly to the back of the head at the base of the brain. In my opinion, the fight should have been stopped, Lewis should have lost at least one point, and Evander should have been given time to recover. Fights move so fast, and referees often cannot see fouls due to positioning, and I thought Lewis got away with the shot to the back of the head. I have no idea whether the punch to the back of the head was intentional, and it could have been that Lewis was trying to land a legal blow, but I did see Michael Grant get hit with a similar shot to the back of the head by Lewis one year later.

HOLYFIELD

*A punch to the back of the head is illegal because the fighter can't see it coming, and it is very hard to recover from. When Lewis hit me at the base of the brain, it felt like my face was on fire and my brain was coming out through my face. I was hurt, but not by a legal blow.*

███████████████████████████████████████████████████

Not taking into account the rabbit punch, Lewis clearly won the fifth round. This was the round scored for Evander by judge Eugenia Williams, which later led to many accusations of wrongdoing. Ironically, had Judge Williams explained that her score was based upon not crediting Lewis with the illegal punch or any of the follow-up shots while Evander was stunned, many experts might have agreed with her upon review of the videotape, but she never did so.

Regardless of how Lewis hurt Evander in the fifth round, Evander was clearly stunned for approximately 30 seconds by the punch to the base of the brain, but Lewis still stayed back and was very cautious, never committing and never taking a chance to end the fight. Later, he said he was cautious because he knew how "crafty" Evander was and he did not want to fall into one of Evander's traps. By making that decision, Lewis was effectively deciding to allow the fight to fall into the hands of the judges rather than taking a chance to decide the fight himself.

In the sixth round, Lewis again played it safe, pawing with his left hand and holding at every opportunity. In my view, neither fighter did enough to win the round, and I scored it even, but I recognized that judges are told to avoid scoring rounds even and that Lewis would probably be given the round based on the lasting and continuing impression of dominance from the fifth round. The seventh round featured more of the same, except that Lewis landed a few effective shots, and, although Evander pursued Lewis throughout the round, Lewis retreated behind his jab-and-hold strategy, and Evander could not get to him with his increasingly cramping legs. At the end of seven rounds, I had the fight scored five rounds for Lewis, one for Evander, and one round too close to call.

In the eighth, ninth, 10th, and 11th rounds, Lewis became even more careful, Evander chased him around the ring while Lewis retreated, *pushing* but not snapping an ineffective jab to hold Evander off of him. Evander was not landing a lot of hard shots, but Lewis was landing almost none, content to push his soft left hand out to slow Evander and grab and hold whenever Evander got in close. Despite the fact that the HBO announcers were providing a one-sided infomercial for Lewis, their in-house fighter, it was clear to me that Evander should be awarded these four rounds and the judges agreed with me. In these four rounds, neither fighter had landed a lot of effective shots, and the total poundage of the punches was about even, but Evander was clearly the aggressor and dictated the action. Even Emanual Stewart, Lewis's trainer, apparently agreed with me as he repeatedly told Lewis between rounds that he was doing nothing and losing the rounds. Later, when asked about the scoring in a New York Senate hearing, Lewis did not dispute the scoring in favor of Evander of these four rounds although he felt they were all close. With one round to go, I had the fight scored dead even. Five rounds to each fighter and one round tied. Later, knowing how bad Evander felt, I considered these four rounds—eight through 11—as some of the most courageous of Evander's career.

Coming out for the 12th round, Evander was confident for the first time that he would get through all 12 rounds, and he came out very aggressively, taking chances in order to have a chance to knock Lewis out. Evander forged ahead, trying to catch Lewis with a dispositive shot while Lewis retreated and repeatedly landed relatively soft left jabs in Evander's face. There was a huge difference in styles and strategies. Evander took the chance to score a knockout by absorbing soft jabs while constantly pursuing Lewis. Lewis, on the other hand, was content to go backward, take no chances, and leave the decision in the hands of the judges. I admired Evander's decision to try to win, but when he did not catch Lewis, I felt Lewis would be awarded the round because of the number of jabs that were not effective punches but did land. With five seconds to go, Lewis raised his hands, apparently delighted that the fight would go to the scorecards.

## HOLYFIELD

*The fact that I didn't raise my arms after the Lewis fight had nothing to do with whether I thought I won or lost. I have never raised my hands at the end of any fight, even when it was obvious I had won. I give the judges more respect than to try to convince them to score the fight for me. Also, I was not happy at the end of the fight, because I had failed to do what I set out to do: knock Lewis out. The fact that Lewis was happy at the end of the fight told me he was happy to have the fight decided by the judges.*

*I am never happy to have the outcome of the fight in someone else's hands.*

████████████████████████████████████████████

I thought the fight was extremely close and extremely even. With the exception of the third and fifth rounds in which Lewis and Evander were rocked, respectively, neither fighter had dominated any round. Evander had been the aggressor, but Lewis had landed more jabs although many were ineffective and in my opinion, meaningless. But I must admit that, as I walked to the ring, I feared Lewis would win an extremely close decision.

When I arrived in the ring, Eliades approached me and offered his condolences.

"What makes you think Lennox won?" I angrily shouted back.

Although I feared the decision would go to Lewis, the fight was so close that I thought it was extremely presumptuous for Eliades to assume he knew the outcome. I was later told that Eliades suggested that my response indicated I might have known the scoring would go Evander's way. Quite the contrary, I knew enough about boxing to know that there is no way to be certain about a close fight that goes to the judges' cards. If anything, I wondered why Eliades was acting like he already knew the result, and I wondered if someone had signaled the result to him from the scorer's table. As it turned out, neither of us knew the outcome, because neither of us anticipated the actual result.

Judge Stanley Christodoulou of South Africa, appointed by the WBA, scored the fight 116-113 for Lewis. Judge Eugenia Williams of the United States, appointed by the IBF, scored the fight 115-113 for Evander. Judge Larry O'Connell, from Lewis's home of London, appointed by Lewis's organization, the WBC, scored the fight 115-115, a draw. The result was a majority draw, and each fighter retained his respective titles. The thousands of British fans in the arena booed, and Lewis and his group were furious.

Although with the exception of the rabbit punch in the fifth round, Evander had not been hit with many hard shots, he had been hit with hundreds of relatively soft, fully extended, pushed and pawing jabs, and in the last round, he was voluntarily walking into some stiffer jabs in an effort to score a knockout. The cumulative effect was significant swelling of Evander's face. That was superficial, however, and the real problem was the cramping of Evander's legs and stomach, which got even worse after the fight. When we got back to the locker room, Evander sat down and was in some distress from the cramping. Dr. Vaughns gave him an ice bag to reduce the swelling in his face, and the room was very somber. We were all so sure Evander would win that we were truly surprised that he had not. We reflected Evander's disappointment, and his disappointment was due not to the result, but to the fact that he had not fought as well as he expected. On the other hand, Evander was very proud that despite his physical limitations from the cramping, he had fought the very best he could under the circumstances and had not quit when almost anyone else would have. Evander was justifiably proud of having fought through adversity and having conquered the pain and temptation to give up.

Evander's older children were in the locker room, and Dr. Vaughns and I tried to assure them that their father was not badly hurt, that his face was only temporarily swollen, that the swelling would go down, and that he would be fine. Evander went to take a shower, and while he was gone I reminded everyone in the room that Evander had not won, but he had not lost and had overcome great adversity with a tremendously courageous performance. We all began to get over our shock, and the mood lightened. When Evander came back into the locker room from his shower, we gave him a sincere ovation. He smiled and clearly appreciated the gesture and support, but he was also still cramping and was in pain. I pulled Evander aside, along with Dr. Vaughns, and offered to go to the press conference and make excuses for Evander's absence so that he could go back to the hotel, lie down, and allow Dr. Vaughns to try to make him more comfortable. Evander would not hear of this. He said part of the job was to go to the press conference, regardless of the outcome, and he would get through it and then lie down.

When we arrived at the press conference, Lewis, Eliades, and Frank Maloney, who was Lewis's manager, were already there and had been lobbying the press with their view that Lewis had been robbed, and a lot of the members of the press were agreeing. What we didn't know was that many in the room had seen or heard about the HBO broadcast, in which the HBO announcers described a one-sided slaughter of Evander by Lewis, and in which the Compubox Punch Stats were shown throughout the fight purportedly "proving" that Lewis landed far more punches than Evander, especially far more jabs. Although Compubox is portrayed as an objective computerized analysis of a fight, it is really nothing of the sort. In my opinion, Compubox is a punch count made by two human beings pushing a button whenever they think they see a punch land, without due consideration to the extent to which the punch was effective, powerful, or did any damage at all. Although they purport to count power punches, the counters merely categorize all punches other than jabs as power punches. Compubox in my opinion is a useful tool in analyzing a fight but should never be considered dispositive of which fighter has won a round.

Some members of the press called for Evander to admit that he had lost. Evander refused to do so, pointing out that it would be disrespectful and harmful to boxing for him to dispute the judges' decisions in a close fight with no knockdowns, especially because they were watching the fight as judges and he was busy fighting. Evander said that when a fighter leaves the decision in the hands of the judges, he must accept the outcome, and that is what Evander had always done. When he had thought he beat Michael Moorer in 1994, he accepted the adverse decision with dignity and grace. He felt that is what Lewis and his camp should do. Evander said that if Lewis wanted another chance, Evander would be happy to give him the opportunity. King jumped on this issue and called for a rematch. The press cited this as an indication that King had somehow manipulated the result to require a rematch in which King would once again make a huge profit. There was one very serious problem with this theory: There was absolutely no evidence whatsoever to support it. In the past, King may or may not have done things in the best interests of boxing, but in this instance, the press was convicting King not only without a trial but without any facts to show any culpability at all. Further, this conspiracy theory made no sense whatsoever based upon one indisputable fact. If the decision had been a victory for Lewis, Evander and King had an absolute right to a rematch. There was no rematch clause in the event of a draw. Therefore, the draw was the worst possible result for King and us, and we all would have been better off with a loss and a right to an immediate rematch.

In addition to the utter lack of factual support or logical premise, there were other problems with the conspiracy theory. If the fight was one-sided, why did none of the judges score the fight that way? Judge Christodoulou scored the fight seven rounds to five in favor of Lewis. Is it unthinkable that one of the rounds Christodoulou gave to Lewis was close enough to be judged the other way? What about rounds four or six, which Christodoulou gave to Lewis? I defy anyone to watch those two rounds fairly and objectively and honestly say Lewis won clearly and indisputably. Finally, Lewis was from London and was the WBC's champion. When the IBF insisted on naming an American as its judge, the WBC insisted on naming a Londoner as its judge. If anything, the London/WBC judge would have been inclined toward Lewis. How and why did the London/WBC judge score the fight even?

Notwithstanding all facts and logic to the contrary, the accusations of a fix persisted, most likely because of King's involvement and reputation. To my knowledge, there was never any hint or suggestion from anyone that Evander, I, or anyone else on Team Holyfield participated in or knew anything about any wrongdoing, but there were rampant suggestions and speculation that King and/or IBF president, Bob Lee, had somehow influenced Judge Williams in favor of Evander. The theory was that even if she were not offered a bribe per se, she knew that prime judging positions, including all-expense paid trips overseas, depended on pleasing Lee, who for whatever reason, wanted to please King, who somehow benefited if Evander won despite the rematch clause in the contracts. It was implausible, but it made a great story, and writers are paid to write interesting stories.

**HOLYFIELD**

*The suggestion of a "fix" in the fight with Lewis made no sense. The outcome of the fight, a draw, was the worst possible outcome for everyone. If I had lost, I had a rematch clause. With a draw, I had nothing. If the fight had been fixed by Don King, it would have been fixed so that the outcome was good for him, and this outcome was not good for him.*

After the press conference, we all returned to the hotel, including Memel and her film crew, who had captured the evening's events on film for Evander's documentary. When Memel and her crew arrived right behind the limo Evander and I were in, she called to me as Evander was on his way up to his suite. She asked me to prevail upon Evander to allow her and her crew to come upstairs and shoot a few minutes of film. I declined the request, saying that Evander had been through enough for one night and needed some time with his children and to himself. She begged me to just ask Evander once, and if he declined, she would leave with no further requests. Memel knew what a warrior Evander is. I went up, asked him, and told him I thought he had had enough and needed to rest.

"Jim, if the documentary is going to be true, it needs to show both sides, the good and the bad. Tell them to come up," he said.

When Memel and the crew arrived, Evander was in bed with an ice pack on his left check. His kids were sitting on the foot of the bed. Evander was telling them that life has ups and downs, and things don't always go the way we want, but if we never give up, that is the ultimate victory, and that night he was victorious because he refused to give up. It was one of the most touching scenes I have ever witnessed, I was so thankful no one listened to me and that we caught this on tape.

## HOLYFIELD

*Victory depends on what the goal is. Once I knew my legs and stomach were all cramped up and once Lewis got past the third round, my goal was to finish the fight without quitting, which I badly wanted to do. When I got to the end of the fight, I thanked God for giving me the strength and courage to finish the fight, and I explained to my children that that was my victory.*

Evander then went to bed, and I went to a dinner party hosted by King at Bravo Gianni's on 63rd Street between Second and Third Avenue to try to learn what was being said about the fight. When I arrived about 2 a.m., King told me that the presidents of the WBA, WBC, and IBF had decided to recommend to their organizations that an immediate rematch be ordered to clear up the controversy, help alleviate the damage purportedly done to the sport by the controversial decision, and finally have an undisputed heavyweight champion. I found it curious that they had acted so quickly, but as it was what Evander wanted, I was pleased.

I then went back to the hotel, but I couldn't sleep. I lay awake wondering what was wrong with Evander. I thought about Turner telling me during the week that he was concerned about all of the nutritional supplements Evander was taking and that Larry Holmes, who was heavyweight champion for more than seven years, took no supplements but instead regulated his nutrition through the food he ate. I also remembered Dr. Harvey Shiller and his wife,

Marsha, stopping by Evander's suite on the morning of the fight. Dr. Shiller, had been a good friend of Evander's for years, dating back to the 1984 Olympics when the doctor had been president of the United States Olympic Committee, and had become a friend of mine. That morning, Dr. Shiller looked at the dozens of bottles and canisters of supplements arranged on the bar in Evander's suite and asked to talk with me privately. Dr. Shiller, who was then president of Turner Sports, told me that he had an advanced degree in chemistry and was very concerned about all of the supplements he saw and worried that they very likely had not been tested in all of their combinations with each other. It began to occur to me that Evander's cramping may have been related to an inadvertent imbalance in all of these supplements. I knew that the supplement program had been carefully developed by Hallmark in conjunction with various experts in the field, and I knew Hallmark cared about Evander as much as anyone, but I suspected there might be some type of reaction or imbalance that had occurred without anyone's knowledge.

The next morning, I met with Dr. Vaughns about this emerging theory, and he jumped all over it. He told me that before becoming a doctor, he had been a pharmacist and kept current as an expert in pharmacology. He said he felt confident we were on to something and that he wanted to give Evander comprehensive tests immediately to try to diagnose the problem if I could persuade Evander to do so.

Later that morning, I asked to meet with Evander. I told him I was once again venturing outside my jurisdiction, and I was sorry if it seemed like I was interfering, but I thought his physical problems in the fight might be related to nutrition and all of the supplements he had been taking. I told him about my discussions with Turner, Dr. Shiller, and Dr. Vaughns. Rather than being annoyed, Evander was very grateful and was excited about exploring this possibility, saying the same thought had occurred to him. He agreed to have Dr. Vaughns conduct the tests he wanted to do, and I asked whether he would mind if I explored the possibility of engaging an expert in sports nutrition, and Evander readily agreed.

**HOLYFIELD**

*I knew something was wrong with me, and when Jim suggested that maybe the problem was in how I was eating and the combi-*

*nation of the supplements I was taking, that made sense to me, so
I asked him to explore it.*

My subsequent research and talks with my friend, Joe Corley, a former
great karate fighter and president of the Professional Karate Association, convinced me that one of the best people, if not the very best person, in the field
of sports nutrition was Dr. Barry Sears, who had written the *Zone* books. I
quickly read each of Dr. Sears's books and learned that he had outstanding credentials, had done extensive research in sports nutrition, and had had tremendous success with the Stanford swimming team and many other athletes. Dr.
Sears's principles were based primarily upon insulin regulation, which kept
one's blood sugar level in the zone, rather than swinging wildly from low to
high and back again. The insulin regulation was accomplished primarily by eating the correct combination of high-quality protein, the right types of fats, and
high-quality, relatively slow-burning carbohydrates eaten in the right portions
at the right times. Although this sounded complicated, Dr. Sears had developed
rules and a system that really made staying in the zone fairly easy.

I called Dr. Sears, and he was extremely eager to help. He told me he had
been a big Holyfield fan and said Evander did not look like himself in the fight
against Lewis. Dr. Sears said that he had an off-the-wall theory that he assumed
wasn't correct, but he wanted to test it anyway. He asked whether there was any
chance Evander had eaten a big bowl of pasta, which is nothing but sugar in
disguised form, about three and a half hours prior to the start of the fight.
When I told Dr. Sears that Evander had eaten a large bowl of pasta at 8 p.m.
just before we left for Madison Square Garden and that the fight began at
11:30 p.m., he said that alone could have had a major adverse impact on
Evander's performance, but might not entirely account for the severe cramping.
He encouraged us to proceed with the tests Dr. Vaughns wanted to perform. I
told him I would call him as soon as we had the results.

I was very excited and called Larkin at Showtime to share this information
with him because we might have found the problem. Larkin thought the news
was great but corrected one thing. He tried to remind me that Evander ate the
bowl of pasta at 5 p.m., not 8 p.m. I politely told Larkin that I was positive it
was 8 p.m. Larkin asked how I could be sure because I wasn't there at 5 p.m.
was in my own room. Eventually, we realized that Evander ate a bowl of pasta

at 5 p.m. before his nap, then woke up with very low blood sugar, and craving a sugar fix for energy, had another bowl of pasta at 8 p.m. when I was there and Larkin wasn't. This created the worst possible roller-coaster effect and had Evander about as far out of the zone as he could be when the fight began, which got worse as the fight went on.

Meanwhile, Dr. Vaughns's tests showed a disturbing excess of one particular supplement that would have the tendency to increase urination and sweating, which would lead to cramping. This triggered my memory of Evander sweating excessively in the stretching warmup in the locker room and his trips to the toilet. I reported all of this to Dr. Sears, who thought the puzzle fit together very well. With Evander's permission, I invited Sears and his brother, Doug, who both lived near Boston, to Evander's estate outside Atlanta to meet with all of Team Holyfield. Everyone was very enthusiastic about Dr. Sears's proposed program based primarily on foods with much less chemical supplementation, and Evander began living and training in the zone, eliminated the suspect supplement, and soon felt much, much better.

Meanwhile, in the weeks and months following the fight, no less than four separate governmental investigations were launched. Senator McCain's senate subcommittee conducted an investigation. The district attorney in Manhattan launched an investigation, as did the New York State Senate, headed by Senator Roy Goodman. Finally, it was reported that a New Jersey federal court grand jury, investigating Bob Lee and the IBF on other charges, had expanded the scope of its investigation to include Holyfield versus Lewis. Evander and I cooperated fully and eagerly in all of these investigations, except the grand jury case in New Jersey, about which we were never contacted. We turned over all relevant documents to the Manhattan district attorney pursuant to a subpoena and met with him and his investigators in New York. We also both testified in Senator Goodman's hearings, and our recommendations on improving boxing were cited prominently in his written report. We also gave Paul Feeney, Senator McCain's chief of staff, our observations. We were eager to participate, because although we were unaware of any wrongdoing in connection with Holyfield versus Lewis, this was an opportunity to focus attention on ways to improve the sport of boxing.

Eventually, when no evidence of wrongdoing was uncovered, the investigations and allegations subsided, and the boxing world began to focus on the prospect of a rematch. Within one week after the first Holyfield versus Lewis fight, I had negotiated and Evander had signed a contract with DKP for the rematch; Evander would receive a guaranteed purse of $15 million. We knew King had a lot of work to do to make a deal with HBO and Lewis, so we knew our contract was the easy piece, but I wanted it to be known to the press that Evander had lowered his purse to maximize the chances of making the fight. Two days later, King and I went to Las Vegas to work on a site deal, because we, and Lewis, had no interest in holding the rematch in New York. A few days later, King and I met with DiBella of HBO to begin negotiations for the rematch, and soon thereafter I began to participate in a round-robin series of telephone calls between all of the principal players to try to make the fight.

Away from boxing, Evander was forced to admit a mistake in his personal life. His marital problems had not been resolved, and Evander filed legal proceedings to divorce Janice. Although this was hard for Evander, he felt that the marriage had been a mistake, and he was determined to put that mistake behind him and move on with his life.

On May 5, Evander and I flew to Nice and then were taken by limo to Monte Carlo for the World Music Awards, where Evander was to present a major award to Will Smith. I had a great time meeting people like Janet Jackson, Will Smith, Pamela Anderson Lee, and Tommy Lee. Some I admired, some I merely found interesting or even bizarre, but it was all fun. We generally went to Jimmyz Disco until 5 a.m., slept late, and participated in activities in the afternoon. Evander took a nap and I worked by phone and fax, and then we went back to Jimmyz.

On the first night, we went to a formal function on the yacht of Mark Hughes, founder of Herbalife and his beautiful wife, Darcy. On another night, Evander and I met with Prince Albert of Monaco, the ruler of Monaco, and five or six of his friends, including Ursula Andress, one of the original Bond girls. We then had dinner in the ballroom at Prince Albert's table. Our table was very interesting. To my right was a beautiful, charming, and very tall model from the Czech Republic named Adriana. To her right were two of the Wayans brothers. Then came a new successful singer named Jennifer Page, then Evander, then Pamela Anderson Lee, Tommy Lee, and Prince Albert. To the Prince's right was a leading singer in Europe, then Val Kilmer, and to my immediate left, Kilmer's girlfriend.

One afternoon I tried to convince Evander to take a 20-minute ride with me to the beautiful hill town of Eze, above the Corniche Moyen between Nice and Monte Carlo, for lunch. It was one of my favorite places in the world.

Evander at first said he didn't want to go, but I finally convinced him, and we had lunch at the Chevre D'or perched on a cliff about 1,000 feet above the Mediterranean. It was a great relaxing afternoon.

**HOLYFIELD**

*I told Jim I didn't want to do too much sightseeing, because I planned to live to be very old, and when I get older, I want to travel around the world and see new places. If I've already seen everything, there will be nothing new left to explore.*

On May 25, Evander and I left New York on Donald Trump's refitted and super-plush 727 for the Miss Universe Pageant in Trinidad. The plane was magnificent, including an original Renoir and a full-size bedroom, where Trump's then-girlfriend, Melania Knauss, was resting when we boarded. Also on board were former Miss America Phyllis George; Victoria's Secret model Stephanie Seymour; model Kylie Bax; Buffalo Bills defensive end Bruce Smith; Cirio Maccione, owner of Le Cirque in New York; Diane Smith, the editor of the *Sports Illustrated Swimsuit Issue*; other celebrities; and a few of us commoners.

While in Trinidad, Diane Smith and I had several glasses of wine together, and I suggested she put Evander in the upcoming *Sports Illustrated Swimsuit Issue*, contending that no one, at least no male, looks better in a swimsuit than Evander. When we were back in the states the next week, Smith called me and asked whether I thought Evander would be willing to appear in the swimsuit issue, and I told her I had already asked him and he had agreed. Smith asked with whom Evander wanted to be photographed. I told Smith I would call Evander and call her back. I called Evander, and he said he had no preference.

"Can I choose for you?" I asked.

"Sure."

I called Smith back and said Evander would accept *only* Heidi Klum. Smith said that might be hard, but she would try. She called back and said she had worked it out. Later, we spent a day with Klum at the photo shoot, and she is as delightful and charming as she is beautiful. She also proved to have a sense of humor. During the shoot she bit Evander on his ear à la Mike Tyson, shocking Evander and resulting in a great photograph for the magazine.

When we returned home, Evander went to training camp in Houston to prepare for the rematch with Lewis, and on November 7, Team Holyfield assembled at the beautiful Mandalay Bay Hotel and Casino. Evander had been exercising his legendary discipline and had been eating and drinking in the zone all through training camp, and it showed. The sugar-based drinks, pasta, and other starches were gone. Lean meats, vegetables, and plenty of water were in. In addition to helping Evander stay in the zone, Hallmark had also made some adjustments to Evander's all-natural food supplements, and it showed. The cramps and excessive sweating were gone, and Evander was moving with more power and speed than he had in at least two years. On Dr. Sears's instructions, Hallmark and I monitored the timing and content of Evander's meals for the 48-hour period prior to the fight and urged him to drink lots of water. As a final touch, I gave Evander two fatty acid capsules an hour before he was to leave the dressing room and half of a Zone Bar 30 minutes later.

Finally, it was fight night, and as Memel's crew shot footage for the documentary of Evander warming up in the dressing room, I felt very confident this would be the night that Evander and Team Holyfield reached the top of the mountain we had been climbing for five years. This would be the night that Evander regained the title of undisputed Heavyweight Champion of the World, would be recognized as one of the greatest heavyweights of all time if not the greatest, and would conquer the last opponent left in his era. And having achieved these feats, Evander would be free to retire, knowing that he never quit until he reached his goals. He could retire on top and in good health as one of the great sports legends of the 20th century—the man who wiped out the entire heavyweight division, no matter how much taller and heavier they were. I was so excited that all of Evander's hard work and discipline would finally land him where he wanted and deserved to be, and I could picture in my mind celebrating in the ring after the fight and all night long.

While Evander was finishing his warmup, I stepped down the hall of the Thomas & Mack Center to watch Lewis's ring entrance, and I got my first sense of foreboding when King was introduced as the promoter of the fight. He was vehemently booed by the crowd. King had been booed heartily at the weigh-in two days earlier, but the weigh-in was attended mainly by a couple thousand of Lewis's British fans, and I did not think much of it. But this was the whole arena booing King unanimously, and everyone knew King was Evander's promoter. I thought that even if the three judges tried hard to be fair and objective, they had to be at least subconsciously aware that a close decision going Evander's way could be perceived by the public as King having manipulated the system one more time. I had thought for weeks that the judges might bend over backward to avoid the criticism and investigations that resulted from scoring close rounds for "King's fighter" in New York. I was afraid that to avoid any similar appearance of impropriety, the judges would be strongly inclined to score all close or debatable rounds in favor of Lewis. Now, listening to the crowd, my fears were much stronger, and those fears only got worse when Lewis entered the arena. One would have thought that in the United States, the American fighter would have the support of the crowd over a Canadian-Jamaican-Englishman. Instead the crowd greeted Lewis as the foreigner who had been cheated in New York and was now going to get his justice. Certainly, there were some Holyfield fans in the crowd, but I was shocked at the warmth of the reception for Lewis. This could only further sway the judges toward giving all close rounds to Lewis to avoid any chance of claims of a robbery and distinguish Nevada as the pre-eminent site of fair play and justice. I had the feeling listening to the crowd cheer for Lewis that Evander needed to knock Lewis out or win a majority of the rounds clearly, convincingly, and without doubt.

When Evander, Turner, assistant trainer Kenny Weldon, Hallmark, and I entered the ring 10 minutes later, I felt a little better. At least a third of the crowd cheered for Evander, not as enthusiastically as the arena as a whole had greeted Lewis, but warmly enough. Even the 7,000 fans from England, to their great credit, refrained from booing the great warrior of so many battles against bigger opponents. It seemed like the crowd was saying, "You might have gotten a favorable result in the fight in New York, but we know it wasn't your fault." I was also heartened by Evander's calm and cool composure. If he was so confident, why should I be worried?

## HOLYFIELD

*Going into the ring, I was relaxed and confident. I had a great training camp, and I felt better than I had for a long time.*

Finally, the fight began, and Evander looked like a different fighter from the one in New York eight months earlier. He was quicker and had better balance, clearly the result of being able to stay down in his stance without pain or cramping. Although Lewis was still scoring with his outstanding jab, Evander was getting to him in a way he had accomplished only occasionally in the first fight. In between rounds, I found myself, for the first time ever, praying during a fight. I was not praying for Evander to win. I don't believe God helps either fighter over the other. I was praying that if the fight went the distance, the decision would be fair. I realized some of the rounds were close enough to go either way, and I hoped and prayed the judges would be able to overcome their unavoidable predisposition to give close rounds to Lewis.

Evander was fighting very well, and his stamina was amazing. Toward the end of the fight, he appeared to have more gas in his tank then did Lewis. Lewis, though, was fighting well also, and he surprised me by how well and courageously he shook off and recovered from some very hard shots from Evander that would have dropped most heavyweights. Although Lewis careful, back-pedaling style was not exciting and gave him virtually no chance to score a knockout, it kept him in the fight by allowing him to accumulate a lot of inconsequential jabs as he backed up. With the exception of one or two hard uppercuts, Lewis rarely hit Evander with any real power. Evander, while not throwing or landing as many touches as Lewis did, clearly landed more effective punches. Halfway through the fight, I had Evander up by two rounds, but then Lewis rallied, and then so did Evander. With one round to go, I had Evander up by two rounds, with one round too close to call, so I had the score at 106-104 for Evander. I knew that the round I scored a tie might go either way, so I thought Evander might be up by only one point, so if he lost the last round Lewis could still tie him. As I watched the final round with my stomach in a knot, I became more and more exhilarated as I became more and more sure that unless Lewis had a late knockdown, Evander would win the round and the fight. Evander fought hard and well until the end, and I was elated. In my mind, he had clearly and undeniably won the fight, with some room to spare. I went into the ring, and Turner, Weldon, Hallmark, and I hugged and celebrated, and we all congratulated Evander on a great performance. I also sincerely congratulated Lewis and his team on a good fight.

After a few minutes, the bell rang, and ring announcer Michael Buffer announced that the judges had reached a unanimous decision.

"Judge Bill Graham scores the fight 117-111."

That meant Judge Graham gave nine rounds to one fighter and only three rounds to the other. I was very surprised by that score, because I had Evander up by only two, or at most three, points, but I was thrilled because I knew beyond any doubt that nobody could have possibly thought Lewis won nine rounds.

"Judge Chuck Giampa scores the fight 116-112."

That meant he gave eight rounds to one fighter and four to the other. This confirmed my certainty that Evander had won, because no one could have possibly given Lewis eight rounds. A later review of the videotape revealed that even Lewis's own corner did not think he had won eight rounds.

"Judge Jerry Roth scores the fight 115-113."

I was standing a few feet directly in front of Evander, waiting to congratulate him when his name was announced.

"For the undisputed Heavyweight Champion of the World—LLLLLLLennox LLLLLLLewis."

I was totally shocked and then devastated. My first thought was, "That can't be," and then I remembered the circumstances, and I realized my worst fears going into the fight had come true. Evander characteristically took the news much less emotionally. When Lewis's name was called, Evander's face broke into a wry smile.

## HOLYFIELD

*I knew I had outfought Lennox, and I knew I deserved the decision, but I was not totally shocked when the decision was announced. Scoring in boxing is subjective, and when you don't knock your opponent out and don't even score any knockdowns, you leave the fight in the hands of the judges, and then anything can happen.*

Later, when I watched the videotape, I saw that loud booming fireworks exploded in the arena, and clouds of confetti came down from the rafters, but I did not notice any of that at the time. I just stood in the ring, oblivious to the pandemonium, thinking about how hard Evander had worked to reach his goal and how unfair it was for it to be taken from him due to the irresistible psychological pressures resulting from the first fight. After a while, as the post-fight interviews were taking place in the ring, Lewis's manager Frank Maloney, a genuinely good guy, saw how disappointed I looked and came over to me.

"Sorry. Evander fought a great fight. I thought Lennox won, but it was close."

"Thanks, Frank, I guess I now know how you must have felt after the first fight."

Eventually, the ring was cleared, and we went to the locker room. After the first fight, when Evander had not fought his best but had received a favorable decision, the locker room was extremely quiet and somber with the mood set by Evander. This time, when Evander had fought a great fight and should have won but received an unfavorable decision, the atmosphere in the locker room was jubilant, again reflecting Evander's mood. Evander went into the fight wanting to fight a great fight. He had done what he set out to do, and no judges could take that away from him. He had overcome a huge size difference and a significant age difference against an outstanding heavyweight fighter. As he said in the locker room in the prayer he led for the team: "Man grants decisions, but God grants victories, and I thank you Lord for this victory." Evander was full of energy and joy, and looked like he could go another 12 rounds.

## HOLYFIELD

*That night my goal was to put on a great performance, and I achieved that goal. The fact that the judges got it wrong could not take anything away from what I had done. I set a goal of outfighting my opponent, and I accomplished that goal. In that sense, I was victorious.*

When we got to the post-fight press conference, Evander was asked at the outset whether he thought he had won the fight.

"It doesn't matter what I think. The fact is that Lennox Lewis is the undisputed Heavyweight Champion of the World."

Everyone in the room applauded for Evander, who was consistent in his belief that one can question but must ultimately accept the judges' decision as the outcome of a fight.

A reporter turned to Lewis and asked, "After the last fight, you said Evander was not acting like a man because he did not admit he lost. Are you going to be a man and admit you lost this fight?"

When there was no answer, and the questioner tried to turn his question over to Evander, Evander waived it off and throughout the press conference refused to criticize the decision or detract in any way from Lewis's victory.

**HOLYFIELD**

*I had said many times in the past, and particularly after my fight with Lewis, that the decisions of the judges must be respected, whether a man agrees with them or not. The fact of the matter is that there was no knockout, so the fight had to be decided by people other than the fighters. For whatever reason, they decided to give the decision to Lewis, and that made Lewis the winner, because that is how the rules of the game work.*

After the press conference, all of Team Holyfield, along with Evander's family and a few friends went back to Evander's suite at the Las Vegas Hilton. When we arrived at the hotel, there was a small crowd waiting to tell Evander that in their opinion he had won the fight. Evander with a spring in his step sang out, "I'm still standing." When we got onto the elevator, Evander joked with a child and his parents, and when they got off the elevator, he turned to the rest of us.

"I keep feeling like tomorrow I'll wake up and they'll say, 'It was a mistake; we read the wrong name.'"

When we got back to the suite at about 11 p.m., Evander was still in a great mood, and we all laughed and joked and talked about the fight as if the decision had gone Evander's way.

Around midnight, Evander went down to the ballroom of the Hilton Hotel where Arthur Goldberg, the president of Park Place Entertainment, which owned the Hilton, was hosting a large post-fight party. Usually, the loser of a fight does not attend, but Evander not only attended but also addressed the crowd in a 10-minute speech in which he graciously thanked everyone involved in the fight for the opportunity to fight for the titles and for their support. Evander received a tremendous ovation and, after mingling with the crowd for another 30 minutes, went back to his suite.

## HOLYFIELD

*After the fight, I felt really great. I had so much energy that it felt like I hadn't even fought.*

A little later, about 1:30 a.m., LL Cool J stopped by the suite and, at 2:30 a.m., Evander and LL went out dancing. They stayed out dancing until morning, when Evander came back to his suite, packed, and went to the airport for his flight to Atlanta. Evander Holyfield, the "old" fighter, went 12 rounds against a bigger, younger opponent recently hailed by some as the best heavyweight in the world, attended a lengthy press conference, gave numerous interviews, hosted friends and family at a party in his suite, gave a speech and mingled with the crowd at a large party, danced all night, and redefined grace and dignity in "defeat." As I said at the press conference, I had never been more proud to be associated with Evander.

When Memel and her documentary film crew asked me for my comments and observations about the fight and what it meant to Evander's career, I predicted that when Evander's career was over, he would be remembered and revered as much for his so-called defeats as for his victories. The Dwight Muhammad Qawi, Buster Douglas, George Foreman, Riddick Bowe, and Mike Tyson victories were certainly impressive, but no more so than the courage and dignity Evander demonstrated in his losses at the Olympics and to Riddick Bowe, Michael Moorer, and Lennox Lewis.

When I returned to Atlanta on the day after the fight, I spent several hours watching a videotape of the fight, stopping at 15-second increments to record what I had seen. When I was finished, I was more convinced than ever that all psychological factors being equal, Evander would have been judged the winner of the fight. It became very clear to me that to the extent the judging in the first Holyfield–Lewis fight had been flawed, the true and ultimate victim had not been Lewis, but instead Evander. If Lewis had been declared the winner of the first fight, Evander would have been at least as gracious in defeat as he was after the second fight in which he fought much better. Evander would have fought Lewis again due to the rematch clause, and Evander would have been perceived to be the beloved American underdog seeking to pull off one more miracle, not the King fighter who had stolen a victory from Lewis. Lewis would have entered the rematch as the physically huge, very cautious, boring, and, to some, arrogant champion rather than the aggrieved and justifiably outraged victim of the politricks of boxing. Under those circumstances, if Lewis and Evander had fought the same fight they fought in Las Vegas, Evander would have been awarded the close rounds, and he would have reached his goal of becoming, once again, the undisputed Heavyweight Champion of the World and would have been free to retire.

After the rematch, because of the way Evander handled the decision, he was once again extremely popular. On December 2, Evander and I went to New York for the *Sports Illustrated* Athlete of the Century Awards. This was perhaps the largest and most accomplished group of elite professional athletes ever assembled in one place, and I must admit it was somewhat overwhelming. Everywhere I turned, there was a world-renowned athletic star bigger than the next. The first thing we did when we arrived was to videotape an opening scene for the show in which Evander was in his boxing trunks and robe, Tiger Woods bounced a golf ball on his club and flipped it to Evander, who caught it and charged onto the stage, while Magic Johnson and I portrayed Evander's trainers, rubbing his shoulders as he made his ringwalk.

Later, backstage I met Jack Nicklaus, Peggy Fleming, Michael Jordan, Joe Montana, Pelé, Mark McGwire, and practically every other top professional athlete in the world. Although I tried hard to be cool, I was like a kid in a candy store. One of the highlights for me was the opportunity to spend a few minutes alone with my favorite actor, Al Pacino. I asked him what he thought his most underrated movie was, and he said it was a very interesting question and one he had never asked himself. When he asked for my opinion and I told him it was *Bobby Deerfield*, he seemed genuinely delighted and said he loved that movie, but that only I and about a dozen other people went to see it.

At the awards ceremony itself, Evander won the award for Boxer of the Decade of the 1990s and was then photographed with all of the other major award winners. After the show, we were invited to a very small private party at a downtown nightclub hosted by Jordan and Billy Crystal. As I sat at a table with Jordan and Evander, it seemed like I was in a dream. I wondered how the kid from Allentown, Pennsylvania, who started out washing dishes on a milk crate in the kitchen of a diner, got here. I had worked hard, but I realized that I was also incredibly lucky, and most of all, I had never given up when things became difficult.

# CHAPTER 10

# 2000: WINNING THE WBA TITLE FOR THE FOURTH TIME

**A**fter the Holyfield–Lewis rematch, Evander and I met to discuss what to do next, if anything, in his boxing career. Evander was very clear and certain from the outset that he was going to retire from the ring only when he became, once again, the undisputed Heavyweight Champion of the World, no matter what or how long it took to do so. He told me his mind was made up when he returned to Atlanta after the fight and after talking to his son Evander Jr.

### HOLYFIELD

*When I returned home to Atlanta after I beat Mike Tyson in 1996 to become the only three-time heavyweight champion other than Muhammad Ali, my son, Evander, Jr., asked me if I would ever be the only four-time champ. I told him I would never have that opportunity because I would need to lose to do that, and I did not plan to lose ever again. When I got home after the second Lewis fight, I was naturally disappointed, but when Evander Jr. greeted me by saying, "Daddy, now you can be the only four-time champion in history." I knew what plan God had in mind for me, and I decided I would not only beat Ali's record but would also once again unify all of the titles and retire as the undisputed Heavyweight Champion of the World.*

The question Evander and I faced was how to get in position to do that. Because the two Holyfield–Lewis fights had consisted of 24 rounds of a smaller fighter chasing a larger fighter and only occasionally catching him, there was no appetite among the public or the boxing press for a third Holyfield–Lewis bout anytime soon. Consequently, it was difficult to figure out what to do next to get in position for another title shot. As noted earlier, in their respective contracts for both the first and second Holyfield–Lewis bouts, Evander and Lewis had agreed that the winner would fight the WBA mandatory challenger in his next bout or give up the WBA title. The WBA mandatory challenger was John Ruiz, who had lost only one bout in his career to the highly touted and high-rated David Tua. The problem with that loss, however, was that Tua caught Ruiz with a devastating punch just after the opening bell, and Ruiz was counted out in 19 seconds. Although that bout had occurred five years earlier and Ruiz had won all of his bouts before and since then, the boxing press would write about little else. Consequently, a Lewis–Ruiz bout would not generate much public interest and would probably flop on pay-per-view. Thanks largely to the press, Ruiz was not a highly regarded opponent, and thanks to his own cautious style, Lewis did not have the drawing power to carry a fight without a top opponent. The Lewis camp, including HBO, decided that Lewis would bypass his contractual obligation to fight Ruiz and instead would fight the extremely highly regarded and undefeated contender, Michael Grant. This was an interesting and complicated development for me, because thanks to the recommendations from Evander and Don Turner, who trained Grant, Grant had engaged me a year earlier to serve as his boxing management adviser, along with Craig Hamilton, who had been working with Grant in that capacity before I was engaged.

Because a Lewis–Grant bout might lead to Lewis losing his WBA title, which would be in Evander's interest and because Grant very much wanted the title shot with Lewis, there was no conflict of interest in making the Lewis–Grant fight. There was, however, a potential conflict of interest regarding the issue of whether Lewis should be forced to vacate the WBA title if he fought Grant. On this issue, Evander might benefit from the WBA title being vacated if he could get an opportunity to fight for the vacant title, but if Grant beat Lewis, he would be better off if Lewis had been able to keep the

WBA title because Grant would then have all three major titles. I carefully and thoroughly explained this issue to Evander, and Grant and discussed it at great length with Hamilton, who understood its implications from the outset. We all agreed that for the moment we would play it by ear, and if the potential conflict ripened into an actual conflict, we would then decide what to do. And it didn't take long for that to happen.

Don King initiated a proceeding before the WBA to have Lewis stripped of the WBA title if he decided to fight Grant instead of Ruiz. The boxing press reacted extremely negatively to this initiative, contending that the titles had been unified for only days before someone started trying to split them up again. Each day I read all relevant boxing articles on the Web, and my review of the articles in the days and weeks after Holyfield versus Lewis II led me to conclude that Evander should stay out of this battle if possible. King was the person who had obtained the commitment from Lewis to fight the WBA mandatory challenger, and the WBA would rule either King's or Lewis's way regardless of what Evander did. I believed that if Evander weighed in on this issue, he would be perceived as trying to win in a hearing what he couldn't win in the ring. Furthermore, Ruiz had the most appealing and compelling argument, and I knew he would be well represented at the hearing by his very able attorney, Tony Cardinale. I felt strongly that with King and Ruiz arguing for Lewis to be stripped if he did not fight Ruiz next, Evander had nothing to gain and much to lose if he got directly involved.

When I informed King's lawyer, John Wirt, that I would not be appearing at the WBA hearing on behalf of Evander, Wirt wrote me a very strong letter accusing me of having a conflict of interest and essentially selling out Evander's interests in favor of Grant's. That was categorically false, and I believed it to be a ploy by King to try to undermine my relationship with Evander and eventually remove my protection of Evander so that King could take advantage of him. I discussed this entire situation at length with Hamilton and Grant, who understood what King was probably trying to do and told me to take care of Evander by eliminating this issue and appearing on his behalf at the WBA hearing. I greatly appreciated their efforts to solve this problem, but I still did not believe it was in Evander's interest to get involved in this issue based upon the increasing and overwhelmingly negative portrayal of King's position in the press.

I took Wirt's letter to Evander personally and went over it with him line by line. I then once again explained my thoughts on every side and aspect of this issue. Evander understood my viewpoint but decided he didn't care about the portrayal of this issue by the boxing press, and if King wanted him to get personally involved, he would do so, because he truly believed Lewis was wrong to breach his promise to fight the WBA mandatory challenger next or give up the WBA belt. I disagreed, but, as always, I was the adviser, and Evander was the ultimate decider. Once he made his decision, it was my job to implement it whether I agreed with it or not. However, as the chairman of my firm's Ethics and Practice Standards Committee, I had a great sensitivity to my ethical obligations to both Grant and Evander.

To avoid even the appearance of impropriety, with Evander's agreement, I engaged one of the top litigators in Atlanta, Bill Clark, to represent Evander at the WBA hearing. I then wrote the argument to be presented on Evander's behalf, reviewed it with Evander and added Evander's suggestions to make sure it reflected his position accurately, and directed Clark to present the argument as crafted by Evander and me. Grant, Hamilton, and I then discussed the possibility of my engaging independent counsel for Grant. They, however, decided that Hamilton could represent Grant's position better than any lawyer we would bring in, and I agreed with them.

At the WBA hearing, Cardinale represented Ruiz's interests, arguing for Lewis to be stripped if he did not fight Ruiz in his next bout. King made the same argument, emphasizing Ruiz's rights and barely mentioning Evander. Clark represented Evander's interests and presented the argument Evander requested and I drafted. Pat English represented Lewis's interests and argued for Lewis to be allowed to fight Grant first and then fight Ruiz and to keep his WBA belt. Hamilton made the same argument on behalf of Grant and questioned Ruiz's credentials as a worthy mandatory challenger. As I predicted, the press reacted extremely negatively to our side and especially to Evander's perceived efforts to win outside the ring what he had not won in it.

In the end, the WBA ruled in favor of Lewis and allowed him to keep his WBA belt and fight Grant if he agreed to fight the WBA mandatory challenger in the following bout. The WBA also ruled that if Grant won the fight with Lewis, he would inherit Lewis's obligation to fight the WBA mandatory bout in his first title defense.

I remain firmly convinced that King's insistence that Evander take part in the WBA hearing may have been good for King but had no upside for Evander. Before the hearing I felt sure that King would get what he wanted from the WBA with or without Evander's support, but the loss by King before the WBA was unprecedented in my memory. The WBA's general counsel, Jimmy Binns, had also served as King's attorney from time to time, and King seemed to me to have enormous influence on the WBA. The only explanation I could come up with for King's loss before the WBA was that the indictment of the IBF's president, Bob Lee, for corruption had caused the WBA to display in a very public manner that it was not controlled by King.

The issue of whether Lewis could avoid his promise to fight the WBA mandatory next or vacate the WBA title, however, was not yet over. Presumably because they were not sure they would win before the WBA, Lewis's lawyers filed a suit on his behalf against Don King Productions in U.S. District Court for the Southern District of New York seeking a declaratory judgment that Lewis's contractual obligation to DKP was unenforceable. DKP counterclaimed, seeking specific performance of Lewis's obligation set forth in the contract between Lewis and DKP. Wirt wrote to me arguing that Evander should intervene in this case to support DKP. I was adamant in my position that Evander should not and could not properly intervene and that this was a contractual matter to be resolved between DKP and Lewis. Although King again accused me of not properly protecting Evander's interests due to a conflict with Grant's interests, Evander agreed with me that he did not belong in a lawsuit about a contract to which he was not a party. Once the WBA had ruled in Lewis's favor, I assumed Lewis's lawyers wished they could have dismissed their suit, but DKP's counterclaim made that impossible under the Federal Rules of Civil Procedure. Eventually, as I predicted, DKP won the suit without Evander's participation, and Lewis was ordered to fight Ruiz in his first WBA title defense or vacate the title. As he had already committed to fight Grant, he had no choice but to vacate the WBA title.

With the WBA title vacant, the WBA ruled that the winner of a Holyfield versus Ruiz fight would be declared the WBA heavyweight champion. With that ruling, Cardinale, Ruiz's trainer and manager Norman "Stoney" Stone, and I met to confirm that Evander and Ruiz wanted to fight each other, and we pledged to each other to try to make it happen. We all informed King, who had the promotional rights for both fighters, that we wanted him to promote Holyfield versus Ruiz. What should have been a relatively easy fight to make was not. Due to the overwhelming negative publicity concerning this fight and, in my opinion, the unfair demeaning of Ruiz's ability, with relentless emphasis on his 19-second loss to Tua, King claimed he could not afford to promote the fight and pay the fighters what they were demanding, which, in Evander's case, was the bare minimum under his contract with DKP. Although a part of these cries of poverty was attributable to King's usual negotiation strategy, the facts were that Showtime was less than enthusiastic about the fight and was not willing to pay a huge licensing fee for it, and there were no sites eager to pay a large guaranteed site fee.

Evander was very excited about the prospect of the Ruiz fight because it would allow him to win the WBA heavyweight title a fourth time. Back when the WBA title was the only title, Floyd Patterson was the first fighter ever to win it twice. Then Muhammad Ali won the WBA title an unprecedented three times when he knocked out George Foreman in the Rumble in the Jungle in Zaire in 1974. Now Evander would have the opportunity to win the WBA title for a record fourth time.

## HOLYFIELD

*Each generation has an obligation to take things to a new level. Floyd Patterson was the first to win the heavyweight title twice, Ali then took it to a new level by winning the title three times. Now I had the opportunity to take it to yet another level by winning the WBA heavyweight title for the fourth time.*

Although some members of the press discounted, and continue to discount, this accomplishment, saying that winning the vacant title is not truly winning the title, Evander could have cared less. If winning a vacant title is not really winning the title, then Tyson, not Lewis, was theoretically the WBC champion when Evander beat Tyson. In that case, when Evander subsequently beat Moorer in 1997 for the IBF title, Evander was theoretically the undisputed Heavyweight Champion of the World. Theory isn't reality, however, and the reality was that Lewis refused to fight the WBA mandatory challenger, was forced to vacate the WBA title, and Evander won that title in accordance with the applicable rules and regulations.

During the first quarter of 2000, while we were working on the opportunity for Evander to win the WBA title for the fourth time, Evander and I also had some fun. On February 14, we attended the ESPY Awards at the MGM Grand in Las Vegas. Although we talked with many great athletes, the highlight of the evening for me was meeting and getting to know members of the U.S. Olympic women's soccer team, which had recently won the World Cup and the hearts of millions of Americans. After the show, there was a private party for the participants at Studio 54 in the MGM Grand. Evander and I sat and talked for several hours with Mia Hamm, Brandi Chastain, Julie Foudy, and other members of the team. We already knew they were great athletes and very attractive, but we also found them to be personable and articulate young women.

The following week, Evander and I attended a small party for the models, including Evander, who would appear in the *Sports Illustrated Swimsuit Issue* to be released on the day of the party. Each model was allowed to bring one guest, and I will be forever grateful to Evander for taking me. Seventeen of the 22 women who appeared in the swimsuit issue attended the four-hour party. In a demonstration of true friendship and a clever way to meet the models and gauge their reactions to him, Evander asked each of the models to have her picture taken with me. It was a great night.

Then, a few weeks later, while I was in Ottawa at my law firm's annual partner retreat, I got a call from Evander saying that he would need to postpone the fight. He explained that he had injured ligaments in his ribs while lifting weights and had aggravated the injury while sparring. He said he might be able to handle the pain of getting hit in the ribs, but the bigger problem was that anytime he threw and landed a punch, he had a searing pain in his ribs like a knife. With the fight still three weeks away, he would not be able to train any further, and even if he were willing to go into the fight unprepared, it still might not heal. I told Evander he was absolutely making the right decision and that I would inform King.

## HOLYFIELD

*I had never before in my life postponed a fight, but I learned my lessons from the first Moorer fight and the third Bowe fight when I fought while injured and sick. I was not going to let my courage overrule my judgment again. Also, Jim and I had promised the Nevada State Athletic Commission that I would not fight again with any undisclosed physical problems, and I am a man of my word. I knew I just needed to be patient, and I would get my chance.*

I called King and gave him the news, and he was surprisingly understanding and supportive. He asked me to help with the publicity of the postponement because the writers' first reaction would be to blame him, and I agreed to do so. King was right, and most of the writers I spoke to wanted to explore the possibility that the tickets were not selling well and King was postponing the fight for financial reasons. I was able honestly to assure the writers that the decision had been made before King even heard about the injury. Although Evander's and my integrity was not questioned by anyone, we nevertheless decided in consultation with King to have Evander examined by the Nevada State Athletic Commission's ring physician, Flip Homansky, to remove any possible doubt. An additional benefit was that this gave all of us an opportunity to say that Evander was taking Ruiz seriously as a worthy opponent. I also called Cardinale and Stone and assured them the injury was real and that Evander had every intention of fighting Ruiz as soon as possible. They once again promised that Ruiz would be there when Evander was ready.

The fight was rescheduled for August 12 at the Paris Hotel. Evander was forced to shut down his camp until he healed, and he planned to resume training in mid-June. I was disappointed about the postponement, because it would be much harder to arrange another fight during 2000, and Evander was not getting any younger. If he was going to keep fighting, I wanted him to get it done as soon as possible, but there was nothing that could be done about this problem so we just had to be patient.

### HOLYFIELD

*Usually there is a bright side to most things if you look hard enough. In this case, the bright side was that I had a few weeks to spend with my kids in Atlanta during their summer break before I went back into training.*

Finally, mid-June arrived, and Evander went back to camp and we made all of the necessary logistical arrangements to reschedule the fight for August. Two weeks before the rescheduled date for the fight, Evander had contracted a fairly serious cold, which was not uncommon for him, because at the peak of his training, his body fat gets so low that his resistance to cold viruses is reduced. This time, however, there was a potentially serious complication. When Evander was blowing his nose, he broke an eardrum. Evander went to a doctor in Houston to get an assessment. He desperately hoped he could go forward with the fight, having already postponed the fight once. The doctor told him that if he was careful, the eardrum would close up before the fight, and about a week before the fight, it did. Consequently, the prefight medical examination did not reveal any problem, and Evander felt fine going into the fight. Watching Evander shadow-box and hit the hand pads during fight week in Las Vegas, I thought Evander looked as good, quick, and powerful as he ever had, and Turner and Hallmark agreed.

On fight night, in the locker room, Evander looked great, and I was very confident of an early knockout. In the first two rounds, Evander was slowly feeling Ruiz out as he often does in the early rounds. Ruiz is an awkward fighter with an unusual style. He fights with his head down low and charges in behind the head, and when he gets in close, he grabs his opponent and holds on. Finally, in the third round, Evander found a weakness and caught Ruiz with a good hard combination. Evander had Ruiz in trouble and then rocked him hard again near the end of the round. When the bell rang to end the third round, Ruiz was still standing, but barely. He was almost out on his feet.

The fight was going as I hoped and expected, and I was sure Evander would finish the fight in the next round. When the fourth round began, Evander was not attacking as I was sure he would. Something seemed wrong. Evander won the round, but Ruiz was coherent again. I was wondering what Evander was waiting for. After the next few rounds, Evander was still winning, but the rounds were much closer than I or anyone else expected. At the end of the fight, Ruiz was still standing. Although I was sure Ruiz had lost, I also had to admit he had by no means been totally dominated. Not to take anything away from Ruiz, who fought a good and courageous fight, but this was not the Evander I had seen in the second Lewis fight or in workouts earlier in the week.

When I climbed into the ring I was certain Evander had won but a little disappointed and worried that Evander had allowed a young, talented, strong, but inferior opponent go the distance, leaving the decision in the hands of the judges. While he waited in the ring for the decision, Stone was angrily berating the referee, Richard Steele, for what he contended was the referee's failure to call fouls against Evander. That led me to believe that not even Ruiz's own corner thought Ruiz would get the decision. When the decision was announced, it was unanimous. All three judges scored the fight for the only four-time Heavyweight Champion of the World, Evander Holyfield.

Unfortunately, the victory was tainted by controversy.

At the post-fight press conference, Stone and Cardinale said they thought Ruiz had been fouled repeatedly and otherwise would have won the fight. They challenged Evander to a rematch. King then jumped on the Ruiz bandwagon, calling the decision controversial and suggesting that there should be a rematch. Put on the spot by King, Evander said he had no problem with a rematch, even though Evander had little to gain from a rematch. I still did not consider the bout or the decision controversial, because I had heard losers complain many times. Also, in talking to quite a few of the ringside boxing writers, I confirmed that although they were totally underwhelmed by Evander's performance, they did think he deserved the decision he got. Later, I learned that 22 of the 26 ringside writers scored the fight in favor of Evander.

During the next few days, it became clear to me that people who had watched the fight from ringside had seen it quite differently from those who had watched it on Showtime. When I watched the videotape replay of the fight, I discovered why. The Showtime announcers, Bobby Czyz and Steve Albert, called the fight as if Evander was being dominated by Ruiz. Czyz seemed particularly prejudiced. According to Czyz, Evander had lost almost every round. After the fight, Czyz called the decision in favor of Evander one of the worst decisions in the history of boxing and clearly implied that the decision was fixed. In my opinion, it was Czyz's distorted broadcast of the fight that was outrageous. I knew Czyz had openly declared all week that Ruiz would win, and he had said the same thing to me in our production meeting two days before the fight. Maybe Czyz was so invested in his own prediction that he could not see the fight objectively.

Maybe Czyz had never gotten over getting soundly beaten by Evander. In any event, Czyz described a one-sided massacre for Ruiz. I have no doubt that Czyz's performance caused many viewers to think they were seeing Ruiz dominate Evander, while virtually no one, not even Ruiz's corner, who saw the fight live at ringside, agreed. I am firmly convinced that casual boxing viewers, and even many avid boxing fans, will tend to see a fight as the so-called experts call it on the air. Scoring boxing is not only difficult, but also highly subjective. Of course a fan at home will defer to someone who is perceived to be such a great expert that he has a job calling fights on television. What the fan at home does not understand is that some of the announcers sometimes are not objective. Czyz and I were in China together a few months earlier, and I truly like Bobby very much, but on the night of Holyfield versus Ruiz, I think Czyz had a bad day at the office.

# CHAPTER 11

# YET ANOTHER SETBACK, RENEWED CALLS FOR RETIREMENT, AND THE CONTINUED REFUSAL TO GIVE UP

In my opinion, largely due to Czyz's and Albert's broadcast, the Holyfield versus Ruiz fight became much more controversial than it should have been. The key boxing Internet sites were filled with fans who watched the fight on Showtime and disagreed with, or were outraged by, the decision of the judges. Armed with the public's protests against the decision in favor of Evander, Tony Cardinale wrote a protest to the WBA asking the WBA to order a rematch. Before doing so, Cardinale called me as a courtesy and told me what he was doing. I told him I understood his position, but that if he really wanted a rematch, he should be careful of the tone of the protest and avoid any excessive accusations of intentional wrongdoing. Cardinale said he had no intention of being overly aggressive, and he wrote a persuasive but respectful protest. I then told him that provided the WBA would sanction a rematch as a mandatory title bout and provided the tone of the protest remained appropriate, we would not resist a rematch. I then wrote a response to the protest stating that although we disagreed with Ruiz's positions, we did recognize that there was some controversy, and if the WBA ordered a mandatory rematch, we would comply.

My thinking was that with the perceived controversy, a rematch with Ruiz might be the best of the various unattractive options available to us, and Evander agreed. Neither Tyson nor Lewis was available, and no one else was of any interest to Evander. I thought Evander had not enhanced his appeal for a third fight with Lewis by his performance against Ruiz, and a rematch would give Evander an opportunity to make amends for his relatively poor performance. Ruiz's stock had gone up, and if Evander blew him out in the rematch, Evander would have a quality win with relatively little risk, making a third bout with Lewis more attractive. On the other hand, I thought that if Evander could not beat Ruiz again, he had no business fighting Lewis or Tyson, and I would be glad he was in the ring losing to Ruiz rather than potentially getting hurt by Lewis or Tyson. Obviously, if I had expected Evander to lose to Ruiz, I would have done everything in my power to persuade him to retire, but the truth was that I still felt he was the best heavyweight in the world.

## HOLYFIELD

*I understood Jim's thinking, but my analysis was much simpler. I planned once again to be the undisputed Heavyweight Champion of the World. To do that, I needed to keep the WBA belt I had and win the WBC and IBF belts held by Lennox Lewis. Lewis was not available to fight me, and no one else had what I wanted, so if the WBA ordered me to fight Ruiz again, that would be a mandatory bout and would extend my time before I had to fight another WBA mandatory bout, which would make it easier to win all three major titles and achieve my goal.*

While we struggled to pull together the Ruiz rematch, Evander and I prepared for a trip literally around the world. Evander had been invited to attend the Olympics in Sydney by the Coca-Cola Company and was allowed to bring one guest. Evander took me as his guest with the thought that we might run across some mutually advantageous business opportunities.

Our two-week stay in Sydney was wonderful. We attended nearly all of the boxing events, which were held in the afternoon and again in the evening of most days, and we got to know the members of the U.S. team. Evander became something of an unofficial coach and motivator for the team, and the team members were thrilled to have his attention, insights, and encouragement. A special section of chairs was set up at ringside for special guests, and on various days we were joined by Australian boxing legend Jeff Fenech, IBF cruiserweight champion Vasily Jirov, and WBC junior welterweight champion Kostya Tszyu. Every time Evander entered the arena, he received an avid standing ovation, and between fights the security guards had to hold the crowd back as Evander posed for pictures and shook hands. Outside the arena without security guards, I was more of a bodyguard than a lawyer, because we had to fight our way through the crowds.

Evander was instantly recognized everywhere. One of the great highlights of the trip was attending the track and field events the night Kathy Freeman, an Aboriginal Australian woman, won the 200 meter gold medal. The entire stadium celebrated, and Evander and I discussed later the beauty and wonder of seeing all of Australia embrace her as one of their own when only a generation earlier that would not have been possible.

After the Olympics, Evander and I flew to Jakarta for Evander to make public appearances and shoot two television commercials for a company named ABC Battery. We were treated like royalty, stayed in the extravagant presidential suite at the magnificent Shangri-La Hotel, and had a great time. As usual, Evander worked by day, took a nap, and then danced the night away at the best R&B clubs we could find. As in Australia, Evander was enormously popular.

One of the highlights of the trip was a seminar at which Evander and I sat at a dais in front of scores of members of the Jakarta boxing community to answer questions. My feelings were not hurt when all of the questions were directed to Evander, because I could see that the people were thrilled to have the opportunity to speak directly to Evander, regardless of what was said. On the previous night, we had attended a boxing event at which numerous Indonesian fighters fought and Evander was asked at the seminar what he thought of the Indonesian boxers. He diplomatically said that he admired their courage, conditioning, and ability and willingness to take punches, but that they needed to learn defense. He said the most important things he could recommend were to keep the gloves up, move the head, and avoid getting hit. The next questioner told Evander that Indonesia was a relatively poor country and that many boxers could not afford medical treatment. The person asked whether Evander had any recommendations about how to stay healthy given these conditions.

"I thought I already answered that," Evander said with a smile. "You've got to keep your gloves up, move your head, and avoid getting hit."

Although I laughed immediately, it was not until the translator was finished that the auditorium erupted into laughter.

We were running out of time to announce the Holyfield versus Ruiz II fight and still could not reach agreement, because King refused to pay Evander the minimum due under his contract, and Evander refused to take anything less than the minimum. Nevertheless, we went forward with a press conference to announce the fight while we continued to negotiate. By the time Team Holyfield assembled in Las Vegas on February 25, six days before the fight was scheduled, we still had no contract, a fact which I did not share with anyone on our team. Finally, less than 48 hours before the fight, we reached a compromise and signed a contract, and the fight was on.

One issue that seemed inconsequential was the selection of the referee. Marc Ratner of the Nevada State Athletic Commission called to ask whether there would be any objection to the appointment of Joe Cortez, who was of Puerto Rican descent, as the referee. Ratner assured me emphatically that Cortez said he could and would be unbiased even though Ruiz was Puerto Rican. I discussed this with Evander, who said Cortez, generally considered the best referee in Nevada at the time, would be fine.

On the night of the fight, as usual, we watched the undercard bouts on television in the locker room, and at 7:15 p.m. Evander had his hands wrapped. The rules require a representative of the opposing camp to be present as each boxer's hands are wrapped, but in this case, we each waived that requirement. As Ruiz's trainer said when Turner asked whether he wanted to watch Evander's hands wrapped, "If you can't trust Evander Holyfield, who can you trust?" Evander went through the usual warmup routine with Hallmark, then got gloved up in the presence of NAC officials, and hit the hand pads held by Weldon, while the gospel music played. Turner and Hallmark paid attention to Evander's combinations on the hand pads, while I kept track of the progress of the undercard bouts and the ever-changing estimated time to leave the locker room and passed it on to Turner and Hallmark. Larkin came by to wish Evander good luck and privately remarked to me that the locker room seemed "flat." I had to agree.

Finally, we left the locker room for the walk to the ring and the preliminary ceremonies and announcements, and then the fight was on. Ruiz, who had complained of Evander's "rough" tactics after the first fight, had vowed to return the favor, and he didn't waste much time fulfilling that promise. Seconds into the first round, he slammed the top of his head into Evander in the first of such countless attacks with his head. Simultaneously, Stone began his non-stop campaign of screaming at Cortez to watch for Evander's fouls, which I thought were nonexistent, but that did not deter Stone, who was doing everything he could to help his fighter. It's the referee's job to distinguish accusations from facts or, better yet, tune out the cries from the corner and make his own judgments about what was going on. Although I was not technically in Evander's corner, I was in the first row adjacent to the corner and was within two feet of Hallmark, Turner, and Weldon, and I must admit I was yelling at Cortez from the outset of the fight to make Ruiz pick his head up, stop using the top of it as a weapon, and to stop holding, which was exactly what I believed was happening.

In the first two rounds, neither fighter dominated the other. I thought Evander landed the cleaner shots, but I saw those rounds as way too close for comfort. I had expected Evander to really jump on Ruiz and blow him out early. I knew Evander typically started slowly and cautiously while studying his opponent's tendencies, but Evander had already gone 12 rounds with Ruiz. If I had been judging the first two rounds, I would have called them both even, but the tradition in boxing has always been to give relatively even rounds to the champion. "The challenger needs to take the title away from the champion" has always been the unofficial rule. Although I did not think Evander had lost the first two rounds, I was worried, because winning another close and debatable decision would not get us where we wanted to be.

In the third round, Evander landed the only effective power punches, and I thought he had clearly won the round. Ruiz was not seriously hurt, but his face was starting to look like he had run into a wall. Stone was screaming to Cortez about how his fighter's face looked, but the tape confirms the only thing hitting Ruiz's face was Evander's gloves. In the fourth round, I thought Evander was marginally better for most of the round but allowed Ruiz to steal the round with a good flurry at the end. In trial work, when playing to a jury, a good litigator pays attention to the principles of primacy and recency. *Primacy* is the phenomenon by which people's opinions are unduly influenced by the first thing they see and hear. *Recency* is the phenomenon by which their opinions are unduly influenced by the last thing they see and hear. In boxing, recency is the predominant phenomenon in judging, and a fighter can often win a close round he was marginally losing for two minutes and 45 seconds, with a very effective final 15 seconds. I feared that was how the judges would call round four.

Evander went back to work in the fifth round, which I thought he clearly won, and he outfought Ruiz in each of the next three rounds. After eight rounds, I had Evander up by two points, worst case, and up by eight points, best case. If the traditional rules applied, I thought Evander would be given every round, but even if the unwritten rules had somehow changed, I thought Evander had undeniably won rounds three and five through eight. Czyz for Showtime, in the past no fan of Evander, had the fight scored consistently with my worst-case scenario.

In the ninth round, Evander dominated Ruiz. He battered him with a barrage and had him staggering, and the only question was whether Ruiz would go down. To his credit, Ruiz showed considerable courage and toughness and got through the round without going down, but when he went to his corner after the ninth, he needed a serious pep talk from Stone to keep going. He was hurt, and he looked like a street gang had worked him over with brass knuckles. In my scoring, Evander was up by at least three rounds, with three to go, and had all of the momentum. The only thing I was worried about was whether Evander would get the knockout that he had predicted, and we needed in order to land a third fight with Lewis. The answer came in the next round.

In the 10th round, Evander was again in control, and it did not look to me like Ruiz would make it through the round. Then Evander hit Ruiz with what appeared to me to be a solid double left hook combination, the first to the body on the belt line and the second to the chin, and Ruiz went down flat on his face and didn't move. Stone was screaming at the top of his lungs that Ruiz was hit with a low blow, and Cortez immediately waived off the knockout count, indicating a low blow, and sent Evander to the neutral corner opposite the one where Ruiz was down. Later Evander told me he saw with his own eyes King screaming at the referee that the punch was low. I could not see where the first hook landed, but the second landed in the area of Ruiz's chin. Ruiz did not immediately hold his groin or ball up as he would have if he had been hurt by a low blow. Instead, he lay stretched out face down without moving for several seconds, indicating to me he had been fairly knocked out by the second hook. Cortez leaned down and told Ruiz he had five minutes to get up.

Because modern groin protectors are so effective that a fighter cannot be permanently injured by a low blow, the rule is that a fighter hit by a low blow must continue within five minutes or he loses the bout. The referee has the discretion to deduct a point, with or without a prior warning, for an obvious, flagrant, and intentional low blow. After several seconds, Ruiz rolled over on his back and moved his gloves down to his waist, which very likely would have been his first reaction if he actually had been hurt by a low blow. Ruiz took most of the five minutes allotted to him to rest on the mat. When he finally got up and was ready to fight after more than three minutes, the fighter, who had been on the brink of being knocked out and then was knocked out, was fully recovered after a rest of more than three times the one-minute period allowed for recovery between rounds. In addition, the referee took a point away from Evander.

When the fight resumed, Ruiz had energy he hadn't had since the fourth round, and he quickly used it to load up and throw a blow from down by his thigh directly into the middle of the cup of Evander's groin protector. It was an obviously intentional retaliatory low blow, and Ruiz later admitted it was intentional. Although it landed right on the cup as Ruiz intended, Evander refrained from faking an injury to get his own five minutes on the mat and have a point deducted from Ruiz. Instead, Evander shook it off and continued, and Cortez merely mildly warned Ruiz. When the round ended, Evander had clearly won the round, but the point deduction from Evander (but not from Ruiz) and the disallowance of the knockdown made the round even. The knockout did not count, and most importantly, Ruiz was allowed to recover when he was ready to go down and out.

Instead of Evander being up by an insurmountable lead or having the fight be over, Cortez's rulings gave Ruiz an outside chance to win a decision. I had already told Evander that I believed the new politics of boxing might make it impossible for him to win a close decision against Ruiz, who had been portrayed as a victim in the last fight. All of this meant that Evander could not afford to simply play it safe and coast into a victory by decision. He had to keep taking risks by seeking a knockout to be absolutely sure victory would not be stolen from him as it had been in the Lewis rematch. When the 11th round began, Evander knew he had knocked Ruiz out in the 10th, and he planned to do it again.

*I knew I had won most of the rounds, but I had also won most of the rounds in the second Lewis fight, and the judges gave the fight to Lewis. It's not my style to play safe when I think I have a lead, but it does affect how much risk I take. When the referee took a point away from me for an accidental marginal low blow on the belt but did not take away a point from Ruiz for an intentional low blow on the cup and did not count my knockdown of Ruiz, the referee changed the round from 10-8 in my favor to 9-9 and gave Ruiz a rest he needed. As a result, I had to go for the knockout to be absolutely sure I would win. If I had been safely ahead as I should have been, I don't believe Ruiz would have had any chance to hit me with any hard shots in the last two rounds. I would have tried to knock him out, but I would not have taken any big risks. As it was, I felt that I needed to take any risks necessary to go for a knockout.*

Ruiz had now had almost four minutes to rest on the canvas and another minute in the corner between rounds to fully recover, and he was in better shape than he had been since the early rounds. Early in the 11th round, Ruiz threw a left-right combination, with the right hand being an unconventional widely arcing, looping punch that Evander never saw. It hit Evander cleanly on the left temple, stunning him. Ruiz then ducked underneath and according to what I saw came up with the top of his head into Evander's left eye, cutting it and knocking Evander to the canvas. Evander had been hit with a hard, clean shot in the temple and then had been hit by Ruiz's head, probably inadvertently. Evander was nearly out on his feet and was taking tremendous punishment. Evander used every tactic at his disposal to survive, and he barely did so. Finally, the round ended, and it was painful to watch, but the great warrior made it back to his corner. As relieved as I was, I was devastated by the turn of events. Before, Evander had the fight won, with the only question being whether he would knock Ruiz out. Now, the question was whether Evander would win the fight. As I had the fight scored, in the worst case scenario if the 11th round were scored against Evander as a 10-8 round, he was still up by one round going into the 12th round. By the start of the 12th round, Evander had recovered amazingly well, but Ruiz probably won the 12th round on an objective analysis. As the fight ended, I thought Evander had won if the benefit of all doubts went to the champion or at worst the fight was a draw, but I was afraid the fight would be stolen from him.

I climbed into the ring incredibly proud of the great warrior but very apprehensive about the result. As we waited for the announcement of the winner, I looked at the two fighters. Evander looked fine except for a small cut just under his left eyebrow. Ruiz, on the other hand, looked like he had been in a car wreck and had gone headfirst through the windshield. Finally, the bell rang, and Jimmy Lennon announced the winner.

"The new WBA Heavyweight Champion of the World and the first Latino Heavyweight Champion of the World, John Ruiz."

I was directly in front of Evander, and he was more demonstrably disappointed than I had seen him after any fight, including the second Lewis fight. Across the ring, I watched Cortez raise the hand of the first Puerto Rican heavyweight champion, and I felt like a fool for believing Cortez could be objective when I saw the huge smile on his face. Then I watched King, Cardinale, and Stone hugging and dancing and celebrating together. Of course Cardinale and Stone should have been celebrating, but I was disappointed, yet not surprised, to see how happy King was because he undoubtedly thought about the many ways to benefit from promoting the first Latino Heavyweight Champion of the World.

## HOLYFIELD

*Even though I got caught with a shot in the 11th round, I thought I was far enough ahead to get the decision. The rule has always been that the challenger needs to clearly and obviously take the title away from the champion. Ruiz had one really good round, and I won nearly all of the rest except for a few that were close. Once again it seemed like I lost because of the new politics in boxing that reward the complainers.*

When we got to the locker room, the atmosphere was very subdued and just got worse when Dr. Vaughns told Evander he needed stitches to close the cut over his eye. Evander lay down on his back, and Dr. Vaughns stitched up the eye while I watched. After Evander showered, gave his post-fight urine sample, and dressed, we went to the press conference. King had Evander speak first, and Evander was gracious as always, saying he would have to get back in line and eventually become the only five-time Heavyweight Champion of the World. When I was then called upon to speak, I followed Evander's lead. I praised Ruiz's courage in taking a beating and not quitting, and I said as disappointed as we were, it was nice to see a group of good people realize their dream. I finished by talking about how proud I was of Evander and challenged anyone to disagree that he was the most courageous heavyweight of all time. It sounded good, and I got lots of praise for my speech, but later I learned that it was not what Evander wanted or needed.

Soon after the fight, I went to see Evander to see how he was doing. He said he felt cheated and set up. He felt that he was not supposed to win. He said that he had knocked Ruiz out just like he said he would, but no one was talking about that. He asked how I felt, and I truthfully told him I agreed.

"If you agree, you should say that," he responded. "Somebody needs to talk about what really happened, and it shouldn't have to be me."

We had talked many times about how, in boxing, the complainer and accuser is assumed to have been cheated while the quiet good sport is assumed to have been treated fairly. It suddenly occurred to me that Evander was exactly right. Someone needed to speak out, and it should not have to be Evander. Tyson had had Horne and Holloway complaining on his behalf; Lewis had had Eliades and Maloney complaining on his behalf; Ruiz had had Stone and Cardinale complaining on his behalf; and, to even the playing field, Evander needed someone to complain on his behalf.

This pointed out one of the problems in being a management adviser/lawyer and not exactly a manager. I was always trying not to overstep my proper bounds and to represent, reflect, and speak on behalf of Evander rather than express my own views. That worked very well on most occasions, but it also had its limits. It was not as if I had failed to speak about unfair treatment of Evander, but that I did it in such a courteous and restrained manner, careful not to be offensive so as not to reflect badly on Evander, that the press did not seem to hear me. With Evander not saying anything, my hints and suggestions of unfairness were ignored. Now Evander wanted and needed a bad guy, someone willing to ruffle some feathers and take some heat for pointing out the truth or at least the other side of the story. Who better to be the bad guy than the lawyer?

I knew just what to say because Evander and I had discussed this topic thoroughly many times and it was all in my head. Although I would tell this story orally at every opportunity, I also wanted to write it down so that there would be some permanent record and to get maximum exposure. The next day, I wrote the following, and soon thereafter, I took it to Evander. Even if the piece were to be totally ignored, it was well worth the effort to see and feel Evander's satisfaction.

"That's what I'm talkin' bout," he said with a smile after I read it to him.

---

HOLYFIELD'S CRIME: Excessive Sportsmanship and Insufficient Accusations and Complaints

by Jim Thomas

As most people in the boxing community know, when I speak or write, I am usually speaking on behalf of Evander Holyfield. This time I am not; this time I am not saying what Evander would say, but instead what he refuses to say. The following are my opinions, not his.

I have finally been forced to conclude that Evander is being punished for violating an unwritten rule in boxing I did not know existed: Evander has committed the crime of excessive sportsmanship and insufficient complaining and accusations. Because Evander has accepted adverse decisions and flagrant fouls without complaint or accusation, the assumption is that he must have been treated fairly, and his accusers must be right, or surely he would have thrown a fit. Similarly, when Evander follows the rules of boxing's governing bodies, rather than openly ridiculing and violating them, he is vilified. As a result of these crimes, the decisions in two of his last three fights have gone against him, and Evander has become the whipping boy of the boxing press and broadcasters. When did the rule become that the champion needs to take the title away from the challenger by dominating the challenger as much as the press and broadcasters have predicted he would? Apparently, today's boxing world is a world in which nice guys and good sports are unwelcome, and boxers who exhibit these qualities are asked to leave the sport by the "experts."

Evander's pattern of crime began in 1984, at the Olympics, when he did not complain about his unjust disqualification. At the amateur level, Evander's dignified acceptance of his mistreatment served him well, and he received great praise. Little did he know that such sportsmanship at the professional level is unwelcome.

In 1992, Evander fought Riddick Bowe in a great fight in which Evander lost the decision. In that fight, Bowe repeatedly hit Evander low, after the bell, and on breaks, and referee Joe Cortez did nothing about those fouls. After the fight, rather than rant and rave about Bowe's fouls and how the fight might have turned out differently if the rules had been enforced, Evander congratulated Bowe and refused to complain.

In 1994, Evander fought Michael Moorer in an extremely close fight that Evander lost by one point. Although Evander scored a knockdown against Moorer in the second round, the round was scored 10-10. Had the round been scored properly, Evander would have won the fight. Again, Evander committed the crime of excessive good sportsmanship and refused to complain.

In May 1996, Evander fought Bobby Czyz at Madison Square Garden. Although admittedly not living up to the expectations of the boxing press, the fact is Evander scored a TKO against Czyz in the fifth round. Czyz's corner accused Evander of "doctoring" his gloves with a substance that got in Czyz's eyes and disabled him. The New York Athletic Commission found no evidence of wrongdoing by Evander or his corner but did find evidence that Czyz's own corner may have been acting improperly. Presumably when Czyz found out what had actually happened, Czyz dropped his protest. Under the unwritten rules of boxing, Evander should have whined and cried about how outrageous the charges were against him and demanded retribution. His crime was to let it go, and no one in the press wrote about how graciously he handled the patently false accusations. The only story was how "shot" Evander was because it took him five rounds to knock Czyz out.

In November 1996, Evander fought Mike Tyson and thoroughly dominated him. To be fair, the press was duly contrite about having written Evander off and praised his performance, but there was an asterisk. Tyson accused Evander of intentional head butting and other dirty tactics. Evander had too much dignity to respond or even point out the fact that it was Tyson who was attempting to head butt Evander and break his arm. Tyson, Horne, and Holloway screamed and whined, and their accusations were reported as reasonable complaints. Did anyone bother to look at the tape and see that, not once, did Evander ever intentionally use his head? Did anyone notice that Tyson repeatedly lunged at Evander with his head and ended up cutting himself with his dirty tactics? I tried to point out that Tyson is used to fighting people who are afraid of him and retreat, which has led Tyson to believe that the "neutral zone" is for his head, and anyone who dares to move forward is invading his space, but no one wanted to hear that story. Because Evander did not complain, there was an assumption in most articles that Evander was guilty, or at least serious doubts were raised about whether Evander had intentionally butted Tyson. Under the unwritten rules of boxing, Evander should have gone on a tirade about Tyson's illegal tactics, but he once again committed the crime of dignified silence, and the allegations grew into assumed truths.

In June 1997, Evander fought Tyson again in the famous "bite fight." Although Evander was duly praised for his grace and dignity after being brutally bitten twice, again Tyson alleged intentional head butts. Because Evander's energy was directed toward forgiving Tyson for what he did, rather than addressing his ridiculous and completely baseless claims of head butts, there was once again an implication that perhaps Tyson was right. Once again, however, there was no evidence whatsoever on the tape of any illegal tactics by Evander. In the press, however, zero plus zero plus zero was beginning to equal one, and the accusations were taking on a life of their own and were growing into assumptions and then facts.

In March 1999, Evander fought Lennox Lewis. Evander was the universally accepted champion, and Lewis was the universally accepted challenger. In the locker room before the fight, Emanuel Stewart dramatically and emphatically complained to referee Arthur Mercante Jr., about Evander's alleged propensity to wear his cup too high, giving him an unfair advantage. This turned out to be a flagrant tactic to divert the referee's attention from the fact that Stewart and Lewis had arranged for Lewis to wear an oversized training cup that protected him halfway up to his solar plexus and gave him a significant unfair advantage against Evander's body punches, which would naturally be an important weapon for Evander against the much taller Lewis. Then, in the fifth round, Lewis used one of his trademark moves and spun Evander to the left with his left hand and hit Evander squarely in the back of the brain with a "rabbit punch" that severely injured Evander and may have been the key to the fight for Lewis. Despite the fact that that was the only round Lewis dominated, and Evander was the champion, all the press and reporters could talk about was how unfair it was for Evander to get a draw. Once again, Evander committed the crime of excessive sportsmanship and refused to complain about the oversized cup and the rabbit punch. Despite my efforts, I could not get one reporter or commentator to discuss the obvious fouls against Evander, but once again, there were stories about head butts by Evander, with no evidence whatsoever.

Evander was then called upon by the boxing community to repudiate the scoring of the judges, and substitute his own judgment for theirs. Evander refused to disrespect the judges and was vilified for doing so. No one, however, called upon Lewis to explain his use of an oversized cup or his blow to the back of Evander's head, a tactic he later also used against Michael Grant. As usual, the complaining party, Lewis, was supported, and the silent party was criticized.

By the time the rematch with Lewis rolled around in November 1999, there was such a feeding frenzy over how Lennox had been so severely "screwed" in New York, that there was no way any of the judges in Las Vegas were about to give any close rounds to Evander and risk the criticism heaped upon the judges in New York for allegedly favoring "Don King's fighter." Many of the best boxing experts thought Evander won the rematch with Lewis. Even those who scored the fight for Lewis thought it was extremely close, 6-5-1 or 7-5. Yet one judge scored the fight 9-3 for Lewis, and another scored it 8-4 for Lewis. Lewis's own corner did not think he had won by that margin and, in fact, were telling Lewis he was losing most rounds because he was too passive and wasn't doing anything. When the fight was over and Evander was shocked and disappointed by the decision, he once again refused to complain. He simply said that he had accepted the first decision and would have to accept the second. In retrospect, he should have lambasted the scoring and talked about Lewis's holding and pulling on the back of his head. Instead, Evander committed the crime of excessive sportsmanship once again. I did not see one article even acknowledging Evander's grace and dignity. Instead I saw calls for his retirement, and for Lewis's coronation, even though Evander and Lennox had fought 24 rounds without either one dominating the other and even though only Lewis repeatedly fouled. Lewis and Panos Eliades were richly rewarded for playing the game right, following the unwritten rules, and screaming and yelling about the incredible unfairness and dirty tactics of the other fighter. Evander failed to point out the oversized cup and rabbit punch in the first fight and how he was robbed in the second fight, allowing the assumption that he must have been treated fairly. Once again, the self-proclaimed victim won, and the accused lost in the world of boxing.

When Lennox Lewis simply disregarded his written contractual commitment to fight the WBA's top-rated contender, John Ruiz, in his next fight, which was an express condition to his getting both the first and second Holyfield fights, the press incredibly condoned his actions and for some unfathomable reason, condemned Evander.

Then, when Lewis was forced to give up the WBA title as he had promised, and Evander agreed to fight Ruiz for the vacant WBA title, Evander was vilified again, and the press unfairly portrayed Ruiz as a "tomato can," which he has proven twice he is not. What did Evander, universally acknowledged as one of the greatest warriors in the history of boxing, do to serve this disrespect and abuse? It's very simple: excessive sportsmanship and insufficient accusations and complaints.

In August 2000, Evander fought Ruiz for the vacant WBA title. In that fight, Ruiz repeatedly and almost without exception, threw a punch, charged with his head, and then held. He did not charge with his head up, which would put him in equal jeopardy of a cut, he charged with the top of his head, so that Evander had to get out of the way or push it down to avoid being hit with the top of Ruiz's head in Evander's face. It is illegal to lead with the head and use it as a weapon, but the referee refused to enforce this rule or the rule against excessive holding. There were only two things Evander could do to protect himself: either push the head down to a place where it could not injure him or push it away with his forearms to keep it from getting to his face. When Evander pushed the head down, as Lennox Lewis had done repeatedly to Evander without criticism, Ruiz fell to the mat, looking for a penalty, and his corner screamed. When Evander pushed Ruiz's head off, Ruiz's corner accused Evander of throwing elbows.

At the end of the fight, it was apparent to almost anyone seated at ringside that Evander had outfought Ruiz. Twenty-two of 26 ringside reporters and three of three judges scored the fight for Evander. But Ruiz and his corner played the game correctly, followed the unwritten rule, and screamed bloody murder about being robbed and head butted and elbowed. Once again, the best defense to Ruiz's headfirst fighting style was a good offense of accusations, and once again, the unopposed accusations against Evander took on a life of their own. I don't fault Stoney and Tony Cardinale for these tactics, they were smart and played the new game well. I fault the people who allowed this tactic to work by accepting the accusations as if they were true. Why was there not one mention in any article about Ruiz's use of his head as a weapon and constant holding?

After the first Holyfield versus Ruiz fight, Evander granted Ruiz a rematch. Although the WBA eventually ordered the rematch, Evander caused that to happen by not opposing Ruiz's request. Evander gave a rematch to a very rugged, courageous, awkward, unorthodox fighter who uses his head as a battering ram and then holds on. Evander allowed the rematch because Ruiz claimed he deserved it. I do not recall seeing one article recognizing Evander's honor in granting the rematch to Ruiz. But apparently honor is not what is rewarded these days.

Evander came to Las Vegas for the rematch in the wake of a relentless crusade of accusations that Evander had gotten away with dirty tactics and Ruiz had been screwed by a biased decision in Las Vegas. I sensed the same type of atmosphere I sensed before the Lewis rematch. The poor challenger was perceived as having been cheated in the last fight, so, somehow the champion needed to overwhelm the challenger or he would lose his title.

In the rematch, Ruiz immediately started slamming the top of his head into Evander from the first round on, and the referee just let it happen. We did not object to a Puerto Rican referee because of assurances he would show no favoritism to a fighter trying to become the first Puerto Rican heavyweight champion. I am confident Joe Cortez did not consciously favor Ruiz, but I must ask myself whether it was a mistake to believe he could avoid a subconscious bias. Despite the complaints from Evander's corner about Ruiz's battering-ram style and holding, Ruiz was allowed to continue. One judge scored all five of the first five rounds for Ruiz. I do not believe there was another person in the arena who thought Ruiz won the first five rounds. This is clear evidence of the psychological pressure not to allow another controversial decision against the underdog in Las Vegas.

In the 10th round, Evander threw a double left hook. The first hook landed on the top ridge of Ruiz's protective cup, on the belt line, not below it, and could not have seriously injured Ruiz. The second hook landed on Ruiz's chin and flattened him. Ruiz did not ball up as one would if hurt by a blow to the testicles. Instead, Ruiz lay flat on the canvas, unable to move at all for at least the count of 10. Cortez, however, called a low blow and told Ruiz he had up to five minutes to recover. Once Ruiz recovered from the knockout blow to his chin, about 15 seconds later, he astutely turned over on his back and raised his knees and put his hands down around his waist. Meanwhile Stoney was screaming about a low blow that never happened and was screaming directly at Evander, which was totally inappropriate. It was apparent to me that Cortez was either intimidated or brainwashed.

Even if the first hook were, for argument sake, deemed low, it could not have incapacitated Ruiz. At worst, it was in the gray zone, on the belt part of the cup, not on the groin protector. Whether or not the first hook was an inadvertent marginally low blow, Evander knocked Ruiz out with a legal hook to the jaw, and the referee did not recognize it as such. Later in the round, Ruiz loaded up and intentionally threw an extremely low blow to the bottom of the cup. Everyone in the arena saw it as retaliation, and Ruiz later admitted that's what it was. Cortez mildly told him not to do it again, but assessed no penalty. Evander's mistake was that he did not fake an injury, fall down, and take a five-minute rest. He just didn't know the unwritten rules. How can an inadvertent, and marginal, at worst, low blow warrant a point deduction but an intentional and flagrant foul does not? Where is the reporting of this irrefutable evidence of bias by the referee? Where is the insightful investigative journalism?

The answer is that there is no energy or space left after the sanctimonious calls for the retirement of a "shot" fighter, who breaks the unwritten rules. What is not reported is that if Cortez had properly called the knockout, everyone would be talking about how Evander started slow, came on strong to dominate the middle rounds, and knocked Ruiz out in the 10th round. Instead, Ruiz got an undeserved five-minute reprieve, and Evander lost a point and could not afford to coast because the decision might go against him. As a result, he had to take risks in the last two rounds and got caught with a shot.

After the fight, despite all of this, Evander still stayed on his crime spree. He refused to complain, refused to accuse, and refused to defend himself against ridiculous accusations by a guy who hits as much with the top of his head as with his gloves. I should have spoken up then, but I followed Evander's lead. I thought some of the "experts" would see through the smoke and report what really happened. In boxing these days the accuser wins and the noble warrior is told to get out of the way and make room for some more accusers and complainers.

These are my opinions. I realize they may not all be shared by everyone, and maybe some are wrong, but isn't there at least some truth here? Why isn't this side of the story being reported by anyone? Was Bobby Czyz the only one who saw Ruiz knocked out with a hook to the jaw in the 10th round? Didn't anyone see Lewis's training cup and rabbit punch? Why is everyone looking the other way? If Evander stopped talking about God, cursed and complained more, and accused others of wrongdoing, would he get the respect and fair treatment he deserves?

---

After Evander lost the decision to Ruiz, there were more calls from the boxing media than ever before for his retirement, but Evander was even more defiant than ever. Evander told me in no uncertain terms that he was absolutely committed to doing whatever was necessary, for as long as it took, to win all three major heavyweight titles before he retired. I had no problem with that position, because I believed Evander had knocked Ruiz out and was still the best heavyweight in the world.

# CHAPTER 12

# GETTING BACK IN LINE FOR ANOTHER COMEBACK, BATTLING KING, AND GETTING ROBBED AGAIN

Now that there was absolutely no doubt that Evander would fight again, we had to consider our options. Without doubt, the only fight that really made sense at that point was a rubber match with Ruiz for several reasons. First, it was the most direct way for Evander to redeem himself for a purported loss to the previously lowly regarded opponent who now would have some respect and prestige. Second, this was the fastest way for Evander to get his WBA belt back and make himself most attractive as an opponent for Tyson, who wanted a title to make himself more attractive to Lewis, or to Lewis, who regretted giving up his WBA belt and wanted it back. Third, Evander really wanted to knock Ruiz out and have it count and be recognized and appreciated.

The biggest problems I saw were (a) I did not think Ruiz would want to fight Evander again because he had escaped a knockout and had been pounded into hamburger by Evander; if I had represented him, I would have wanted a much easier opponent and the chance to keep the WBA title for a while, and (b) I was afraid King would not want to make the rubber match; I thought King would want to ride the first Latino heavyweight champion as long as possible and feed Ruiz relatively easy opponents signed to King without having to deal with me and my annoying habit of fighting for the athlete to make the bulk of the money. Despite my concerns, I called King and told him Evander was committed to fighting again and wanted no other fight than Ruiz in a rubber match.

I was right about my concerns, but I got two important breaks. First King badly wanted to promote the first professional world title fight out of China, and the local sponsors in China couldn't care less about John Ruiz; they wanted Evander Holyfield, who was known throughout China. The Chinese wanted a title fight and Evander. The only way to do that was a rubber match between Evander and Ruiz. Second, Tony Cardinale, who now represented the WBA Heavyweight Champion of the World rather than an obscure wanna-be, was rapidly becoming nearly as big a pain to King as I had been for the last five years.

I continued talking to King, but I was also talking directly with Cardinale. As I suspected, the Ruiz camp had strong reservations about fighting Evander again. Recognizing that we were in negotiations, so all statements must be taken with a grain of salt, I still thought there was some amount of truth in Cardinale's contention that they thought Evander was the toughest opponent in the world for Ruiz, so why would he want to fight him again and risk losing the title within a matter of months? Cardinale also expressed concerns about a fight in China, where Evander was a well-known and much loved hero and where the site would be tantamount to home turf for Evander. I told Cardinale I was considering appealing to the WBA, as he had done on behalf of Ruiz, to seek a mandated rubber match on the ground that Holyfield versus Ruiz II was highly controversial due to the blown call on the knockout and the disparate treatment on low blows. I also told Cardinale I felt Ruiz owed Evander a rematch under these circumstances, because when Ruiz had complained after the first fight, Evander gave him a rematch. Then Cardinale got to the point. He said Ruiz would give Evander a rematch, but he would need to be paid "big bucks." I told Cardinale he needed to work that out with King, but we would do what we could to help make that happen, including, if necessary, reducing Evander's minimum purse under his master contract with DKP.

I then called King, told him about my discussion with Cardinale, and asked him to work on putting the rubber match together. King said he was already hard at work on it. He said there were two conditions. First Evander

needed to take less than his minimum purse. Second, the Ruiz camp was insisting that Ruiz, as champion, be paid more than Evander. I told King I did not think those conditions would be a problem, and that Evander wanted the fight. Within days, King and I, with Evander's approval of course, had reached a tentative agreement on Evander's purse, and things seemed to be moving in the right direction. King, however, reminded me that he would have to get the approval of the WBA for the rubber match. Somehow I believed King would get what he asked for from the WBA; I just had to hope he really asked for approval of the rubber match. Although it was difficult as always, we eventually reached agreement on Ruiz versus Holyfield III in Beijing to be held on August 4, 2001.

On April 27, something unexpected happened in the heavyweight division. When efforts to make a Lennox Lewis versus Mike Tyson fight failed, at least in part due to the fighters' exclusive television contracts with HBO and Showtime, respectively, Lewis was scheduled to fight Hasim Rahman to stay busy until a significant fight could be arranged later in the year. Rahman was once considered to be a promising contender but had slipped a bit when he was knocked out by David Tua in December 1998 and dropped further to journeyman status when he was literally knocked out of the ring by Oleg Maskaev, who was then himself knocked out by Kirk Johnson. The Lewis versus Rahman fight generated virtually no interest among the boxing media or the public, and it was eventually sent to a site near Johannesburg, South Africa, presumably because of a lack of interest among sites in the United States.

The fight was expected by everyone to be a nonevent in which Lewis would dispatch Rahman quickly, easily, or both as he had all of his opponents since Evander. During the week before the fight there was finally a minor buzz in the boxing press, because Lewis seemed to be taking Rahman lightly. The site was about a mile above sea level, and Rahman had set up camp there a month before the fight to acclimate himself to the altitude. Lewis, on the other hand, came to the site only 12 days before the fight, having decided to make a cameo appearance in a movie being shot in Las Vegas. The movie was a remake of *Ocean's Eleven*, starring Julia Roberts, George Clooney, Matt Damon, Brad Pitt, and others, and the boxing reporters speculated that Lewis seemed to be more focused on hanging out with the stars than taking care of his real job.

Then at the weigh-in, Lewis was heavier than he had ever been although by only a few pounds and looked less toned than usual. Upon reading these reports, I began to let myself dream about the possibility of a Rahman upset, which would shake things up and perhaps get Evander a chance to fight for the IBF and WBC titles after he got his WBA title back from Ruiz. I believed that Lewis would duck Evander for the remainder of his career, knowing in his heart Evander had outfought him in their second battle, but if Lewis lost, Rahman might fight Tyson, and the winner—most likely Tyson—might then fight Evander, which would be perfect.

As the Lewis versus Rahman fight began, I saw that it did appear that Lewis was disdainful of Rahman and did not respect his ability. By the fifth round, however, Lewis began to look a bit ragged. When Rahman tagged him with a hard right, Lewis just smirked, but when Rahman tagged him with another hard right, Lewis hit the canvas—and he did not get up. It was a stunning upset, but then again almost predictable. An underdog's greatest weapon is arrogance of the favorite, especially when joined with a lack of preparation. That is why Evander reminds me from time to time that there are no easy fights. After the fight, I called Evander who had been watching in Florida.

"It looks like the plan is unfolding," I told him.

Evander, who knew that I meant his vow to retire as undisputed Heavyweight Champion of the World had just become a lot more likely, simply responded, "You're exactly right."

Rahman's improbable victory over Lewis and the ensuing scramble to take advantage of this development created a greater level of interest in boxing in general and in the heavyweight division in particular than had existed for quite some time. Before Rahman knocked out Lewis, the general consensus among the boxing writers, and consequently also among the public, was that (1) Holyfield was fading as evidenced by his loss to Ruiz; (2) Tyson was the only guy with a real chance to beat Lewis, but that fight would never happen due to the television networks; (3) none of the younger guys was capable of competing seriously with Lewis; and (4) we were stuck with the big, boring, cautious Lewis for the foreseeable future. Rahman's stunning knockout of Lewis changed all that, and suddenly new equations were possible, but a rematch clause in the Lewis versus Rahman contracts had the potential to send everything back to the *status quo ante*.

When Lewis was beaten, HBO's dominant hold on boxing was suddenly in jeopardy. HBO had apparently thought so little of Rahman's chances that it did not lock Rahman up on HBO if he won. Showtime had Tyson locked up, and both Ruiz and Evander had the right to fight on either network but preferred Showtime. If Showtime could somehow lure the new IBF and WBC champion to Showtime and into a fight with Tyson, Showtime would suddenly have control over all three of the major championship belts, and HBO would be essentially out of the heavyweight business.

This scenario was obvious to HBO and the Lewis camp, and they had no intention of allowing things to play out that way. Immediately Lewis announced that he had a contractual right to a rematch and would insist upon exercising it as soon as possible, and HBO, of course, backed him. Rahman and his co-managers, Stan Hoffman and Steve Nelson, however, contended that the rematch clause required an agreement on a rematch to be made within 150 days of the first fight, with the fight to occur within a reasonable time thereafter, and that the clause did not preclude an interim bout. The press reported, however, that the rematch clause did not expressly rule out an interim bout but did require the actual rematch itself to occur within 150 days on a date to be set by Lewis. Under this interpretation, the rematch would need to occur no later than the end of September, and Lewis, through legal counsel, designated the date of August 18 in an obvious move to preclude an interim bout, because the interim bout would need to occur no less than 60 days before the rematch, which meant it had to occur by mid-June—only six weeks away. Even if an interim fight could be promoted in such a short time, Rahman had suffered a cut in the Lewis fight and would not be ready to fight by mid-June.

Showtime, on the other hand, studied the contracts with its in-house and outside counsel and concluded that an interim fight for Rahman was a possibility. Meanwhile, Tyson, who was the No. 1 rated heavyweight in the WBC, sued WBC seeking to force the WBC to enforce its rule against rematch clauses, and the WBC immediately stipulated in court that it would not sanction a rematch between Lewis and Rahman. Tua then sued the IBF to enforce the IBF's rule against rematch clauses. HBO, apparently recognizing the potential legal problems in forcing an immediate rematch with Lewis, made a huge offer to Rahman to fight Lewis. Showtime countered with an even bigger offer to Rahman to fight Tyson. Suddenly, Rahman, considered a journeyman a week earlier, was the most sought-after heavyweight in the world.

On May 15, Evander and I and a group of about 20 others left for Beijing. The group included Don King, Charlie Lomax, Bobby Goodman, Dana Jamison, and Alan Hopper of Don King Productions; Norman Stone, Tony

Cardinale, and John Ruiz; Evander and me; and the president of the WBA, Gilberto Mendoza and his wife. We flew from New York to Los Angeles and then on to Beijing, arriving on at about 5:30 p.m. local Beijing time, which was 5:30 a.m. Eastern. Upon landing, there was an elaborate welcoming ceremony, and at about 8 p.m. we eventually arrived at the beautiful and very modern Beijing Hotel, 26 hours after we left our hotel in New York. We had a welcoming banquet and went to sleep.

On May 17, we spent most of the day inspecting the arena where the fight would be held and then had a banquet hosted by the head of the Sports Agency of China, who was also the vice-president of the Beijing 2008 Olympic Bid Committee. After a round of speeches, our hosts brought a cake and sang "Happy Birthday"; I turned 50. Apparently, someone had picked up the date on my passport.

The next day we visited the Great Wall of China at the Badaling section, then had lunch, and played golf at a new country club resort with a Jack Nicklaus-designed golf course. We then went to tape a television talk show promoting the fight and then were hosted at a party by the People's Insurance Company of China. Later, our group had the honor of lighting Tiananmen Square for the weekend.

The next day we visited Mao Zedong's tomb at Tiananmen Square and then walked through the Imperial Palace within the Forbidden City. We then had a banquet featuring Peking duck at the Duck King Restaurant.

After sightseeing for a day, we visited the offices of our local fight promoter, Great Wall International Sports Media Company, Ltd. and then had a very welcome western meal at the new Outback Steak House. That evening we had yet another 12-course Chinese banquet at the TJ Plaza Hotel, one of our host hotels for the fight.

Everywhere we went in China, at least hundreds and in many instances thousands of Chinese people surrounded us and pushed and shoved along with dozens of still and video photographers to get close, while our security guards and local police tried to hold the crowds back. Many of the people seemed to recognize King, either from previous exposure on television or from the current news coverage. There was absolutely no doubt, however, that the crowds turned out to see Evander, and he was openly worshipped as a hero. For his part, Evander patiently had his picture taken with literally thousands of his local fans, often to the frustration of the security guards who tried to manage the crowds. When we emerged from the building that housed Great Wall's offices, a crowd of about a thousand people waited for Evander. The security guards told us to run with them through the crowd to our limo. We reached the car and got in, and the crowd pressed up against our car while the guards unsuccessfully tried to hold the crowd back. As the crowd called for Evander, he opened the sunroof and stood up through it, and the crowd surged forward. Evander then handed a pack of several hundred cards with his picture to one of the security guards. When the crowd swarmed the guard, he threw the pack of pictures in the air, and the crowd got completely out of control. They were rocking the car, and there was serious danger of an outright riot, so the driver began blowing the horn and finally just drove through the crowd to get away. We were all extremely relieved and surprised that no one was injured.

## HOLYFIELD

*It was thrilling to me that so many people so far from the United States showed how much they admired and cared for me. The Chinese people, and their warmth and hospitality, were truly beautiful.*

We returned home, Evander went to training camp, and in two months, we were on our way back to China. I left for China on July 24 and landed in Beijing in time to deal with all fight tasks that might occur during the next 12 days leading up to the fight. On July 26, King told me we had a serious problem. He explained that Great Wall had deposited the money it was obligated to, but that the Chinese government had put a tax lien on the funds, which would give the government the first right to part of the funds ahead of DKP, which would make the fight financially unfeasible. King told me he had a meeting scheduled with the appropriate government officials on July 30 to try to get the lien removed.

Early the next morning, nine days before the fight, Turner told me there was a rumor that Ruiz was sick. Rumors of a fighter being sick or injured are common. Reporters had often called me to ask whether Evander was injured when there was no truth to the rumor at all, so I did not worry. I thought that even if Ruiz was not feeling well, he undoubtedly had the same type of upset stomach nearly everyone on our team experienced in Beijing and that it would last only a day or two. But, at 11 a.m. DKP's public relations director, Alan Hopper, called and read me a proposed statement to be released to the news media in which Evander sympathized with Ruiz's need to postpone the fight, because Evander had needed to postpone his previous fight with Ruiz due to an injury. Hopper and I had always gotten along very well, and he assumed I would approve Evander's statement automatically. I said I wasn't about to approve anything. I angrily told Hopper that the previous day King had told me there was a financial problem and now suddenly Ruiz had a stiff neck. I said that if King didn't even have the courtesy to tell me what was going on, the only thing I was going to do was start an investigation. Within two minutes King called, apologized, and said he thought I had heard the news about Ruiz and asked to meet with me right away to explain everything he knew.

When I met with King, he explained that Ruiz developed serious stiffness in his neck and had gotten a long, hard massage, which made the neck worse. I was told that the next day Ruiz had received extensive acupuncture from Chinese doctors that ran for about an hour, and his neck then seized up in a painful spasm, preventing him from turning his head. Then, earlier that morning, a doctor examined Ruiz in the presence of King and DKP's director of boxing operations, Bobby Goodman. The doctor declared Ruiz unfit to fight. I told King I wanted another opinion and some tests to substantiate the injury. King said he had already ordered, for his own protection, an examination by the best doctors available, along with an MRI. I then went to Evander's suite, to break the bad news, but he had already heard it. Evander took the news calmly as he had on previous occasions of postponements, but this time he was openly skeptical. I told him I would conduct my own investigation.

### HOLYFIELD

*I always give people the benefit of the doubt, but this whole thing seemed very questionable. I was extremely sure I would knock Ruiz out. He did not look to me like he was in good shape and ready to fight, then suddenly his neck hurt.*

The doctors confirmed that Ruiz had herniated discs between his fifth and sixth, and sixth and seventh cervical vertebrae and could not train or fight. One of the doctors told me that the neck spasms could clear up in a matter of a few days with rest and muscle relaxers, but that Ruiz would then need to wait at least a week before resuming training or he would very likely re-injure his neck. Finally, I had a very long talk with Cardinale, whom I had come to know well and for whom I had a great deal of respect. Cardinale explained that hours before Ruiz began experiencing the neck spasms he had been doing wrestlers bridges, an exercise with which I was extremely familiar from my high school and college wrestling days. This exercise concentrates the bulk of one's weight, in Ruiz's case about 220 pounds, on the neck and could easily cause an injury according to Evander's strength and conditioning coach, Tim Hallmark.

It is certainly possible that Ruiz's injury was faked to help King out of a financial jam as King's long-time rival Bob Arum reportedly was telling anyone who would listen, but, based upon the facts I gathered in my investigation, this conspiracy theory is highly unlikely, because the postponement of the fight was going to cost someone hundreds of thousands, if not millions, of dollars and that cost almost surely exceeded the amount of the tax lien King was concerned about. Furthermore, rescheduling the fight would be extremely difficult because there were no good pay-per-view dates available in the next three months.

King would have had to persuade Ruiz, Stone, Cardinale, and Ruiz's trainer to fake the injury. Everyone else in Ruiz's camp would have had to go along. All of them stood to make a lot of money if the fight went forward. Ruiz himself was scheduled to make almost $4 million if the fight went forward, and any time there is a postponement, there is a chance the fight won't happen, for example, Holyfield versus Tyson in November 1991 and Holyfield versus Akinwande in June 1998.

Although there was some speculation that Ruiz was out of shape and would benefit from a postponement, my own very reliable source within Ruiz's training camp confirmed that Ruiz had been sparring 12 rounds three times a week before coming to China and was in great shape. Ruiz was in shape and now would have to break training and start over without any additional compensation. Furthermore, Ruiz risked missing a chance to fight the winner of Lewis versus Rahman rematch if Ruiz eventually won but his bout with Evander was delayed too long.

Cardinale would have had to risk losing his license to practice law if the fraud were ever uncovered. Why would he do that? How much of a bribe would be required to get him to do that?

The doctors I talked to would have had to risk losing their licenses if the fraud were uncovered. Why would they do that? How much would it cost to bribe them, along with all involved hospital personnel?

Someone would have had to provide an MRI of a patient with herniated discs, and that MRI would have had to be fraudulently identified as Ruiz's.

Everyone involved would have had to risk criminal prosecution if the fraud were discovered. King had been extremely worried about going to prison in 1999 and had no intention at age 70 of putting himself at that risk again.

King also risked losing Evander's promotional contract if the fraud were discovered. I would not have hesitated in terminating the contract if we learned of fraud in the postponement.

My experience of over two decades as a trial lawyer told me that if this were a conspiracy, there would have been a much better story about how Ruiz hurt his neck. When stories are too good, they are often made up. This story was too suspicious to be the product of a conspiracy to defraud.

Cardinale spent over an hour with me discussing every detail of the events leading to the postponement. That was a totally unnecessary risk. Cardinale knew I was a good cross-examiner and would look for inconsistencies. He could very easily have been unavailable.

In summary, too many people, including outsiders, would have had to have been in on the conspiracy, and there would be no way to keep the truth from leaking eventually with so many people involved. I explained my analysis to Evander and recommended that he authorize me to have an independent medical examination performed on Ruiz or accept the postponement as an unfortunate accident about which we could do nothing. Evander said he had already gone beyond the postponement and was looking forward to knocking Ruiz out whenever the fight could be rescheduled.

Within the next few days everyone on Team Holyfield, except Evander, returned to the United States. I spent the next few days doing interviews with reporters about the legitimacy of Ruiz's injury and Evander's reaction. Then I started pushing King to reschedule the fight as soon as possible. I solicited and received the support of the Ruiz camp for a date later in August, but King said there was no way to reschedule the fight that soon. September was out because King had a big pay-per-view event in the Felix Trinidad versus Bernard Hopkins fight scheduled for September 15. Conventional wisdom teaches that it is difficult to hold two pay-for-view boxing events in one month, because most potential viewers will not pay a total of $100 ($49.95 twice) to watch boxing in one month.

October was a possibility, and we were initially targeting the date of October 6. Then we learned that Arum already had that date, so King began exploring October 20 and 27, but those dates would result in the fight competing with the World Series. King was planning to put the Lewis versus Rahman rematch on November 10 or 17, knocking out November for us. I was becoming extremely concerned about a postponement until December or later, and King stopped taking or returning my phone calls. Finally I pinned King down, and we rescheduled the fight for November 24 in Beijing.

With our fight rescheduled for Beijing for November 24, two days after Thanksgiving, Evander began his strength and conditioning training on the day after Labor Day and planned to leave for Houston for his boxing training in mid-September. On September 10, I went to New York for meetings the next day, intending to return to Atlanta the next evening. The next morning my wife called me in my hotel room, where I was preparing for my meetings, and told me to turn on the television. I did so just in time to see the South Tower of the World Trade Center attacked. When the towers collapsed, I ran as close to the site as I could to volunteer to help but was turned away. Later, Evander called to make sure I was okay.

So many people were so tragically affected by the September 11 attacks that the direct impact upon Evander and me was relatively inconsequential, but there was a direct effect upon our fight. I was stuck in New York for four additional nights due to the suspension of air traffic, and while I was in New York, I visited with Kery Davis of HBO and discussed the impact of the attacks upon HBO's plan to broadcast the fight from Beijing approximately two months later. I argued my case for staying with the plan to go to China, explaining my belief that the security measures I observed in China and the apparent absence of any due process of law constraints on the government there under these circumstances would result in our being safer in China than in the United States. Davis did not seem convinced but had an open mind.

The following week, when I had returned to Atlanta and Ross Greenburg, the president of HBO Sports, had made it back home to New York; I called Greenburg and made the same argument. Like Davis, Greenburg was skeptical but open-minded. Two weeks later, when the United States started bombing Afghanistan and our State Department issued an advisory warning regarding foreign travel, HBO announced that it would not send its film crew to China to broadcast our fight. I called Greenburg to argue our case for going to China, but he stopped me by explaining that the decision had been made at the highest level of AOL/Time Warner based upon liability concerns if the company ordered its employees to travel to China and they were harmed or detained.

Moving the fight to the United States would not have been a major problem under most circumstances, but in this case it was. November 24 was a very important date to HBO, because it was one week after the Rahman versus Lewis rematch on pay-per-view, and HBO wanted to package the free tape delay of Rahman–Lewis for the WBC and IBF belts with the live broadcast of Holyfield versus Ruiz for the WBA belt. If the fight were in China, that would be no problem, because the seats could be sold without any complications. In the United States, however, there were two major problems with the date. First, it was the Saturday of Thanksgiving weekend, and it would be hard for many fight fans to get a "pass" from their families to leave for Las Vegas that weekend. Second, it is generally not practicable to stage two major fights on back-to-back weekends in Las Vegas because the seats would not sell, and the Rahman versus Lewis fight was to be held at the Mandalay Bay Hotel in Las Vegas on November 17.

That meant for the fight to be held on November 24 it would need to be held outside Las Vegas. DKP went to work trying to find a site that would be willing to pay a significant guaranteed site fee for a fight on Thanksgiving weekend, and no one was very eager to step up to the plate. HBO then made a major concession and agreed to a backup date of December 15, provided that a deal was reached by October 30. With a deadline of October 30 from HBO facing us, King called me only days earlier and told me he could put on the fight, but only if both fighters took a substantial cut in pay.

For the next few days, King and I engaged in some of the most difficult and hostile negotiations in our long and contentious relationship. King was insisting on further reducing Evander's purse, and Evander was refusing to take any more cuts. As was so often the case in these disputes, I sent to King and his attorneys a detailed brief on our legal positions and how we planned to proceed with litigation if King persisted in his efforts to cut Evander's purse even further below the contractual minimum Evander was entitled to. In the past, on some occasions, I had advised Evander to be flexible in order to get the fight he wanted, but this time I fully agreed with his decision not to take one dollar less than King had already agreed to pay him. King first gave me an ultimatum, and when that didn't work, asked me to put the demand for a cut to Evander as a request from King for a personal favor.

**HOLYFIELD**

*I had already voluntarily taken a huge cut in pay to make the fight happen. I was not about to allow Don King to take more money out of my pocket and put it in his. I did not believe he would lose money on the fight, but I also didn't really care. I was tired of not getting what I was promised, and I wasn't about to stand for it anymore. Jim told me we had a good chance to get out of the contract with Don King if he failed to do what he promised, and I was ready to take my chances. It was real simple. If he wanted to do what he promised, there would be no problem. If not, I did not want to be with someone I could not trust to keep his word.*

I was very pleased that Evander had decided not to give in to King. Now it was my turn to posture this whole situation in a way that would allow King to accept Evander's position without losing face. I called King.

"I have Evander's position," I said.

"Give it to me."

"Just as you have politely and respectfully asked Evander to help you by changing the agreement, Evander politely and respectfully asks you to help him by not changing the agreement."

King laughed and said, "You put it that way, and I'll do it; I'll make the fight, but make sure you explain to Evander I am doing this for him."

I assured King I would pass his words on to Evander. As usual, King wanted credit for simply doing what he had already agreed to do as if he were doing Evander a favor. At about 4:45 p.m. on October 30, 15 minutes before the deadline, we had a deal. The fight was on for December 15, 2001, at the Foxwoods, a Native-American casino in Connecticut.

About one month prior to the fight date, I called Evander to go over the status of every item on my prefight checklist. One of the items we discussed was who the referee would be for a fight in Connecticut. I told Evander I had heard and read rumors that the referee would be Steve Smoger and that I had checked Smoger out, and he seemed to be okay. Evander said he knew Smoger and he would be fine. I then told Evander that I had not yet been able to determine who any of the judges would be. Evander said to forget about the judges and not spend any time on the judges, because they would not be involved in the outcome and if they were, he would be in trouble no matter what I did.

Finally, more than four months after we had left China without a fight due to Ruiz's sore neck, it was fight week once again. Evander wanted to leave for the Foxwoods at the latest possible time. Because the prefight press conference would be held on Thursday, and the weigh-in was scheduled for Friday, I arranged for Team Holyfield to arrive at the Foxwoods on Wednesday night. At the press conference the next day, Ruiz's team was unusually aggressive and derisive, especially toward me. I did not know where that was coming from, but I took it as a sign of tension and insecurity.

On Friday, the fight rules meeting with the commission was scheduled immediately after the weigh-in. Usually the rules meeting is a perfunctory meeting of a few minutes at which the local commissioner goes over the rules we all know. On the previous day, I had asked Peter Timothy, the Mashantucket Pequot Tribal Nation Athletic Commissioner, to make sure Smoger, the referee, would be at the meeting. Prior to the rules meeting, I met with Don Turner and Kenny Weldon to discuss our strategy for the rules meeting. I planned to ask the referee about his interpretation and application of the rules in various circumstances. This was the best and most appropriate way to sensitize him in advance to the tactics we believed Ruiz and his corner would attempt to employ to gain an unfair advantage. At the meeting, Ruiz's manager, Norman "Stoney" Stone was furious about our questions, such as what action the referee would take if one fighter faked a low blow and pretended to be hurt, but we came away very satisfied that the referee was aware of Team Ruiz's tricks, and after the meeting, Smoger told Turner, Weldon, and me that we had done a good job of looking out for Evander.

Finally, it was fight night. In the first round, Evander showed that he was really tired of Ruiz as he loaded up and tried to take Ruiz's head off. Ruiz, as usual was able to smother Evander's attacks with his incessant holding, but halfway through the round, Evander caught Ruiz on the top of the head with a crisp shot that put Ruiz on the canvas. The referee, however, called it a *slip* and waived off the knockdown. Without the knockdown being called, the first round was fairly even. Had it been called a knockdown, Evander would have been up a minimum of one point but more likely two points on all three judges' cards.

Rounds two and three were similar to round one, except that Evander did not score any further knockdowns. In round four, Evander boxed instead of trying to take Ruiz out with one shot, and Evander started to score effectively. Evander's father and I touched fists after the fourth round, because, after three indecisive rounds, it was obvious to us that Evander won the round. The fifth and sixth rounds were two more good rounds for Evander, but Ruiz came back in the seventh to keep it relatively close. Evander then undeniably won rounds eight and nine by wide margins, and I was sure he was up by a minimum of three rounds with three to go, and I had him up by five rounds, 7-2. The 10th and 11th rounds were again close, with no clear advantage in effective punches for either fighter. If those rounds were scored for Ruiz, Ruiz, in my book, could be within one round of getting even. I still had Evander up 9-2 on my card. In the 12th round, Evander absolutely pounded and overwhelmed Ruiz, and Ruiz had to hang on even more than usual to avoid being knocked out. Everyone at the fight who was for Evander was celebrating, and Team Ruiz looked like its dog had just been run over.

Our team was in the ring celebrating while Team Ruiz hung their heads and Stoney griped and moaned about the referee. Finally, Jimmy Lennon announced the scores.

"Judge Julie Lederman scores the fight 116-112 for Evander Holyfield."

"Judge Don O'Neil scores the fight 115-113..."

I was already jumping up and down for joy.

"... For John Ruiz."

I absolutely could not believe my ears. I looked at Evander, and he had that same wry smile on his face he had after the second Lewis fight, as if to say, "Why should I be surprised that they are cheating me again?"

"Judge Tom Kazmarek scores the fight 114-114, a majority draw, and John Ruiz keeps the WBA heavyweight title."

I was so upset I could hardly breathe. To know how hard Evander had worked at age 39 to defy the odds and the critics and dominate a fighter 10 years younger, only to have the fight stolen from him broke my heart and made me furious.

Knowing I was in no condition to talk to anyone, I backed away to Evander's corner and looked away from the center of the ring. For some reason, Stoney came all the way over to me and shoved the WBA belt in my face. It was all I could do to stay in control.

Cardinale came over and pulled Stoney away and said to me, "It's not worth it."

I told him to keep Stoney away from me, and he promised to do so. We left the ring and went to the locker room, and I was asked to do several interviews, but I was too upset to think clearly, so I went off by myself to calm down. I came back to check on Evander, who looked like he had not done anything strenuous.

"Let's go to the press conference," he said.

After the last fight—where Evander had knocked out Ruiz in the 10th round but the referee called it a low blow, stealing the fight from Evander—I was extremely polite and complimentary just like Evander always is, and Evander said I had let him down. I was not going to make the same mistake twice; I knew what my marching orders were. It was my job to point out that Evander had been robbed, so that Evander could be noble and stay above it all.

We arrived at the press conference, and King took the microphone and was soon proclaiming that we all had to accept the decision of the judges who were trained professionals. He said that no one should second-guess the judges, and he certainly would not. Apparently something must have changed since the first Holyfield versus Ruiz fight, after which King called for a rematch to clean up the "controversial" decision by the judges. He then tried to bypass me and called Evander to speak, but Evander directed me to speak first. I took the microphone and stood up. King tried to get me to sit down and not speak, but I refused. I said that I would like to be polite, get a pat on the head for being a good sport, and say everything that had just happened was fair, but I could not do so in good conscience. I said everyone else could do what they wanted, but I was not going to play the game of "The Emperor's New Clothes." I said that the decision in the fight was a travesty of justice, and everyone who saw it knew that. I asked all boxing writers in the room to indicate by their applause how many felt Evander had dominated Ruiz. Almost every writer clapped. I then asked how many professional writers thought Ruiz had won, and none of them clapped.

King then jumped in again and said we could not second-guess the judges, and we all needed to accept the decision and move on. I was sick of King pretending to be on Evander's side but undercutting him at every opportunity.

"I am disappointed that the man who calls himself 'Evander Holyfield's promoter' thinks what happened tonight is okay," I said into the microphone.

King went ballistic and started screaming at me about how ungrateful I was.

"Evander would not even be here if it weren't for me," King said. "How dare you vilify me."

"I am not vilifying you," I replied. "I am asking Evander Holyfield's promoter to say that this is not okay."

King tried to shout me down, but I said I would tell the truth about what happened and would not be intimidated by him or anyone else. That set off another round of screaming by King. Evander nodded to me indicating that I had done my job, so I sat down, having said what I needed to say.

When the press conference finally broke up, the police offered to escort me back to my room.

"This would not be a good night to try to hurt me," I told them. "I'll be fine."

The police laughed, and I made my way back to Evander's suite alone. On the way, I couldn't help asking myself what I could have done to avoid this latest injustice. I had been directed by Evander not to do anything about the judges. I had violated that direction a bit by calling the local commission on the day before the fight and asking for the names and states of the judges. I knew Julie Ledermen and Tom Kazmarek, but I did not know the name Don O'Neil. I had asked where he was from and was told he had been out of Florida, and I accepted the representation without further questioning. At the post-fight press conference I learned that Don O'Neil was from Ruiz's hometown of Boston and had only moved to Florida part time in recent years. I wondered whether I should have investigated further about the judge I didn't know. I raised this issue with other members of the team, and they were good enough to try to convince me that if someone was trying to influence the outcome of the fight, it was going to happen whether I objected to O'Neil or not.

When I got to Evander's room, Sharon Steuart was giving him a massage. I sat down beside him so our heads were at the same level and told him I thought he fought a great fight and that I was sorry he got cheated. Evander said he knew he needed to knock Ruiz out and tried but didn't quite get him. I asked how he felt about the post-fight press conference, and he said I did a good job. I asked whether he thought I should have confronted King.

"All you did is ask the man to say it was wrong," Evander said. "That was the right thing to do."

I told Evander I was extremely proud of him and proud to be with him, and I got ready to leave. On my way out, Evander's father put his big arm on my shoulder.

"I want to thank you, Jim, for standing up for my boy."

I walked back to my room in tears of frustration, and I never slept one minute that night.

On December 20, I sent letters to the local commission and the WBA notifying them that I would be protesting the conduct and outcome of Ruiz versus Holyfield III. I then filed our protest with the WBA, and with Evander's agreement I also published the protest on one of the leading boxing websites because I felt that we needed the WBA to understand that the public was watching how the association would respond. Evander and I received tremendous response to our protest from boxing fans and boxing media, unanimously in favor of our position. The overwhelming sentiment was that there was no way the WBA could deny us relief.

I sent a copy of our protest to King along with a letter explaining that we would welcome his support for our position but understood that he had a conflict of interest due to his promotional contract with Ruiz. Therefore, I put King on notice that we expected him to remain neutral. I realized, of course, that there was nothing I could do to control any maneuvering by King behind the scenes, but I at least wanted to prevent any open or public opposition by him to our protest. I received a letter back from King's attorneys assuring me that due to the conflict of interest, DKP would remain strictly neutral and would have no involvement with our protest or Ruiz's defense.

Soon after I filed our protest with the WBA, Cardinale responded on behalf of Ruiz, but there was very little substance in the response. Basically, the response merely generally alleged that the facts in our protest were not true, with little or no factual support for Ruiz's contentions. Cardinale did the best he could with the facts he had, which were not good for Team Ruiz.

In mid-January, I received an e-mail from Gilberto Mendoza Jr., the son of the president of the WBA, who was then the WBA's executive director. Mendoza informed me that the WBA had received our protest, would give it due consideration, and had set it for a hearing in Caracas, Venezuela, where the WBA is headquartered, on February 16. I then met with Evander to discuss and review where we were. One of my points was that Evander could expect King to try to get Evander to split from me.

"He can't get rid of anybody," Evander stated matter-of-factly.

"All I'm saying is he's going to try," I responded.

"He already has," Evander replied.

### HOLYFIELD

*Jim didn't need to tell me how Don King works. I knew he would try to separate me from Jim, because Jim was willing to stand up to Don to help protect me. I had no intention of allowing King to dictate who I had on my team. All I wanted to know from him was whether he was going to offer me a fight for $5 million within six months, which he owed me under my contract. I wasn't about to let things completely break down, though, until the WBA had ruled on my protest.*

On January 30, I learned from one of my sources that HBO had made an offer to King to televise Holyfield versus Rahman for a license fee of $5 million. Predictably, within one hour, Evander called to tell me King had called him.

### HOLYFIELD

*King called and offered me $3 million to fight Rahman. I told him I had a contract that guaranteed me at least $5 million per fight. He said the fight would not generate enough money for me to be paid $5 million. I told him I wasn't concerned about that, and that I needed to be paid $5 million. I understood that the fight between me and Rahman might not generate enough money for me to get paid $5 million, but I either wanted to get paid $5 million or be free from my contract with King. Once free, I would accept whatever the market would pay for my fights. I was not about to accept less than $5 million and be tied exclusively to King.*

When Evander explained his conversation with King and his thinking, I gave him my full support. Evander said that if King called again, he would have

King call me. I reminded Evander that we had the WBA hearing in Caracas coming up on February 16, and we agreed to try to avoid a war with King until after the WBA had ruled. We were very concerned about King's potential ability to adversely affect the outcome of the WBA hearing if we went to war before the hearing.

On the morning of February 15, Evander and I traveled to Caracas, and I worked on refining my oral argument to be presented the next morning. Meanwhile, King was already in Caracas, presumably meeting with the WBA's leaders. At the hearing on February 16, I presented a very detailed and passionate case for why Evander deserved relief because he had been robbed of the victory he should have received in his fight with Ruiz. I had virtually every member of the 15-member executive committee clearly nodding in agreement with virtually every point I made. I argued that Evander deserved an immediate rematch but candidly recognized that I did not realistically expect the WBA to order a fourth consecutive bout between Ruiz and Evander. Therefore, I argued that the very least the WBA could due to restore justice was to allow Ruiz to fight his mandatory bout against the No. 1-rated challenger, Kirk Johnson, and order the winner of that bout to fight Evander next.

I had heard a rumor that there had been some talk among various executive committee members and King about ordering Ruiz to fight Johnson and Evander to fight Rahman with the winners to fight each other. I argued vehemently that ordering Evander to do anything would constitute the imposition of a penalty upon the victim of the transgression for which we were seeking restitution. I was adamant about this point, because Evander wanted to fight Rahman, and I knew from Rahman's managers that Rahman wanted to fight Evander, and I was hopeful we could negotiate a fight with Evander being paid his $5 million minimum purse and Rahman receiving somewhere between $1 million and $2 million. I knew that if the WBA ordered the Holyfield versus Rahman fight, Rahman would be in position to refuse to fight for less than Evander received, forcing the fight to a purse bid in which each fighter would receive 50 percent of the winning promoter's bid, which would cost Evander millions of dollars if he agreed to go forward. If he did not proceed with the purse bid, he would be dropped from the WBA ratings and would lose any hope of fighting for the WBA title in the foreseeable future. I explained this whole scenario in detail, and the committee members seemed to understand fully.

When Cardinale had finished his presentation on behalf of Ruiz, and Johnson's attorney had made his presentation, I was allowed to reply, and then the executive committee announced it would recess for deliberations and would return with its decision within 30 minutes. When the executive committee had left the room, many people who had been in the audience came over to me and congratulated me on the strength and presentation of my argument, many opining that the committee had no choice but to do what I had asked for. I was feeling quite confident and proud of myself when I was snapped back into reality by another well-known boxing attorney, Leon Margulies, who was there for a protest on behalf of another fighter.

"Jim, you're looking pretty confident."

"I am," I replied.

"I'm surprised at you, after all these years, are you really allowing yourself to believe you have any influence on the outcome? Are you really allowing yourself to believe this issue was not decided before you got here?"

I realized the awful truth in what Margulies was saying, but continued to delude myself.

"This time they have to do the right thing. Our position is too strong, and there are too many people watching," I said.

Margulies smiled, shook his head, and said, "Good luck."

It was obvious that he was really saying, "Get a grip on reality."

When the executive committee returned, longtime WBA general counsel, James "Jimmy" Binns, who from time to time had represented King, read the WBA's decision. The WBA decided that: (1) Ruiz would fight Johnson in the mandatory bout; (2) Evander would remain in the top challenger spot; (3) the top four boxers behind Evander would participate in a tournament to see who would fight Evander; and (4) the winner of the bout between Evander and the tournament winner would be the mandatory challenger and would fight the WBA champion for the WBA title. The only good thing in the decision for us was that Evander was allowed to fight anyone rated in the top 15 heavyweights while the tournament proceeded or could simply wait for the tournament to be concluded. This convoluted decision meant that Evander was at least a year away from a title bout.

Without a word, Evander and I stood up and left the room and went to Evander's suite. I was so furious I couldn't speak.

"They really didn't do anything for me, did they?" he asked.

"They did very little, but at least you're free to do whatever you want. It is a completely unfair decision."

I then told Evander I thought we should leave immediately, rather than staying for the dinner and awards ceremony as planned.

"I don't want to do that," Evander replied. "What good would it do? I accept people for how they are. This isn't the first time this has happened."

I said I hated the thought of smiling at and shaking hands with people who had just cheated Evander all over again.

"You just need to learn to accept people as they are," Evander responded.

## HOLYFIELD

*Jim was angry and upset. He had worked hard and done everything necessary to win, and the result was unfair. I was disappointed, but I can't say I was truly surprised. We were not on a level playing field, and I knew that just as I knew it when I went into the ring with Ruiz in his own backyard. I knew what happened was wrong, but I was not about to allow these people to drag me down and lose my dignity by complaining about the result or by leaving before the awards ceremony. I was no happier about having to deal with the hypocrisy of shaking hands with people who had just treated me so unfairly than Jim was, but I realized all people are flawed and that I just needed to forgive them and move on.*

When I overcame my anger, I realized Evander was right about staying, and I went to the cocktail party, dinner, and awards ceremony determined to follow Evander's advice. At the cocktail party, I was approached by nearly every member of the executive committee and was told privately that I had made one of the best presentations they had ever seen, that they were convinced that Evander won the fight against Ruiz, but that they thought the tournament for the No. 1 challenger spot was the best thing for the WBA. I smiled, shook hands, and tried to forgive them, but it was difficult, and it must have been extremely difficult for Evander, too, because he left the cocktail party soon after he arrived and asked me to come and get him in his room when his award for Boxer of the Decade was about to be presented.

# CHAPTER 13

# 2002: ANOTHER BIG WIN, A TITLE SHOT, A COURAGEOUS LOSS, AND MORE CALLS FOR RETIREMENT

When we returned from Caracas, Don King and I began negotiations for the Rahman fight, with King predictably opening by explaining that there would not be enough revenue generated by the fight to allow Evander to make $5 million. I told King I did not believe Evander would fight for less than $5 million. King explained why the Rahman fight was good for Evander, but I told him he was preaching to the choir. I was strongly in favor of the Rahman fight. In the end, I told King I would discuss the whole situation with Evander, but that I doubted he would come off his contractual minimum. I discussed the situation with Evander, and he told me he would not fight for less than he was entitled to under his contract with DKP.

## HOLYFIELD

*For me, it was very simple. I had a contract that said Don King would be my promoter as long as he did certain things. He had two choices: He could do what he agreed to do or he could let me go. I had sacrificed in the past and taken less than what my contract provided for. That was over. I was tired of being the one to*

*sacrifice and having nothing to show for it. This was not an emo-
tional issue for me. It was simply business. I already had a contract, and I had consistently lived up to my part of the bargain. I
didn't care about how much money the fight would make. I was
either going to receive what my contract said or I was going to be
free.*

I explained Evander's position to King and told him I did not believe it
would change. King asked to speak directly with Evander, and I told him that
was fine but that it would do no good. I explained that one option was for him
to agree to terminate the promotional agreement between DKP and Evander
and then attempt to negotiate a purse for the Rahman fight without any constraints or purse limits. King eventually offered to pay Evander $4 million for
the Rahman fight and set Evander partially free, retaining only a right of first
negotiation and last refusal for future fights. I actually recommended this compromise to Evander because I felt it was very important for him to move on
with his career as quickly as possible and, more importantly, because I had
determined that as a practical matter, the terms King had asked for would have
no adverse effect on us.

**HOLYFIELD**

*I felt no time pressure whatsoever. Although other people might be
thinking I was getting older and needed to compromise to save
time, I did not feel that way. I had made up my mind that I was
either going to get exactly what my contract provided, or I was
going to be completely free to do whatever I wanted. If the market dictated that I could not get $5 million for a fight, I would
accept that, but I was not going to stay under contract with someone who was not living up to what the contract said.*

Evander rejected King's proposal, and to my surprise, soon thereafter I
received a proposed contract from King offering to pay Evander $5 million to
fight Rahman.

The Holyfield versus Rahman fight was scheduled for June 1, 2002, Evander began strength and conditioning work in March and held his full-scale boxing camp in Houston during April and May. The site of the fight was the newly renovated Boardwalk Hall in Atlantic City. Big-time boxing had been absent from Atlantic City for several years, and this fight was heralded as a renaissance. Park Place Entertainment, the owner of the Bally's and Caesar's Palace hotels, was the site host for the fight. We received great hospitality, and the refurbished Boardwalk Hall was an excellent venue.

Team Holyfield moved to Atlantic City on May 26, which was Memorial Day weekend. The long-awaited Lennox Lewis versus Mike Tyson fight was scheduled for June 8, one week after our fight, and to some extent, our fight was overshadowed by it. However, there was a fair amount of attention paid to Holyfield versus Rahman by the boxing press because it was widely speculated the winner would probably fight the winner of Lewis versus Tyson, if not immediately, then eventually. Most of the boxing writers and commentators expected Rahman to beat Evander, and I spent most of my time and energy during fight week attempting to convince the press that Evander was going to win and then fulfill his destiny to retire as the undisputed Heavyweight Champion of the World.

I believed Evander would be in good position for another title shot for the following reasons. First the IBF had already agreed to rank the winner of Holyfield versus Rahman No. 2, so if Evander won and Lewis failed or refused to fight his mandatory bout against No. 1-ranked Chris Byrd, Evander would be in position to fight Byrd for the vacant IBF title. Second, only Tyson, Vitali Klitschko, and Rahman were ranked ahead of Evander in the WBC ratings. I felt that if Evander beat Rahman and Lewis beat Tyson, I had a good chance of convincing the WBC to rank Evander No. 1 in the WBC, which would guarantee him a WBC title shot within one year. Third, I was continuing to object to the WBA's ruling on our protest of the Ruiz fight because no progress was being made on the proposed tournament for the No. 1 ranking, and days before our fight, the WBA finally agreed that the winner of Holyfield versus Rahman would be ranked No. 1 behind the winner of Ruiz versus Kirk Johnson, guaranteeing a WBA title shot within a year.

On June 1, Evander put on his best performance in the ring since the Michael Moorer fight almost five years earlier. Evander completely dominated Rahman during all but one of the first six rounds. Evander outfought and outthought Rahman. He was quicker on the outside, had better position and more power on the inside, and landed combinations of punches better than he had in a long time. In the seventh round, when it looked as if Rahman was in trouble from the battering he was taking from many power punches Evander was landing, the two fighters were battling for position on the inside and their heads collided. Rahman developed a pronounced egg-sized contusion on his forehead. The referee correctly ruled the event an unintentional head clash, and the fight went on. Evander landed several hard punches on Rahman's head, and the contusion began to swell as the round ended.

In the eighth round, Evander was dominating the fight even more, and Rahman was being hit repeatedly and was in trouble, and the contusion on his forehead was continuing to grow. At about one minute into the eighth round, the referee stopped the fight to allow the doctor to look at the contusion, which had grown to the size of a fist and looked grotesque. The doctor determined that it was a mere hematoma, or blood sack outside the skull, and not dangerous, but Rahman said his vision was impaired, so the fight was stopped. According to the rules, because the injury was caused by an accidental head clash, the scorecards would determine the result of the fight. The rules provided that if there was substantial activity in eighth round, it should be scored, and in my opinion there was more than ample activity to require the eighth round to be scored.

The scores were tabulated and given to New Jersey commissioner Larry Hazzard. I then went to Hazzard, who had already reviewed the scorecards, to make sure the eighth round had been scored. When he said it had not been, I became very upset but calmed down when he quietly told me to relax because it didn't matter. I knew, of course, that the fight should not have been close, but we had been unpleasantly surprised in three of Evander's last four fights so I was taking nothing for granted. The ring announcer then announced the results. The first judge scored the fight six rounds to one for Evander, which was reasonable, although I would have given all seven of the first seven rounds to Evander. The second judge scored the fight four rounds to three, which I though was absurd enough, and then I heard the ring announcer say, "for Hasim Rahman." I was shocked and must admit I was bracing for Evander to be "cheated" one more time. Fortunately, like the first judge and unlike the second, the third judge saw the same fight everyone else in the arena saw and scored the fight six rounds to one for Evander, and Evander won.

Evander fought a brilliant fight and looked like a young fighter, but once again the victory was somewhat marred by controversy. I was extremely disappointed to hear Rahman and his managers contend that Evander had repeatedly and deliberately head butted Rahman, claiming that Evander should have been disqualified and did not legitimately win the fight. Although this upset me, almost no one who actually saw the fight was buying Rahman's story, and predictably it had virtually no effect on Evander, who knew with absolute certainty that he had not intentionally head butted Rahman.

## HOLYFIELD

*I always try to be honest and realistic about my performance in the ring. When I have been disappointed by how I performed, I have said so. In this fight, however, I fought very well. I moved well, had excellent endurance, threw combinations, and most of all I outthought my opponent. I was able to see what Rahman was trying to do, and I was able to prevent him from doing it by beating him to the best position inside. Because we were competing for position inside, our heads collided several times, which is not unusual in that type of a fight. With respect to Rahman's claim that I was intentionally hitting his head with my head, I have two responses. First, I know that I never tried to hit him with my head, and that is what is most important to me. Second, Rahman's claim makes absolutely no sense. I truly believe I am going to win every fight I am in, so I am never going to take the risk of getting cut or getting disqualified. In this particular fight, I was dominating the fight and was sure I would knock Rahman out. There is no way to hit another man's head with your head and predict which man will get cut. In my fights with Mike Tyson, he did try to head butt me, and he was unlucky enough to get himself cut. In the Rahman fight, when I was doing so well, why on earth would I risk cutting myself or getting disqualified?*

After Evander defeated Rahman, Rahman and his managers filed an official protest with both the WBA and the New Jersey State Athletic Commission. The thrust of the protests was that Evander had injured Rahman with an intentional head butt and should have been disqualified. I had a distinct approach for defeating each of these protests, but I was very confident of the outcome in both and told Evander not to worry about them. Once again I was defending Evander against the persistent allegations that he systematically and intentionally used his head as a weapon. Once again I explained how illogical these allegations were. When two heads collide, whether one fighter or both fighters is injured is beyond anyone's control. There was a theory, however, that if a fighter knew the secret technique of how to head butt without getting hurt, it could be done. This theory was openly articulated soon after the Rahman fight when Sugar Shane Mosley was getting ready for his rematch with the great Atlanta Welterweight Champion of the World Vernon Forrest, who had dominated Mosley in their first bout. Mosley alleged that Forrest had beaten him in their first fight by intentionally butting him with his head and that Forrest had taken head butting lessons from Evander, who conducted clinics on successful head butting at his estate south of Atlanta. I could only hope this was as funny and ridiculous to everyone else as it was to me. Mosley, however, cited proof that there is a way to head butt without getting hurt. He pointed to martial artists, who broke boards and even bricks with their heads without getting hurt. This was even funnier to me, because when I was younger and doing karate exhibitions as a fourth-degree black belt, I used to break objects with my head until I became the highest-ranked member of the exhibition team. At that point I made someone else do the head breaks because I had no control over whether I hurt my head doing the breaks and knew that hitting a hard object with one's head and not getting cut or developing a hematoma was only a matter of luck.

In any event, these newest allegations of head butting by Evander were no more true than Tyson's lame excuses for why he was dominated by Evander. In addition to the factual dispute over whether Evander had intentionally butted Rahman, I had developed good, solid, and in my opinion irrefutable legal arguments to defeat Rahman's protests to the WBA and the New Jersey State Athletic Commission, and both organizations eventually dismissed the protests.

## HOLYFIELD

*I had no doubt that if I got the opportunity to fight for the undisputed Heavyweight Championship of the World, I would win and retire in that position. Now it looked like I would get that opportunity, and things were beginning to develop according to God's plan for me. Once again I was in position to show the children of the world that if you work hard, have faith and patience, and never give up, you can achieve any goal, no matter how many doubters there are.*

Once the Rahman protests were dismissed, I wrote to the WBA in an effort to lock Evander into the WBA mandatory challenger position. At the time, there was no question that Evander had earned the right to be the mandatory challenger, but I knew there was always the risk—if not the chance—of a dispute with King down the road, and I feared some representatives of the WBA might develop amnesia if and when Evander was no longer on the King team. I wrote to the WBA with questions about the deadline for the champion's defense against Evander, but I was not so much concerned about the deadline itself as getting a written acknowledgment that Evander was, and would remain, the mandatory challenger. When this mission was accomplished, Evander and I began focusing on his next bout.

The situation in the heavyweight division was as follows:

- Lennox Lewis was scheduled to fight the WBC mandatory challenger, Mike Tyson, to maintain his WBC title (and make about $20 million).
- John Ruiz was scheduled to fight the WBA mandatory challenger, Kirk Johnson, to maintain his WBA title (and fight someone other than Evander for the first time in about 18 months).
- Chris Byrd had defeated David Tua to become the IBF mandatory challenger to Lennox Lewis's IBF title and was not about to fight anyone with a pulse until he got his title shot.

On June 8, Lewis totally dominated, punished, and knocked out Tyson, who would need to be rehabilitated with at least one quality win before he would be viewed as a top rank contender. Lewis had firm control of the WBC belt and would have until June 8, 2003, before he had to defend it. The No. 1 contender was Vitali Klitschko, the former WBO champion who had been beaten by Byrd, and the No. 2 contender was Evander.

On July 27, 2002, Ruiz fought Johnson for the WBA title. Johnson appeared to be winning until he was disqualified for repeated low blows. Johnson must have somehow missed Ruiz's Academy Award performance when

Evander hit him with what I thought was a legal shot. What made him think he could get away with punches that actually were low? The win gave Ruiz until July 27, 2003, before he had to face Evander again, although I was arguing that the deadline should be earlier because Ruiz delayed fighting Johnson beyond the deadline for that fight imposed by the WBA rules.

In the IBF ratings, Byrd was the mandatory challenger, and Lewis's mandatory bout with Byrd was due almost immediately. Lewis would need to decide fairly soon whether to fight Byrd next or lose his IBF title. The decision would have been an easy one for Evander who never failed to fight a mandatory challenger in his career, but it was predictably more difficult for Lewis, who had already lost his WBA title by refusing to fight Ruiz when Ruiz was the mandatory challenger. Byrd was a slick, quick southpaw with a difficult slap-and-move style that could make Lewis look bad. Compounding the problem was the fact that Byrd was not very well known, and consequently the money for Lewis versus Byrd would not be big.

Meanwhile, I began the familiar process of documenting our right to terminate Evander's promotional contract if King failed to offer Evander a bout for at least $5 million to occur no later than December 1. My letters on this occasion did not even bother reciting all of the relevant facts. Instead, I merely attached copies of my letters from the last time we did this dance. Once again King explained that the money simply wasn't there to pay Evander $5 million, and once again I responded on Evander's behalf that no one was trying to force King to lose money; he had the option to free Evander from his contract.

We were essentially at a stalemate when King woke me up at 1 a.m. one night and told me that he was with Lewis and had just done something wonderful for Evander. King reported that he had just paid Lennox $1 million to give up the IBF title, which would leave Byrd and Evander to fight for the vacant IBF title. I wasn't prepared for a confrontation, and it was unnecessary at the time anyway, but I had every reason to believe based on my sources that Lewis was going to give up the IBF title regardless of this deal with King, so I simply asked King to call me within the next day or two. My true thoughts were that I wondered (and still wonder) what King had really gotten in exchange for his $1 million.

Within a few days, King called to tell me: (a) how lucky Evander was to have him, because he could now put Evander in position to be the five-time

Heavyweight Champion of the World and (b) that Evander could not possibly expect to make $5 million to fight Byrd, especially after King had already paid Lewis $1 million on Evander's behalf. King said he could make the fight and pay Evander $3 million. I told him that he already knew Evander's position and that nothing had changed. The right number might be $3 million, and Evander might fight Byrd for that amount, but if he did so, it would be as a free agent going forward.

This new stalemate lasted until we were almost out of time for King to meet the condition of presenting a $5 million bout to Evander to occur by December 1. King then went to work on a new element. He was trying to convince the great light heavyweight champion Roy Jones Jr. to fight Ruiz for the WBA title, with the winner to fight the winner of Holyfield versus Byrd to consolidate the WBA and IBF titles. King presented this to me as a godsend for Evander, and it might have literally been so, but Evander's price did not, and would not, change.

I began to feel a great opportunity for Evander, and possibly the last opportunity while he was young enough to take full advantage, slipping away. I met with Evander and discussed my concerns, and he and I came up with a proposition for King involving licensing rights to Evander's fights in King's film library that we thought could potentially be of more benefit to Evander than cost to King. I was very proud of this solution and presented it to King, who summarily rejected it for reasons he could or would not explain. I relayed all of this to Evander, who accepted it in his typical fashion.

### HOLYFIELD

*I understood and appreciated Jim's concern, but I felt no pressure at all. I had always been patient, but at almost 40 years old, I had become a very patient man. If King did not or could not pay the amount necessary to fulfill his contractual obligation for a fight with Chris Byrd for the IBF title, I would wait and fight the WBA champion, whether it was Ruiz or someone who beat him, by July 2003.*

I fully understood, and in fact admired, Evander's position, but I had less faith than he did that if and when we announced that Evander was free of King, the WBA mandatory position would still be his. I went to work to find a way to make the Byrd fight. Eventually I came up with a slight compromise on the timing of the payment of a portion of Evander's purse that would cost Evander little if anything and would allow King to put the fight on. The usual death throes of the negotiation followed, with King protesting every last step of the way but eventually we had a deal. Evander would be paid his $5 million contractual minimum, but $2 million would be deferred until specific dates in 2003. These payments were absolutely unconditional.

The Holyfield versus Byrd fight was scheduled for December 14 at Boardwalk Hall in Atlantic City. Evander began training in early October and had an excellent training camp, sparring very effectively with two southpaws who tried to mimic Byrd's style. When Team Holyfield arrived in Atlantic City for fight week, I debriefed each of Evander's trainers and was consistently told that he was ready for the fight, with one relatively minor problem. Evander had been having trouble with his left shoulder, on which he had arthroscopic surgery a few months earlier to "clean it out." Evander's final sparring session before a fight was typically on Tuesday. On Tuesday, when I arrived at the training facility and told Don Turner I was looking forward to seeing Evander spar, Turner said Evander was not going to spar because his shoulder was sore. I asked Evander about this, and he assured me it was not serious, and that he would be fine by Saturday.

On Saturday Evander entered the ring at age 40 looking spectacular. He was a bit more muscular and therefore heavier than usual, which for him means he had trained extra hard because he trains up in weight, not down. Evander weighs about 208 when he is not in training and had packed on 12 pounds of muscle training for this fight. Byrd, 10 years younger, looked extremely fit and seemed to be as confident as Evander. After the usual announcements, the fight we had been waiting for finally began, and I was very confident we would soon be celebrating Evander's fifth world championship.

Evander fought extremely well in the first round and rocked Byrd in the final seconds. All three judges scored the round for Evander, and I felt very good about the great start to the fight. In the second round, however, Evander seemed to throw fewer punches, and Byrd landed some of his lightning-quick jabs, which Evander had successfully blocked in the first round. For the next few rounds, Evander landed by far the heavier punches, but Byrd was racking up points with quick, jabs. Evander seemed to throw fewer punches in each round but did catch Byrd on the ropes several times, and when he did, he landed some power shots, but Byrd took them well. During the sixth round I was extremely frustrated watching Evander fail to throw any left jabs, and I asked Tim Hallmark what was going on. I got some very bad news. Hallmark told me Evander's left shoulder was shot, that Evander could not lift his left arm higher than his chest, and that Evander had apparently torn a ligament. That meant that not only was Evander unable to throw his own left jabs, but he was also unable to block Byrd's right jabs.

## HOLYFIELD

*I knew that I had the option to stop fighting and that no one would have criticized my decision under the circumstances, but I did not want to disappoint all of the people who had come or tuned in to see me. I had shown those people over many years that nothing could ever make me quit. Even more than that, though, I could not quit, because that is not who I am. I would rather lose trying even if it was hopeless than quit.*

Not only did Evander not stop the fight, but he also concealed the injury throughout the fight. Turner was wearing a microphone, so when Evander returned to the corner after each round, he whispered to his corner that his shoulder was shot but no one said anything out loud. Hallmark just put ice on the shoulder and everyone tried to conceal the injury. If the television commentators and the public would have known about the injury, they would have been able to appreciate how courageous Evander's performance was. Instead, Evander just looked ineffective, with no apparent reason other than the assumption of age and declining skills.

## HOLYFIELD

*Of course I could have revealed the injury and got a lot of sympathy and praise, but that was not my goal. My goal was to give myself the best possible chance to win, which meant trying to conceal the injury to the extent I could.*

As the fight wore on, the only way Evander could block Byrd's constantly flicking jabs was to use his right hand instead of his left. This, however, took away Evander's only remaining weapon and his only chance to win. Realizing this, Evander stopped using his right hand to block the jabs and simply allowed Byrd to land them with the hope that Evander could counter with a big right hand. Byrd, however, getting no resistance from Evander's left hand, kept slipping to Evander's left out of reach of the counter-punches. This caused Evander to over-extend and reach to catch Byrd with a right, straining his back. Thus, the first injury led to a second less serious but nevertheless troublesome injury. As a result of the back strain, Evander was unable to sit down between rounds for the first time in his career.

As the fight continued into the late middle rounds, it was apparent that Evander was being outpointed even though he was not being hit with any punches that hurt him. Evander then tried another tactic for the first time. He turned and tried to fight southpaw, but he had never trained to fight that way and it was not a solution. As the fight entered the 10th round, it was clear Evander was losing on points and needed some big rounds. In both the 10th and 11th rounds, Evander somehow summoned up the will and courage to trap Byrd against the ropes and hit him with some combinations. Although he could not lift his left arm, he could throw left hooks to the body, and he scored with those hooks and right crosses to the head. Somehow, without being able to lift his left arm, Evander won the 10th and 11th rounds of the fight, but it was too little too late, and after the 12th round, the decision was announced for Byrd.

In the locker room, Dr. Vaughns examined Evander's shoulder and gave a preliminary diagnosis of a torn rotator cuff. Evander was in a great deal of pain. We went to the post-fight press conference as quickly as possible to try to get Evander back to his room to lie down, but King was in the hallway giving interviews. I went to Turner and told him Evander was in severe pain and that we needed to leave if the press conference did not begin immediately. Turner came to the podium and allowed Evander to speak. Evander said very little, because he wanted to leave. I then spoke and told the crowd and the press that I was not going to be specific and was not making any excuses, but that someday they would all realize what a courageous performance they had just seen. We then left. I told Evander he had done the best he possibly could under the circumstances and that was all any man can ask of himself.

*Once again I did not get the result I had been hoping for, but once again I overcame adversity and the temptation to quit. My boxing record suffered another loss, but I kept my record as a man intact by continuing to never quit no matter what happens.*

Two days later Evander saw two of the world's leading orthopedic surgeons who are shoulder specialists, Dr. Xavier Duarte and Dr. Marvin Royster. These two doctors had successfully saved the careers of many professional athletes, including Atlanta Braves pitcher John Smoltz, and Atlanta Braves catcher Javier Lopez, both of whom had made full recoveries from torn rotator cuffs. The doctors ordered an MRI on Evander's left shoulder, and the following day they explained their findings to Dr. Vaughns, who immediately passed the diagnosis on to Evander and me. The pain Evander experienced in the first round of the fight was, as suspected, from an acute tear of the super spinatus tendon of the rotator cuff. The MRI also revealed some longer term damage and potential bone spurs. The doctors were unwilling to speculate on the prospects of recovery until they had a look at the damage during surgery, which was scheduled for the morning of December 21.

Because Evander had received some criticism in the press for, in their view, making an excuse for losing by saying his shoulder hurt, I immediately posted the following press release on the leading boxing websites:

Evander has undergone an MRI procedure on his left shoulder, and the MRI was analyzed today by two of the finest shoulder specialists in the country, Doctors Javier Duarte and Marvin Royster who have performed successful shoulder surgery on many athletes, including John Smoltz and Javier Lopez of the Atlanta Braves. The doctors have confirmed that the pain Evander experienced in the first round of his fight with Chris Byrd on Saturday night was caused by an acute tear in his rotator cuff, specifically the super spinatis tendon. Evander will have surgery to repair the tear on Saturday. We are hoping for a complete recovery, but will know more after the surgery.

It took great courage for Evander to fight eleven rounds without the ability to lift his left arm above chest level, and many fighters would have stopped the fight, but Evander did not want to disappoint the fans at the arena and on television and he has never stopped a fight in his life due to an injury, so he was committed to finishing the fight.

These facts are in no way intended to diminish Chris Byrd's accomplishment in defeating Evander fairly and winning the IBF Heavyweight Championship of the World. Chris fought a great fight, proved he is a worthy champion, and deserves great respect and admiration. Evander makes no excuses, and no one is suggesting that the outcome would necessarily have been any different had Evander not been injured. I am simply reporting the objective facts about the injury because so many people have asked why Evander threw almost no left jabs, threw no left hooks above the waist, tried to block Byrd's jabs with his right hand, and tried to fight southpaw at one point. We feel that the boxing world is entitled to know the true facts, rather than be forced to speculate.

---

At 6 a.m. on December 21, I met Dr. Vaughns at Piedmont Hospital in Atlanta, and a few minutes later Evander arrived. As usual, Evander was in good spirits and was looking forward to putting the surgery behind him. Although we were all hopeful that what the doctors found would be fully repairable and I was outwardly confident, inside I was worried. I consoled myself with the thought that if the doctors determined that Evander could not, or should not, fight again, that would be the sign Evander would need to know it was time to retire. I was fully prepared to accept that result, although I still believed that if he could recover, Evander could still achieve his goal of retiring as a champion.

Dr. Duarte and Dr. Royster were gracious enough to allow Dr. Vaughns to observe the surgery, and Dr. Vaughns was kind enough to postpone a family holiday vacation to do so. I waited nervously in the family waiting area. And a little over two hours after the surgery began, the doctors came out to give me their report while we waited for Evander to wake up. As usual, there was good news and bad news, but this time, there was also great news. The bad news was that the doctors found extensive damage. The good news was that they were able to repair the damage completely. The great news was that the doctors were able to determine and eliminate the source of the problem.

Over the years, Evander had developed two significant bone spurs under the shoulder bone. When Evander was not training for a fight, these bone spurs caused little problem and little pain. Unlike most heavyweights, who lose weight to get in shape, Evander bulks up to get ready for a fight. Out of training, he walks around at about 208 pounds. When he goes into intensive weight training and eats much more protein getting ready to fight, however, he gains from 10 to 14 pounds of pure muscle. This increase of size caused the muscles and tendons in his shoulder to rub against the bone spurs causing abrasions, which make the tendons more susceptible to tearing, which is what happened in the first round of the Byrd fight. The doctors were able to remove the bone spurs completely and felt confident Evander would recover completely, and when he did, his shoulder would feel better than it had in years. The doctors predicted that given Evander's incredible work ethic, he could potentially be in unrestricted training within three to four months and could potentially fight within six to seven months.

At the end of our debriefing, the doctors told me they were absolutely amazed that Evander had kept on fighting after the injury. I mentioned to them that a very talented and highly regarded heavyweight, Vitaly Klitschko, fought Byrd in a title fight, was winning on all three judges' cards after 10 rounds and merely needed to avoid a knockout by the light-punching Byrd to win but tore his rotator cuff in the 10th round and could not continue. The doctors said they understood, and it made sense. What none of us could understand, however, was how Evander fought 11 rounds with the same injury.

When Evander woke up, the nurses allowed me to see him. Evander was surprisingly lucid. I told him what the doctors had said and he said it all made sense.

**HOLYFIELD**

*For years, every time I went into training for a fight, the more prepared I got and the harder I trained, the more my shoulder hurt. I just decided I had to learn to deal with and fight through the pain, and that's what I did. Now I finally knew what was causing the pain.*

# CHAPTER 14

# 2003: EVANDER PASSES UP A TITLE SHOT ON PRINCIPLE; THEN SUFFERS HIS WORST LOSS EVER, BUT REFUSES TO QUIT

The next big fight in the heavyweight division was the John Ruiz versus Roy Jones bout for Ruiz's WBA heavyweight title scheduled for March 1, 2003. Several years earlier, Jones had met with Evander and me to discuss the possibility of Jones fighting Evander for the WBA title. Jones was now scheduled to challenge Ruiz for the same title. The fight generated a substantial amount of speculation about the outcome among fight fans. Many felt that despite Ruiz's limitations, he was simply too big for Jones. Others felt that Jones was too quick for Ruiz. Unfortunately, this intriguing fight was overshadowed by a sideshow.

Mike Tyson was scheduled to fight Clifford "The Black Rhino" Etienne on February 22 in a bout designed to resurrect Tyson so that he could fight Lewis again in their contractually obligated rematch. Etienne was carefully selected to play his role. He was a big tough-looking heavyweight with what many described as a glass jaw. Etienne had recently fought Fres Oquendo, a competent heavyweight who had knocked Etienne down seven times before the fight was mercifully stopped. Not many people knowledgeable about boxing suffered from any delusions that Etienne had a chance, but as always, there was the Tyson factor to generate some interest in the fight. One never knew what craziness might arise. After training hard for weeks, Tyson suddenly stopped training 12 days before the fight, spent a night out partying, and then had a large tattoo put on his face. For the next three days he reportedly left his trainer, Freddie Roach, waiting at the gym and then claimed to be suffering from flu symptoms.

Tyson's close friend and assistant trainer, Jeff Fenech, was so distressed by Tyson's behavior that he went home to Australia. On the Sunday before the fight, Tyson missed his flight to Memphis where the fight was to be held, and speculation was rampant that the fight was off. When Tyson again missed his flight the next day, the fight was called off. The next day, Tuesday, February 17, Tyson woke up, said he felt fine and flew to Memphis, saying he was ready to fight. Etienne then said he had been told the fight was off and was not going to be jerked around by Tyson, so Etienne was not going to fight. So the fight was on and off one more time. On Wednesday, Etienne agreed to fight, and the fight was back on. Everyone was suddenly talking about a fight that should have had a foregone conclusion. Meanwhile, Don King was fuming about the fact that his champion, John Ruiz, was fighting an historic fight against a light heavyweight the next week and no one was paying any attention.

On February 22 Tyson entered the ring with an aboriginal warrior tattoo covering half of his face, while the audience wondered what new bizarre twist would occur. There was nothing bizarre, or even all that interesting. Tyson simply hit Etienne with a very hard right hand 39 seconds into the fight, and Etienne hit the canvas, pulled out his mouthpiece, and closed his eyes; the referee counted to 10, and the fight was over in 49 seconds. Suddenly, "Iron Mike" was supposedly back.

Next up: Ruiz versus Jones on March 1 at the Thomas & Mack Center in Las Vegas. I went to Las Vegas on the Thursday before the fight for two specific purposes: (a) to talk to Chris Byrd and his representative, John Horneuwer, about a possible rematch for the IBF title and (b) to talk to Murad Muhammad, Roy Jones's promoter, about a bout with Jones if Jones were to win. I had both meetings and felt very good about Evander's options, especially if Jones won. Byrd continued to show that he was a class act by telling me he had always admired Evander, that Evander had agreed to fight Byrd, and that Byrd felt that he owed Evander a rematch. Muhammad made no commitments but indicated he and Jones would be interested in exploring a Jones versus Holyfield bout if Jones beat Ruiz.

The Ruiz versus Jones fight was spectacular entertainment. Jones, at a 22-pound disadvantage, peppered Ruiz throughout the fight with quick, accurate, effective shots. There was nothing to rock Ruiz, but Jones had him off balance all night. Jones won a clear decision and was suddenly the unrivaled hero of the boxing world. More important to Evander and me, we now had an alternative to the Byrd rematch, which would be offered to us by King, because King had promotional rights to Byrd's next fight.

On March 3, King called me and suggested he, Evander, and I meet to discuss our alternatives. I discussed this with Evander, and he wanted me to handle any meetings with King. Three days later, I flew to King's offices in Florida to discuss his thoughts on Evander's future. We actually had a fairly pleasant meeting for about three hours, including lunch. I laid out five options I said I was considering for Evander (only three of which were truly viable). King said he had promotional rights to Jones's fight if Jones fought as a heavyweight. King said he did not believe a Jones versus Holyfield fight could be made in the foreseeable future, but a Byrd rematch for the IBF title could be made quickly. King offered Evander $1 million for the opportunity to win back the IBF title. King also offered to pay Evander the $2 million he already owed Evander for the last fight for a total purse of $3 million. I told King I would discuss his offer with Evander and flew back to Atlanta.

## HOLYFIELD

*My goal was still to win the IBF, WBA, and WBC titles and retire as the undisputed Heavyweight Champion of the World, and the order in which I won those titles was not important, so if a fight against Chris Byrd for the IBF title could be made, that was great, but I was not about to fight for a title for $1 million. I was also not about to let Don King pay me $1 million, give me $2 million he already owed me from my last fight, and call it a purse of $3 million.*

In preparation for my response to King's offer, on March 10, I called Mark Taffet, head of marketing operations for HBO Sports to get some idea of the size of the licensing fee HBO would pay for Holyfield versus Byrd. I knew that HBO had paid $5.5 million for the first Holyfield–Byrd fight and that fight did a rating of more than 10, which was excellent. If HBO would pay the same amount for a rematch, I knew there would be enough in the pot for Evander to make at least $2 million. Taffet said HBO had not decided what it would do about a fee for Holyfield versus Byrd but asked why we were not working on Jones versus Holyfield. I explained that the signals we were getting from Jones indicated that he would demand too much money to allow Jones versus Holyfield to be made. Taffet said he was not as pessimistic about making Jones versus Holyfield and said that was the fight HBO really wanted.

Later that day, I got a call from Kevin Wynn, head of the boxing program at Madison Square Garden, who told me he had just met with Jones and Muhammad, and that MSG was very interested in hosting Jones versus Holyfield. Wynn wanted to know whether Evander and I were interested in that fight. I told him that we were interested but that I didn't want to waste my time and Evander's time working on that fight if Jones was not going to be realistic about his purse. I pointed out that Jones was being quoted as saying he would want a guarantee of $50 million to fight Evander and that was obviously far from realistic. Wynn said he was having dinner with Jones and Muhammad that night and would feel them out and call me the next morning.

The next day Wynn called me and said he believed there was a realistic chance of making Jones versus Holyfield. I told Wynn to tell Muhammad that if Jones was serious about making the fight, Muhammad should call me. Within hours, I got a call from Muhammad, who suggested we get together to talk, and Muhammad offered to come to me, and we scheduled a meeting at my firm's offices for the following afternoon. I considered Muhammad's willingness to fly to Atlanta on such short notice to be a very strong indication that Jones and Muhammad were serious about making the fight.

The next day Muhammad and I met in a conference room at my firm's offices from 3:30 p.m. to 6 p.m. I mostly listened for the first two hours until I felt I had a firm grip on where Muhammad and Jones were coming from. I then told Muhammad we needed to agree on one central concept or we would be wasting our time—if he and Jones thought we were negotiating the terms of the Roy Jones Show, we would never reach an agreement. I explained that in my view Jones versus Holyfield could be a huge event because of both fighters, not either one. I pointed out that Jones had beaten one heavyweight in his career, whereas Evander had beaten more current and former heavyweight champions that any fighter in history. I was pleasantly surprised that Muhammad said he agreed in principle. I then asked him what King's role and rights were with respect to a Jones versus Holyfield fight. He said that King was entitled to be a part of the promotion but that Muhammad had the right to negotiate with Evander and me. Muhammad and I both laughed when I told him I would be more than happy to leave the negotiations of what King's role would be to Muhammad. We both knew King would not be happy not being in control, but Muhammad assured me there was nothing King could do to prevent us from going forward.

For the next 30 minutes we discussed our respective views of the estimated revenue streams (pay-per-view, site, foreign television, closed circuit, sponsorships, merchandise, etc.) and costs of the fight. Muhammad then explained that in the Ruiz versus Jones fight, Jones had a $10 million guaranteed purse, and Ruiz had no guarantee. I told Muhammad that Evander was not Ruiz and was not going to fight a huge money fight without a substantial guarantee. I did tell Muhammad, however, that I believed it was possible that Evander would agree to the concept of allowing Jones's guarantee to be substantially larger than Evander's provided that Evander would have the opportunity to close the gap in compensation from the pay-per-view upside. At that point, Muhammad said he felt we were conceptually in the same ballpark, that it would be worthwhile to pursue negotiations, and that he would talk to Jones and get back to me within a few days.

A few days later, on March 22, I received a letter from King's in-house attorney, Charlie Lomax, accusing me of "interference with DKP's contractual rights" and demanding that I cease and desist from any further discussions with Muhammad concerning a Jones versus Holyfield bout. On March 24, I received a copy of a letter from Muhammad's attorney to Lomax taking the position that Muhammad had the right to discuss Jones's career decisions with anyone he wanted. On March 25, I wrote back to Lomax explaining that I had only had general discussions with Muhammad and informing him that I would continue to do so whenever I felt it was in Evander's best interest. I also explained that the issue of whom I should be dealing with could be resolved if I could see the contract governing the promotional rights for a Jones versus Holyfield bout. I then received a copy of a letter from Muhammad's attorney to Lomax ordering Lomax not to show the contract to me.

Two months then passed while I tried to get King and Muhammad to meet with me to negotiate the terms for a Jones versus Holyfield bout. I also asked for assistance from HBO in getting this done. Finally, thoroughly frustrated, I sent an opening offer to King on May 23. Despite follow-up phone calls to King, I heard nothing until June 10, 17 days later, when I received a counterproposal from King offering a fixed purse of $7 million (inclusive of the $2 million, which was owed for Holyfield versus Byrd) with a guarantee of $5 million plus an upside to be negotiated and agreed upon. I called King and asked what this meant, and he told me it meant that he would pay Evander the $2 million he owed him plus a guaranteed purse of $5 million for the Jones fight. I told him I thought that was a ridiculous offer and that unless it changed very substantially, it was clear to me that he did not want to make the Jones versus Holyfield fight. I was well aware that King was reportedly trying to settle the lawsuit brought against him by Tyson, and it occurred to me that King might be dangling a Jones fight before Tyson to entice Tyson to drop his suit.

When I received King's so-called offer, I became extremely concerned about being strung along by King and Muhammad and having Evander forced to take a completely unfair deal because nothing else was available. To me that appeared to be King's strategy. Consequently, I went to New York to meet with Jay Larkin, the head of boxing operations at Showtime, to explore whether there were any other possibilities for Evander. Despite my pleas, I had not received any significant support for Evander from HBO in making a fair deal on Jones versus Holyfield, and I knew I would not receive any support from HBO for another bout, so my only alternative was to explore other possible options with Showtime.

I met Larkin in mid-June at the bar of a great Italian restaurant named Gabriel's at 60th Street and Columbus Circle, where he and I regularly met and where many of the financial czars of the world and celebrities regularly meet. I explained the trap I felt Evander and I were in. I made it absolutely crystal clear to him that by far Evander's and my preference was to fight Jones, and that if Larkin and Showtime were going to feel used by exploring alternatives, we should change the subject. Larkin said he understood completely and wanted to help, knowing full well that he might be simply helping us make an acceptable deal with King. Larkin said he would do some thinking overnight and that we should get back together the next day.

The next day, he and I met at Showtime's offices at 50th Street and Broadway. Larkin had come up with a very attractive idea. He suggested trying to arrange a fight between Evander and "Baby Joe" Mesi. Mesi was a good-looking, articulate Italian-American undefeated heavyweight, who was incredibly popular in his hometown of Buffalo, New York. In light of Mesi's popularity in Buffalo, we speculated that a Holyfield versus Mesi fight could generate a huge gate, and Showtime would be willing to pay an attractive license fee for the fight. I liked the fight because (a) Evander would make somewhere between $3 million and $4 million; (b) a victory over Mesi would be considered a quality win against a tough young heavyweight; and (c) I was sure Evander would beat Mesi, who had never fought anyone of Evander's quality.

While Larkin and I were discussing this possibility, Larkin's colleague, Ken Hershman, stopped by Larkin's office. When we told Hershman what we were working on, Hershman said he had heard the negotiations for a fight between cruiserweight champion, James Toney, and middleweight champion, Bernard Hopkins, were breaking down, and that a Holyfield versus Toney fight might be a possibility. Larkin then called Dan Goossen, Toney's promoter, and asked about the status of the Toney versus Hopkins negotiations. Goossen said the negotiations were absolutely irretrievably dead and he was looking for a new opponent. Larkin carefully explained that I was trying to make a fight between Evander and Jones, and that if that fight could be made, Evander would take it. Larkin also explained, however, that I was concerned that King and Muhammed may try to force Evander into an extremely unfair deal, and if that happened, we wanted a backup deal. Goossen said he would be very interested in Holyfield versus Toney, and he understood it would merely be a backup plan in case Jones versus Holyfield could not be made. I then called Evander and asked whether he would be interested in fighting Toney if we could not make a fair deal with King and Muhammad for the Jones fight. Evander said he wanted the Jones fight, but if a fair deal could not be made, he'd fight Toney if the money were right.

## HOLYFIELD

*Of course I wanted to fight Roy Jones for the WBA heavyweight title rather than fighting James Toney, who was a very good fighter and a cruiserweight champion but had never before fought as a heavyweight, but I was not going to let anyone take advantage*

*of me. If a fair deal could be made for the Jones fight, I would*
*fight Jones, If not, I would fight someone else.*

████████████████████████████████████████

Larkin and I then ran some numbers and discussed how much financial support Showtime would provide for this backup plan. We eventually concluded that Evander could make somewhere between $5 million and $6 million for a pay-per-view deal on the Toney fight, which at that time was more than the $5 million King was offering for the Jones fight. Larkin then checked Showtime's master calendar and concluded the only remaining date available for a pay-per-view bout was October 4. He explained that Bob Arum of Top Rank Promotions was trying to lock up the October 4 date for an event on HBO but had not yet been able to do so. I told Larkin I would try to force the Jones versus Holyfield negotiations to a conclusion as soon as possible before Arum was able to set up his fight.

The next day, I wrote King a letter. One of the two promissory notes from DKP to Evander had been due on June 14. Having not received payment, I threatened collection of the note through legal process, and on June 16, I finally received a call from Muhammad inviting me to meet with King and him on June 18 to try to negotiate the Jones versus Holyfield bout.

I met with King and Muhammad at DKP's offices. I arrived at 11 a.m. as expected, and Muhammad was expected to arrive at approximately the same time, but the meeting did not begin until about 1 p.m. And so I waited. When the meeting began, it appeared to me that King and Muhammad had been talking to each other for some time before the three of us met. Before the meeting, Muhammad, talked to me very boldly about not being intimidated or controlled by King. At the meeting, however, Muhammad's attitude had changed dramatically and he could not have been more deferential to King. After extensive negotiations, King offered to pay Evander $8 million for the Jones fight and repay the $2 million owed to Evander from the Byrd fight with an upside of $7.50 per pay-per-view buy over 1.2 million buys. The offer was conditioned upon Evander's agreement to grant to King his promotional rights if he won the bout for as long as he was WBA champion with a further agreement that Evander and Jones would fight an immediate rematch if Evander won. For the rematch, Evander would be paid the same as Jones. I told King and Muhammad that I had another offer for a fight for less money but without future promotional obligations that needed to be accepted within 24 to 36 hours and that Evander planned to accept it unless he received a true $10 million guaranteed purse for the Jones fight, plus a reasonable upside. King said we should go take the other fight because their offer was not going to get any better. I said that before I left, I wanted to make sure I had written down the offer correctly, because, even though I believed Evander would reject it, I would nevertheless take the offer to him. We then went over the terms of the final offer one more time. I then told King and Muhammad I would take the offer to Evander as soon as possible and let them know his response. Muhammad then told me something very disturbing. He said that even if he and King reached an agreement with Evander, he would then meet with Lennox Lewis's representatives and negotiate a deal with them and then present both proposals to Jones for his decision. Obviously the plan was for Muhammad to get Evander committed to a deal with no commitment by Jones, King, or Muhammad, and then shop our deal and see if Lewis would beat it. Meanwhile, we would lose our other fight opportunity and would have no alternative but to take what was then offered to us or not fight at all, and Evander had already been inactive for longer than we would have preferred.

When I landed in Atlanta at about 8 p.m. the next day, I went immediately to meet with Evander. When I presented the terms of the offer to him, he was upset. I pointed out that even though the offer for the Jones fight was obviously unfair, it was still more than we could get for the Toney fight and it was for the WBA title. Consequently I recommended Evander take the Jones fight. Evander said that as a matter of principle, he would not fight at all or fight for free before he allowed someone to take advantage of him to this extent. I then worked out with Evander what the absolute worst terms were that he could accept. Late that night, I put those terms in writing to King and Muhammad. We offered to accept a $10 million guarantee for the Jones fight with an upside of $7.50 per buy, starting at 800,000 buys. King would control Evander's promotional rights as long as Evander was WBA champion, but with a limit of one year as required by law. Evander would fight a rematch whenever it was allowed by the WBA, and for the rematch, Evander would receive at least as much as Jones and no less than $15 million.

I faxed my letter to King and Muhammad the next morning; I put a deadline of 5:30 p.m. on the deal. I then called both of them repeatedly but received no return calls. At about 3 p.m., I reached Muhammad on his cell phone, but he said he had to hang up and would call me later. Finally, at about 6 p.m., King and Muhammad called me. Both had read my letter and neither disputed its accuracy or the description of their offer in my letter in any way. They simply both told me that the offer they had made, which was outlined in my letter, was non-negotiable and Evander's choice was to accept it or lose the Jones fight. I told them that I believed there was no chance Evander would accept their offer without changes. King then went on a diatribe, telling me what a fool Evander was, how King had made him what he was, and that Evander should be happy to have the opportunity to fight for the WBA championship regardless of what he was paid. Muhammad echoed these same points.

The final offer to Evander was $8 million to fight Jones with very important and burdensome conditions. On the surface one might ask: "How can an offer of $8 million be exploitative?" Obviously, $8 million is a lot of money. The unfairness of the offer was not in the amount offered, but rather in the division of the net revenues from the fight.

Holyfield versus Tyson II had approximately two million pay-per-view buys. Muhammad, based upon his many years in the boxing business, adamantly projected a minimum of 1.5 million buys from Jones versus Holyfield in his discussions with me and was absolutely positive the fight could not possibly do less than one million buys. When the time came to negotiate an upside for Evander, King wanted to cut Evander in for additional revenues above the 1.5 million level. Muhammad offered an upside at 1.3 million. In the end, King and Muhammad were willing to allow Evander to have some upside when sales reached the 1.2 million level, and they would not go below that level. Unless King and Muhammad thought the fight would do a minimum of 1.2 million buys, they were offering Evander no upside, so they must have thought the fight would do close to or more than 1.2 million buys. That means at 1.2 million buys at $49.99, the cable operators would get half and the remainder would be $25 per buy, or $2.5 million per 100,000 buys. At 1.2 million buys, there would be $30 million in the promotional pot. Muhammad told me that Madison Square Garden had made an opening offer of $10 million to him, but he was certain he could get it to $12 million or more. Using the conservative number of $10 million, that puts $40 million in the pot. A reasonable, and in fact conservative, number for the remaining income streams of international television sales, closed circuit television, sponsorships, fight merchandise, etc., is $5 million. That takes the pot to $45 million. Kery Davis of HBO confirmed to me that HBO would cover all of the marketing expenses for the fight in return for the delay broadcast rights for the HBO broadcast a week after the fight. Davis also projected international television sales, alone, at more than $5 million, so my estimate of $5 million for ancillary revenue streams was probably low. With a pot of $45 million, the only expenses the promoters would incur would be the purses of the undercard fighters and travel and other incidental expenses, which would be somewhere between $500,000 and $750,000, but I will estimate $1 million. That leaves at least $44 million in the pot for distribution to the two fighters and the promoters. Even if my estimates were off by 10 percent, there would be $40 million available to be split between Evander on the one side and Jones and his promoters on the other side. The question, then, is how should that money be divided.

Evander was the only four-time Heavyweight Champion of the World and a ring legend known for his aggressive, exciting style. He has proven repeatedly (Foreman, Bowe, Tyson I, Tyson II, Lewis) that he is a big draw on pay-per-view when he has a good opponent. Jones was an exceptionally skilled fighter who has suffered in popularity and recognition due to a lack of top opponents in the light heavyweight division. Jones's style is more evasive and defensive than aggressive. Jones had not been a pay-per-view attraction. Jones was the WBA heavyweight champion, but most of boxing's so-called experts considered Lennox Lewis the true heavyweight champion. Under these circumstances, a split of 60 percent to Jones and 40 percent to Evander would be more than fair to Jones. Evander wanted the Jones fight badly enough, however, to accept a two-thirds to one-third split, which would have been extraordinarily fair to Jones.

Under the take-it-or-leave-it offer from King and Muhammad, if the fight did 1.2 million buys, putting $44 million in the pot, Evander would have received $8 million. If Jones received twice that much, the total paid to the fighters would have been $24 million. That would leave $20 million for the promoters! Even if Jones were to be paid three times what Evander received, there would be $12 million left for the promoters, meaning the promoters would receive 50 percent more than Evander. It should be duly noted that under King's way of doing business, he takes very little, if any, business risk in doing fights. The money to pay the fighters and other expenses is guaranteed by the television distributor and the site. Moreover, the vast majority of the marketing efforts and virtually all of the marketing expenses are borne by the television distributor and the public relations and marketing firms it engages to help. What could possibly justify that amount of payment to the promoters? Or were they going to pay Jones four times what Evander made and still keep $4 million for themselves? In either scenario, the offer was grossly unfair to Evander. Under these circumstances, when I told Evander that King and Muhammad had said their offer was final and non-negotiable, Evander ordered me in no uncertain terms to decline the offer, cease all further discussions with King, and try to make the Toney fight. I followed my marching orders. The following morning I told King Evander declined his offer. King did not give any indication whatsoever that he was willing to increase his offer in any respect. He simply said he was disappointed we could not make a deal and that Evander was making a huge mistake.

Evander's decision to fight Toney instead of Jones was made entirely on principle and upon Evander's confidence that he could and would defeat whomever he fought. From a purely objective perspective, the Jones bout was a better fight to accept. Evander would have made $8 million for the Jones fight but would make $5 million with a potential upside of up to $2 million more for the Toney fight. Also, the Jones fight would have been for the WBA title, whereas the Toney fight would be for no title. Furthermore, although he was the reigning IBF cruiserweight champion, Toney had never fought at heavyweight, whereas Jones had established himself as a viable heavyweight by soundly defeating Ruiz to win the WBA heavyweight title. Finally, although Toney was known by boxing insiders to be one of the best boxers in the world, most casual observers did not know much about Toney, whereas Jones was widely considered the best boxer in the world and was enormously popular. The cumulative effect of these factors was that Evander had more to gain by fighting Jones and much more to lose by fighting Toney. Evander, however, did not think Toney had any chance to beat him, so there was little risk.

## HOLYFIELD

*I completely understood Jim's reasons for suggesting that the Jones fight was the better fight even though the terms were unfair, but I was not about to let Don King take advantage of me, so for me, it was a matter of principle. I am a student of boxing, and I knew that James Toney was one of the best fighters in the world, but I did not believe he could beat me. I was willing to be patient. I figured after I knocked out James Toney, the Roy Jones fight would be even bigger, and I would then get that fight on fair terms. If that fight was not available, I would still be coming off a quality win, and a rematch with Chris Byrd would be a good option. Overall, at this stage of my career and after all I had accomplished, I was not about to let anyone bully me or mistreat me. I was going to fight on fair terms or not at all.*

After Evander made his decision to fight Toney, I called Goossen in Los Angeles to negotiate a deal for Holyfield versus Toney. Goossen and I had a discussion about basic terms at midmorning Eastern time, and we agreed Goossen would send me a written proposal as soon as possible. By early afternoon, I had a written proposal. By mid-afternoon, I had sent to Goossen a request for approximately 10 substantive changes with a written explanation for each requested change. When Goossen had reviewed my response, he called and thanked me for obviously only asking for things that were fair. Goossen said he could not deny the fairness in my explanations for the changes I wanted and that he wanted to make a deal that was evenhanded for both sides. We made a few minor compromises and agreed upon all deal points. By early evening Eastern time, Goossen sent me a redraft of the proposed contract and it accurately reflected all of the points we had agreed upon. I called him and told him that subject to Evander's approval, which I believed was a foregone conclusion, we had a deal. Goossen sent me a signed copy of the contract. I then faxed the contract to Evander and went over it with him point by point. Evander then signed the contract and faxed it to me, and I faxed it to Goossen, and we had a deal. Throughout this process, Goossen and I both talked to Larkin to get the necessary support and approvals from Showtime.

I had not had the opportunity to do a fight deal for Evander with anyone but King for more than seven years. I realized that day how immune I had become to the excruciating and totally unnecessary pain of doing a deal with King. This was the polar opposite of making a deal with King. In my opinion King's goal is always to beat the party he is negotiating with, not to make a fair deal. All Goossen, Showtime, and I wanted was a deal that was truly fair to all parties. Under those circumstances, there was never a need for a raised voice, a threat, or any other discord. Three reasonable, fair-minded parties made a balanced deal and documented it in less than 12 hours.

The next day, word of Holyfield versus Toney began to leak out, and Arum tried to claim the October 4 date for his proposed pay-per-view event, but Larkin had already notified the cable operators that we had a signed deal for Holyfield versus Toney and they could not deny us the date. Had we made our deal one day later, we very likely would have lost the date, and Evander would have been out in the cold or at King's and Muhammad's mercy, which would not have been a good place to be.

When King learned about the deal for Holyfield versus Toney, he immediately started spreading misleading reports of our negotiations to anyone who would listen. To set the record straight and protect Evander, I published an article on the major boxing websites entitled "The Truth About Why Jones vs. Holyfield Didn't Happen," which was exactly what the title promised and explained the events that I mentioned above.

King responded with an interview with boxingtalk.com reporter, Greg Leon, in which King repeatedly proclaimed, "Jim Thomas sold Holyfield out." King falsely claimed that I had blocked the deal because of a personal vendetta I supposedly had against King. King also ridiculously claimed that he would have given Evander anything he wanted if Evander had only called him personally. The most insulting statement King made was that he forgave Evander because Evander suffered from the "wounds and scars of slavery." In other words, King cannot even conceive of Evander having the intelligence, courage, and integrity to make his own decision to reject King's effort to exploit him.

In response to King's defamatory statements in the press and directly to Evander that I had sold Evander out, I wrote the following letter to King on July 25.

---

Don:

You have crossed the line. It is one thing to characterize negotiations in a way favorable to yourself, but it is quite another thing to publicly announce that I "sold out" my client and friend, Evander Holyfield. You knew that statement and others you have recently made about our negotiations were blatant lies. You knew perfectly well that Evander made every decision regarding the negotiations for Jones v. Holyfield. You knew that I had absolutely nothing to gain, and a lot to lose, from failing to reach agreement on that fight, but you nevertheless announced to the public that I "sold out" Evander, which means I got something in return for harming him. What you have accused me of is a crime, an act that, if proven, would cause me to lose my license to practice law, and the most serious breach of the ethical rules for lawyers. In making these false statements, you have very seriously hurt me. For some reason, some people still believe your allegations, and unlike you, I have a reputation that can be seriously damaged. My future, and that of my family, depends upon being engaged by athletes and other clients. That future has been harmed by your blatant lies. I am sure your lawyers will tell you that this amounts to slander per se. Your public repetition of your false accusations at the Mayorga vs. Forrest fight have increased the damage and confirmed the malice in this attack. Furthermore, your obvious efforts to induce Evander to terminate his relationship with me is also actionable.

You and I have argued in negotiations many times as should be expected when we were doing our jobs. I have never cursed or threatened you, but you have done both to me numerous times, and I have always let it go. When you were in trial for alleged criminal activity, at your request, I attended part of the trial in an effort to show support from Evander Holyfield. When you were under investigation after the first Holyfield vs. Lewis fight, I testified repeatedly in your favor. When negotiations broke down with HBO and you were under attack, you asked me to state publicly that you were not to blame, and I did so. Despite all of that, you have chosen to make the worst possible accusations against me, knowing they are blatant lies, all because you want to avoid a public dispute with Evander Holyfield. You apparently do not have the courage to have a dispute with Evander, so you have tried to make this something between you and me. In the process, you have launched a vicious personal attack on me without any regard for the consequences.

Because I have always been direct and honest with you when I have disagreed with what you were doing, I am writing to let you know that you have left me no choice but to defend myself against your slanderous remarks.

---

Very soon thereafter, I received a letter from King.

---

Dear Jim:

As you say in your letter, we have had many battles and I don't know anyone who has more vigorously defended the interests of his client. Indeed, we have successfully survived our many battles since Evander first fought Tyson and I believe Evander's interests have always been well served both by you and by Don King Productions, Inc.

As I was sure you and everyone else understood, including Evander, what I said about you and the decision to fight James Toney meant only that I felt the decision was not the best when compared with DKP's offer. Given your reaction, I obviously should have been more careful with my words, but, as you know, I was terribly disappointed and hurt when DKP's deal was rejected.

In any event, you have my strong personal regret and apology.

Sincerely,

Don King

---

I then met with King privately and told him what he did was wrong and that if it happened again, there would be no letters or conversations. King said he had misspoken and understood why I was upset. We shook hands and agreed to put this latest battle behind us.

Fight week finally arrived, and on September 28, Evander and I flew from Atlanta to Los Angeles for two days of promotional activities. When we landed, we went to a local television studio and Evander did an interview with the very popular sportscaster, Jim Hill. Next Evander did an in-depth on-camera interview with Jim Gray, one of the best and most prominent and respected sports reporters in the business. After the interview, Evander and I had dinner with Hill and his lovely wife, Fran.

The next morning, Evander worked out with Hallmark, who we flew in to make sure Evander did not miss any training. Then we went to a press conference at a local restaurant. After the press conference, Evander appeared on *The Best Damn Sports Show, Period*. We were both happy to see former Georgia Tech and NBA basketball star John Salley, who was one of the hosts of the show, a huge Holyfield fan, and a guy who had been a supporter of mine. Later, Evander appeared on *The Jimmy Kimmel Show* along with fellow guest, Daryl Hannah, who was promoting her new movie, *Kill Bill* directed by Quentin Tarentino. Finally, at 10:30 p.m., we boarded a private jet and made the 45-minute trip to Las Vegas.

Fight week in Las Vegas was relatively uneventful. Evander sparred the next day and looked very sharp. We had the usual press conference on Wednesday, and the weigh-in on Thursday. Evander worked out Thursday night and Friday night, and finally it was Saturday. About 2 p.m., Evander took his usual nap, and at 5:15 p.m., Team Holyfield walked to the locker rooms at the Mandalay Bay Convention Center. The locker room was quiet, but not somber. The team watched the preliminary bouts on a closed-circuit television monitor. At 6:30 p.m., Turner wrapped Evander's hands. At 7 p.m., Hallmark stretched Evander out. At 7:15 p.m., Evander worked on the hand pads held by Weldon, and finally, it was time to walk to the ring.

As we walked to the ring and the trainers, Evander, and I climbed through the ropes, I was very confident we were in for a very good night. Evander was finally healthy, and he had worked hard in training camp according to Turner and Hallmark. Toney seemed to be a perfect opponent. He was not a huge puncher; he was smaller than Evander and not as strong; although he had good head movement, he did not run around much; and he was respected as an extremely talented and tough fighter, so a victory would be impressive.

As I climbed out of the ring and took my usual seat next to Dr. Vaughns, I felt more relaxed than I had in a long time going into one of Evander's fights. The bell rang, and round one began as I had hoped. Evander was active and assertive and dictated the pace. He landed his jab well and avoided Toney's quick jabs. Toward the end of the round, Evander hit Toney with a double hook that Toney felt, and the round ended. It was clearly Evander's round, and I felt great. I thought we were in for a relatively easy night.

Round two began a lot like round one. Evander was moving and jabbing, but Toney was starting to defend and counter better than he had in the first round. Evander landed a hook or two but could not land anything really solid. Toney landed a few quick jabs. Although the round was competitive, I thought Evander won and that it was only a matter of time before his superior power wore Toney down.

Round three was a lot like round one. Evander was quicker and more powerful than Toney and again landed some good left hooks. It was clearly Evander's round, and I was even more confident. As round four began, I was looking for Evander to finally land a shot that would hurt Toney and signal a beginning of the end. Instead, Toney landed a hard right to Evander's head that momentarily shook him. I was surprised, because I didn't think Toney had the power to stun Evander with one punch. That one punch seemed to give Toney a big boost, and Toney became more active and aggressive. Toney started landing left jabs and an occasional right hand behind the jab, and Evander was definitely receiving more than he was giving. As the round ended, it was undoubtedly Toney's round.

Evander had won the first three rounds, but Toney had won the fourth and was obviously feeling more confident. It was time for Evander to go back to work and regain the momentum, but in round five, Evander threw very few punches, and Toney was landing his punches consistently. Round six was even better for Toney, and after the sixth round, Turner told Evander that he needed to fight back because Toney was doing all of the punching. The next round, Toney began landing left jab, right cross combinations with apparent increasing ease. After the seventh round, Turner told Evander that if he did not fight back or at least defend himself better, Turner was going to stop the fight. Toney dominated the eighth round, and Evander looked tired and noticeably slower and was absorbing a lot of punches. After round eight, Turner told Evander very emphatically that if Evander could not do any better, Turner would stop the fight, because Evander was not able to defend himself or fight back. Toney continued his domination in the ninth round, and halfway through the round, Toney hit Evander with a body punch and Evander fell to his hands and knees. Evander slowly got to his feet and looked very tired. Referee Jay Nady checked Evander and then suddenly stopped the fight when Turner stepped through the ropes, indicating that he wanted the referee to stop the fight.

As I climbed into the ring, I felt profound sadness as I realized that Evander's performance in this fight had dealt a serious blow to his goal of winning all three major heavyweight titles before retiring. It would now be difficult to even get a chance to fight for any of the heavyweight titles. When we reached the locker room after the fight, Evander sat down and hung his head in a way I had never seen before, indicating to me that Evander also knew what effect this result would have on his plans.

Evander went into the private shower area. When he did not come out after the time it would have taken to take a quick shower, I went in and told him the post-fight press conference was about to begin. Evander told me to go to the press conference and get started, and he would be there later.

Larkin and I walked to the press conference together.

"You are going to be asked two questions: Are you going to recommend retirement, and if you do and Evander refuses, will you resign?" he told me.

When I arrived at the press conference, those were the first two questions asked.

"First, I will advise Evander to do exactly what I believe is in his own best interest without regard to the interests of anyone else, including myself," I began. "Second, I will provide my advice, Evander will make his own decision, and I will stay with him as long as he wants me. I realize that, if my advice is inconsistent with Evander's decision, it may cause him to want a new adviser; but I have always accepted that, and it has never influenced my advice and never will. That is all I have to say on this topic."

Soon after this statement, Evander arrived and I handed the microphone to him. Evander complimented Toney on a great performance. He also said that he saw openings but could not get his punches off in time to land them and that he saw Toney's punches coming but could not react quickly enough to block them. He said that Toney had simply beat him up and that he had always said that he would not retire until someone beat him up. On the other hand, Evander said he wanted to see a tape of the fight, and he would put off any decision about what to do with his boxing career so that the decision was not an emotional one. Evander thanked all of his fans for their support over the years and left the dais to a standing ovation from everyone in the room.

Later that night, Evander and his family flew back to Atlanta on a private jet offered to him by a friend so that they could go to church on Sunday morning. I left Evander to his family on the day after the fight, but on the next day, October 6, I asked to come and see him at his office to share some thoughts about the future. We spent a couple of hours together talking, and Evander listened without comment and allowed me to get all of my points out before responding.

"Evander, I think you are confusing 'retiring' with 'quitting,'" I told him. "I know you have never quit in your life and never will, but retiring isn't quitting. Cal Ripkin played his heart out every day of his career for the Baltimore Orioles. He never even took a day off and he certainly never quit. At the end of his career, he wasn't quite as good as he was at this peak, but he was still good, and he retired. He retired with pride and dignity and in many ways on top.

"You need to face the fact that you will retire. The alternative is a lot worse. Your concern is about retiring on top. Just like Cal Ripkin did, you can retire right now on top. Everybody loves and admires you, and you have done all you can do in this sport. You are on top. You have already done so much in boxing that winning the titles one more time will not significantly enhance your legacy. On the other hand, one more performance like this last one, and you will lose some of your current ability to finish on top. You have tremendous support and good will right now. You can lose that if you go on too long and that would adversely impact your endorsement and appearance revenue after boxing.

"Showtime has offered to throw you the biggest athlete retirement party in history and televise it, which can be a springboard to your post-boxing projects.

"As a practical matter, I do not think you will be able to get another title fight at any time in the foreseeable future due to the current state of the heavyweight division, unless you re-sign with King. We have fought for years to get free from King, and I would hate to see you put yourself back in a situation where he has any control over you or your career.

"You are still, and always will be, the one who makes the decisions. You know what I think you should do, but you need to decide. Whatever you decide, I will be with you, and whatever your goals are, those will be my goals, but I think it is time to move on to other things."

I then described a long list of things I felt we could do together very successfully in the post-boxing era. When I had finished, Evander said he appreciated what I had said, but he was not ready to retire. He said he believed there were adjustments he could and would make to get better, and any obstacles in his way could be overcome.

"I will retire as the undisputed Heavyweight Champion of the World, and anyone who does not believe that does not need to be with me when I do it."

After my meeting with Evander, he decided he wanted a management team that fully believed in and supported his goal of regaining all of the major heavyweight championships before retiring from boxing. Evander announced at a press conference in New York that to manage his quest to win the WBA, WBC, and IBF heavyweight championships and manage his various business-es while he pursued his boxing career, he had selected Alex Krys and two other men I had never heard of. I knew Krys well and liked and respected him very much. Krys also had no prior experience in boxing, but I knew from serving with him on the board of directors of the Holyfield Foundation that he was a very intelligent and successful businessman and someone who could be trusted to do his best to help Evander.

I was disappointed and hurt when I heard that Evander had selected a new management team, but I was not shocked. I knew that when I decided to rec-ommend to Evander that he retire, the likely result would be that I would no longer represent Evander. Evander's position has always been that the people around him need to believe in his goals or they need to leave. I understood how Evander could view my recommendation to retire as a loss of faith in him despite my explanation that it was not, but my conscience told me I had no choice but to provide my honest opinion, which I had promised to do from the day Evander and I began working together.

After the press conference to announce Evander's new management team, Evander, Krys, and I met for breakfast. Evander said he was not angry with me at all but realized I did not truly support his goal of fighting until he won all of the heavyweight titles and that he felt he needed to have managers who sup-ported that goal. We mutually agreed that to allow a fresh start for Evander and his new management team and to avoid confusion, it was best if we had a clean and complete break in our business relationship. I told Evander that I could handle losing my client, but it would be much harder to lose my friend, and that I hoped we would stay in touch. For the remainder of 2004, however, we did not see much of each other. Evander had been an extremely important part of my life for many years, and I felt a great sense of loss.

# EPILOGUE
# HE NEVER GAVE UP

**A**s of the spring 2004, Evander was closing in on 42 years of age, had lost his last two fights in lopsided defeats, had won only two of his last eight fights, and was unranked by any of the rating organizations, except for the WBA, which ranked him No. 15. Yet Evander still insisted and fervently believed that he would win all of the major heavyweight titles once again before he retired, no matter how long it took. To any ordinary man, the obstacles facing Evander would be obviously insurmountable, and they appeared to be insurmountable to virtually everyone other than Evander. So why did Evander continue to tilt at windmills and seek the impossible dream like a modern-day Don Quixote? Was it unbridled ego, irrational denial, or selfish disregard for his own well being and the care of his family as many in the press proclaimed? The answer is none of the above. Evander chose to pursue his quest so that he could inspire people of all ages and backgrounds all over the world to believe that anything is possible if one works hard, has faith, and never gives up. Answering the question of his motive, however, does not answer the question of what caused Evander to honestly believe he could and would reach his goal if he never gave up. In my opinion, there were three forces deriving from his life experiences that coalesced to make Evander believe he could achieve the seemingly impossible.

First, Evander was taught by his beloved mother as a young boy that he was allowed to quit only on top and that if he never gave up, he would eventually reach his goal, at which point he could quit. When Evander suffered his first boxing defeat against Cecil Collins at age 10, he wanted to quit boxing, but his mother adamantly refused to let him quit until he beat Collins. I think this lesson became a secret for success for Evander in all things, and his refusal to quit until he reached his goal of winning all of the heavyweight titles was at least in part fulfillment of his commitment to his mother never to quit until he reached his goal.

Second, Evander believed it was his destiny and calling to achieve the seemingly impossible and retire as the undisputed Heavyweight Champion of the World, which had been done only twice before in the history of boxing. Evander saw his recent losses as part of God's plan, because the losses would make achievement of the goal all the more amazing and inspiring. Because Evander felt he was destined to reach his goal, the only thing that could prevent him from reaching the goal would be quitting before he got there, so he was obligated to stay the course.

Third, Evander felt not only entitled, but obligated to disregard other people's opinions as to whether he could reach his goal. Evander felt that all his life he had been told directly and indirectly all of the things he could never achieve. He felt he had been told over and over that he was just another black kid from the projects who would never achieve anything worthwhile. By refusing to accept other people's limitations, Evander

- made the 1984 U.S. Olympic boxing team and won a bronze medal;
- became the first and only undisputed cruiserweight champion in boxing history;
- knocked out Buster Douglas, who had knocked out "the Baddest Man on the Planet," Mike Tyson, to become the undisputed Heavyweight Champion of the World;
- became the only four-time Heavyweight Champion of the World in boxing history (Ali won the title three times);
- compiled from 1984 through 1998 a record of 33 wins (25 by knockout) and only three losses (to heavyweight champions Riddick Bowe and Michael Moorer) against arguably the highest quality of opponents in heavyweight history;
- never fought an opponent with 10 or more losses (Ali fought nine such opponents);
- fought opponents who cumulatively had won over 95 percent of their bouts when Evander fought them (Ali's opponents had won 84 percent of their bouts);
- earned more than $200 million in the ring, allowing him to help thousands of others in need; and
- fought and defeated 10 men who won major heavyweight titles (Ali defeated eight such opponents).

Evander felt that if he had listened to other people's opinions on what he could do, he never would have achieved any of these things. If he had retired when there was broad consensus among experts that it was a time, he would have retired in 1992 after the first Bowe fight, in 1994 after the Michael Moorer fight, and in 1996 after the third Bowe fight; he never would have defeated Mike Tyson or won the heavyweight title more than once.

So, despite the unanimous opinion of boxing experts and myself that Evander should retire after the Toney fight in October 2003, he refused to do so. Because King promoted John Ruiz, Chris Byrd, and Lamon Brewster, who held the WBA, IBF, and

WBO heavyweight titles respectively, Evander re-signed with King reportedly based upon a commitment by King to provide Evander with a heavyweight title bout before the end of 2004. When King did not do so, Evander accepted a bout against Larry Donald on the undercard of Ruiz's and Byrd's respective title bouts. Donald was a fighter who had compiled a very good record against mediocre opponents but had never won a bout against a top-ranked heavyweight. Donald was supposed to be an opponent respectable enough that a win by Evander would lead to a top 10 ranking by the sanctioning bodies, leading to a title shot—but not a serious threat to beat Evander.

Prior to the Holyfield versus Donald bout, Evander's new trainer, Ronnie Shields, repeatedly said Evander was in great shape and had had an outstanding training camp. Shields, who had worked with Evander in the early years of his career, opined that Evander had declined in recent years because he had not sparred enough and did not have a trainer who believed in him. Shields said he had been able to push Evander very hard in his training sessions, and that Evander was back to fighting the way he had fought in his early years and was totally healthy for the first time in a long time. Evander was very confident and once again predicted that even at age of 42, the best was yet to come, and I am sure he believed it with all his heart.

On the night of November 13, 2004, Holyfield versus Donald was the first of four heavyweight bouts on a Don King Productions pay-per-view show aired on HBO. In the first round, neither Evander nor Donald landed any significant shots, but Donald simply threw and landed more scoring punches. The following 11 rounds were more of the same. Donald jabbed, moved, and threw combinations, while Evander threw, for the most part, one punch at a time. Compubox counted 286 punches landed by Donald to 78 for Evander. One judge scored the fight 10 rounds for Donald and two for Evander; the other two judges scored the bout 11 rounds for Donald and one for Evander. If there was anything positive for Evander, it was that he went 12 rounds without noticeably tiring and was never seriously hurt. After the fight, Evander and Shields reported that Evander suffered back spasms from the second round on.

After the bout, there were the usual cries from the boxing press for Evander to retire, but this time, there was something more. The commissioner of the New York State Athletic Commission, Ron Scott Stevens, announced that he had placed Evander on indefinite medical suspension due to his poor performance against Donald. Because all state athletic commissions must respect a medical suspension from any other commission, the suspension in New York was in effect a nationwide suspension.

I had known Stevens for years. I respected his integrity and felt sure that his decision was motivated by a genuine concern for Evander's well being. As a legal matter, however, I had a big problem with the stated rationale for the suspension. There are numerous objective rules any commission could adopt to further protect fighters that would not infringe the legal rights of fighters. For example, a commission could adopt a rule that any fighter over the age of 40, any fighter with more than 40 professional fights, or any fighter who had lost three fights in a row was required to pass a predetermined battery of medical tests in order to be allowed to continue fighting. In my opinion, what a commission cannot do legally is retroactively adopt a subjective standard for taking away an athlete's livelihood based on a poor performance.

A year earlier after the Toney fight, I had explained to Evander that in my opinion his best course, on a cost-benefit analysis, was to retire from boxing, but absent medical evidence of increased risk of harm, I did not feel that I or anyone else had the right to make that decision for Evander. In my view, the issue of what any person thinks another ought to do must be very carefully distinguished from the issue of who gets to make the decision. I personally think Tyson, who is 38 years old and was totally destroyed by Lennox Lewis and then was knocked out by a journeyman named Danny Williams, should retire. If I were his adviser, I would be obligated to tell him my opinion. But if I represented Tyson, I would nevertheless fight for his right to make his own decision on retirement unless there was medical evidence to justify suspending his license. The same might be said of the great Roy Jones, who has suffered devastating early-round one-punch knockouts in his last two fights. When I asked boxing insiders why everyone seems intent on forcing Evander to retire but not Tyson, Jones, or others, they uniformly responded, "We care more about Evander." In my opinion, no one should have the right to take away a fighter's right to pursue his livelihood because they care about him more than they do about others, or, for that matter, because they perceive that he already has enough money and doesn't need any more.

Two days after the Larry Donald fight, I called Krys to see how he and Evander were. Krys told me that Evander was adamant about challenging the suspension of his boxing license and that Krys had already informally informed the New York State Athletic Commission that Evander intended to appeal the suspension. I told Krys that I would be willing to help Evander and him with this issue on an informal and confidential basis. Krys said he was certain Evander would appreciate and would be touched by my offer to help and asked me to give Evander a call directly.

I called Evander and asked how he was feeling. He said he was fine. He was curt and cool, and I sensed a suspicion that I might be calling to say, "I told you so." I told him that Krys told me that he planned to appeal the suspension of his license and that I just wanted to call and offer my help wanting nothing in return. There was an abrupt and dramatic change in Evander's tone. He said he was happy I called and really appreciated my offer to help. I asked whether he might want to have lunch and hear my ideas on how to get his license back. Evander said he would like that very much, and we agreed to meet the next day.

I chose an informal sports-themed restaurant named Champions, feeling it was appropriate for meeting someone I would always think of as a champion. We sat down to lunch and discussed the forthcoming appeal.

"I still think your best option is to retire, Evander," I told him upfront, "but I will support and assist you in gaining the right to make that decision for yourself."

I then pulled out a multipage outline of the legal arguments and procedural strategy I recommended for challenging the suspension and explained each one to Evander.

As he looked over the points, Evander looked at me and asked, "When did you do this?"

"I have accumulated the information over many years, but I organized it and wrote it down last night."

"I really appreciate you doing this for me," he said looking up from the document.

"What are friends for?"

We both smiled broadly.

There was no doubt in my mind that Evander realized that whatever my past advice—right or wrong—had been, it had come from a true friend. We talked about our families and all that was going on in our lives and about sports and music and movies, and I felt like something that had been broken was fixed.

As the conversation waned and the lunch meeting came to an end, I felt I had to say one more thing.

"Evander, I have one more idea," I said.

He looked at me and waited for me to continue.

"I think a great way for you to finish on top would be to win back your license, call a press conference the next day, and announce that now that the decision is yours to make, you have decided to retire."

Evander smiled warmly.

"You never give up, do you?" he said shaking his head.

I smiled and looked at him.

"I learned it from you."

# INDEX